THE AEGEAN

A SEA-GUIDE TO ITS COASTS
AND ISLANDS

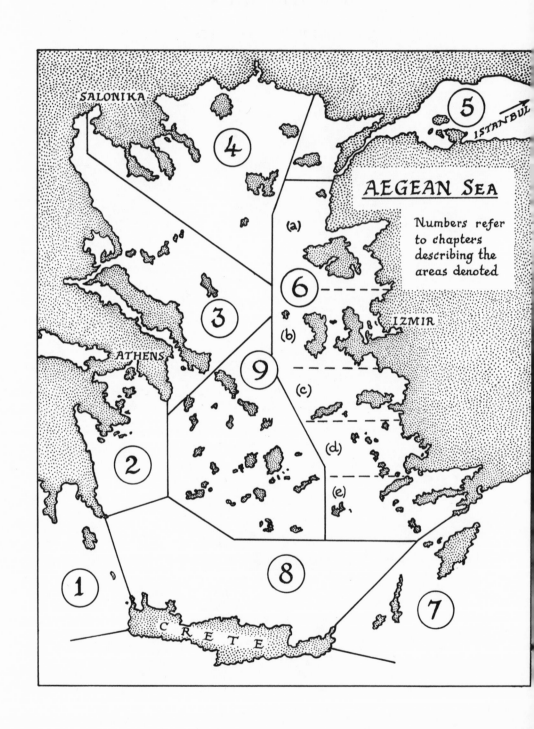

AEGEAN SEA

Numbers refer to chapters describing the areas denoted

SALONIKA

ISTANBUL

IZMIR

ATHENS

CRETE

(a)

(b)

(c)

(d)

(e)

THE AEGEAN

A Sea-Guide to its
Coasts and Islands

H. M. DENHAM

W · W · NORTON & COMPANY · INC·
New York

Sea-Guides by H. M. Denham

THE AEGEAN
THE ADRIATIC
THE IONIAN ISLANDS TO RHODES
SOUTHERN TURKEY, THE LEVANT AND CYPRUS
THE TYRRHENIAN SEA

First American Edition 1976

ISBN 0 393 03197 7

1 2 3 4 5 6 7 8 9 0

Contents

Illustrations

SOURCES OF ILLUSTRATIONS

Sketch maps by Elizabeth Scott and Aydua Scott-Elliot. Drawings
by Elizabeth Scott and Madge Denham. Title page drawing by David
Knight. Photographs: 1, 2, 3, 8, 9, 10, 11, 12, 13, 15, the Author;
4, Nikos Kontos, Athens; 5, 22, Spyros Meletzis, Athens; 6, Nick
S. Stournaras, Athens; 7, 19, 21, Yannis Scouroyannis, Athens;
14, D. A. Harissiadis, Athens; 16, 17, 20, Mustafa Kapkin, Izmir;
18, T. Amorghianos; 23, Voula Papaioannou, Athens.

ERRATA

p. 37, para. 3, line 3: for 'xxii' read 'xx'
     last line of page: for 'xxviii' read 'xxvi'
pl. 12, fac. p. 63: caption to read 'See p. 233'
p. 221, para. 5, last line: read 'opposite p. 225'
pl. 21, fac. p. 224: caption to read 'See p. 208'

The grand object of travelling
is to see the shores of the Mediterranean.
On these shores were the four great empires of
the world—the Assyrian, the Persian, the Greek and the
Roman. All our religion, almost all our arts,
almost all that sets us above savages
has come to us from the shores
of the Mediterranean.

DR SAMUEL JOHNSON

Preface to Third Edition

Having received helpful information from so many sailing friends I find it difficult to mention them all by name or even to refer to their contribution which has either confirmed what I have written or pointed out recent changes. I prefer to mention Mr Anthony Butler and Mrs Jehane West who have consistently kept me on course and also to convey my gratitude to Captain Paizis Paradelis of the Hellenic Navy who has helped me with the proofs. I am, however, most grateful to them all.

H.M.D.

Preface to First Edition

This book is the result of various cruises, both under steam and sail, as well as periods of camping, mountain scrambles, shooting and shore excursions.

During these years I have kept a record of local conditions, sailing craft, ports and anchorages, the latter having been recently collated for fellow members of the Royal Cruising Club.

Although I always had a latent enthusiasm for sail, my interest in the Aegean began the hard way. At the age of 17, when a midshipman in a battleship at the Dardanelles during the First World War, my action station was normally in the crow's nest, a waist-high canvas structure mounted on the head of our topmast. When the bugle for action sounded, I had to struggle up a swaying Jacob's ladder to reach my lofty perch; armed with a telescope and part of a chart, I then waited for the guns to go off. My duty was to report where our shells had fallen, and any signs of enemy activity.

It was in the intervals when our guns were silent that the Aegean landscape gradually grew on me. History seemed to spread itself out on a gigantic map around me; from my crow's nest on the Hellespont I could see the Plain of Troy to the southward, Gallipoli (often too close) to the north, the islands of Tenedos and Imbros and, sometimes, the tall rounded summit of Samothrace. In the vicinity were one or two of the alleged tombs of Homeric heroes and other historic landmarks, all of which, with the aid of my scrap of chart, could be identified.

During the years between the Wars, when I was serving with the Mediterranean Fleet, a proportion of our time was spent in the Aegean. There were many opportunities for rough shooting in the winter, for scrambling over mountains and exploring under sail in ships' boats many of the small coves and sheltered anchorages which I was subsequently able to visit again some years later.

Twenty years ago, when I was able to cruise in my own yacht, I became captivated by the Aegean—not only for the beauty of the country and the liveliness of the small ports, but for their association with the past. Many places have Hellenic and medieval remains and here the link with ancient history is evident and vivid. Even without these remains, it needs only a little research in museums, libraries or early writings to link what you see today with the great events that once took place there. Thus, by recreating the past, what had perhaps appeared to be an uninspiring anchorage becomes once more alive.

To clarify descriptions of some of the more remote places considered suitable for yachts, a number of sketches and rough harbour plans are provided. With few exceptions these are not published elsewhere, the data having been obtained from early surveys corrected for recent physical changes and based on my own soundings.

1963

Since the first edition of this book was published eleven years ago, many changes affecting yachts have taken place. Both Greece and Turkey have provided better facilities, but in different ways. In Greece these are mainly the construction of yacht marinas and, in addition to physical changes in the ports, better arrangements for supplies have been organized. In Turkey, where difficulties discouraged yachts from returning to these pleasant shores, measures have been taken to put things right, and an increasing number of yachts now visit Turkey each year. This book has therefore had to be expanded to bring information up-to-date and also to describe the hitherto unvisited shores of Turkey.

I must make it clear that none of this information is meant to take the place of official publications, *Sailing Directions* or charts. It is intended only to augment them to help those coming to the Aegean by sea; to choose where to go and how to get there; what to do and how to go about it after they have arrived.

1970

Introduction to Greek Waters

GENERAL CRUISING INFORMATION

Spelling of Greek and Turkish Names. During recent centuries, names used for islands and ports were very often those given by the Venetians, e.g. the island of Telos was called Episcopi: Piraeus, Porto Leone; Chios, Scio; etc.

British charts used either:

(*a*) the British conception of the phonetic spelling of Greek names, e.g. Euboea, for Ευβοια, or
(*b*) a transliteration of the sound of the Greek name, e.g., Evvia, or
(*c*) a mixture of the two, Evvoia, or
(*d*) The Italian name, e.g. Stampalia for Astipalia.

In the last year or two the Greeks have disagreed with the English spelling and have persuaded the English hydrographer to conform to their ideas on how a place should be spelt. For example, you may still find on a Greek steamer's stern 'PIRAEUS', but on an English chart you must now seek this port under the name 'Pireefs'.

The Turkish Government has now given Turkish names to places known for centuries by their Greek or Venetian ones, and on the new British charts the names of places are now printed to agree with their modern Greek or Turkish counterparts. Throughout this book I have observed the following system:

Such well-known places as Athens, Rhodes, Crete, Salonika, I have written according to our English custom, but to make sure that every place may be easily found in the Index I have in most cases inserted its alternative name. For the less well-known places I have used the spelling of the modern Greek chart.

A guide to the pronunciation is given in the index where the accented syllables have been indicated.

Port Officials are not mentioned at each place, since at every small Greek port there is normally both a Customs Office and a Port Authority. In very small places the local policeman sometimes acts on their behalf. The harbour officials dress like the Navy, though they are not sailors, nor are they administered by the Admiralty. On a yacht's arrival from a foreign port a *transit log* is issued at the Port of Entry (see list on page xxii) on presentation of the Ship's Papers.

For the remainder of the yacht's stay only this log and a crew list, indicating the last and next port of call, are required by the authorities. Dues are imposed on a yacht at only the modern yacht harbours where special facilities are provided, e.g. Vouliagmeni, Zea, etc. The formalities on entering and leaving Turkey are described in the 'Introduction to Turkish Waters', page 79.

Fuel and Water being an important concern for a small cruising yacht, the Tourist Organization has now issued a list of 'Supply Ports' where these commodities can be obtained. At some of these places water and fuel have always been obtainable, but fuel* can usually be provided from a diesel fuel pump on a section of the quay marked by blue and yellow zebra stripes; this pump also supplies the fishing craft. Caution, however, is necessary because sufficient depth cannot be depended upon, nor is the berth necessarily a safe one.

Fuelling stations in Turkey are restricted to the larger ports.

When visiting Turkey, unless one is sure of the quality of the fresh water, it is advisable to wait and replenish on return to Greece. As far as possible observations on the quality of the fresh water have been made at each port listed.

Gas. As the British fittings are different it is more convenient to land these cylinders for the duration of a yacht's stay abroad and purchase Greek cylinders together with a reducing valve and a short length of tubing. Agencies are to be found all over Greece for the exchange of cylinders. A recoverable deposit is charged originally on each cylinder.

Food and Drink. As the enjoyment of cruising in Greece can be so easily marred by stomach troubles, a few notes on the local food and drink are necessary. Very few English digestions are immune to Greek cooking, which has strong Greek olive oil added to almost everything.

In all the small restaurants it is quite in order for the customer to enter the kitchen and choose his dish from the wide copper pans spread out on the charcoal stove—generally there are chicken, lamb stew, stuffed tomatoes, savoury rice, and fish soup etc., all looking most inviting, as well as the Greek dishes such as *Dolmades* (meat and rice in vine leaves), *Moussaka* (a sort of shepherds' pie with cheese and aubergine) and *pasticche* (baked macaroni with meat and cheese). These should be avoided in the evening as they were probably cooked for the mid-day meal and have been re-heated. Usually there is a charcoal grill, and lamb cutlets or fish cooked on this is a safe bet; but be sure to say 'without oil' (*ohee Ládhi*) when ordering or you will find cold olive oil has been poured over your

---

* The Transit Log enables a yacht to buy fuel out of bond; a great concession applicable only to Greece.

grill. Fish is almost invariably good and fresh. Nearly all restaurants have little dishes of *Yoghourt*, and also delicious *Baklava* (honey-cakes with almonds). Never order your whole meal at one time, or you will find that the dishes will be brought all together, and by the time you have eaten your first course the second will be congealed. [For Turkish food see 'Introduction to Turkish Waters', p. 79.]

The following are usually available:

Fish

Gilthead bream	*Tsipoúra*	Whitebait	*Marídes*
Sea bream	*Sinagrída*	Anchovy	*Antsoúya*
Common bream	*Lithríni*	Mackerel	*Skoumbrí*
Red mullet	*Barboúnia*	Spanish mackerel	*Kiliós*
Grey mullet	*Kéfalos*	Prawns	*Garídes*
Sole	*Glóssa*	Squid	*Calamári*
Bass	*Lavráki*	Lobster	*Astakós*

Meat

Lamb } —usually good	*Arnáki*	Steak (fillet)	*Bon Filet*
Pork }	*Hirinó*	Veal	*Moskári*
Chops	*Brizóles*	Kidney—usually good	*Nefró*

Butter is obtainable at most of the towns frequented by tourists.

Fruit and Vegetables—Early in the season are:

Apples, oranges, cherries, loquats, beans and peas, courgettes, artichokes and lettuces.
Some of these begin to go out of season in May and are followed by tomatoes, cucumbers, aubergines, peaches, apricots and figs. Later there are melons and grapes.
Anything eaten raw should be washed with a few grains of permanganate of potash.

Wines—Should be bought in a 3 kilo *galloni* which can be bottled off and exchanged anywhere: Red and white K.A.I.R., *Neméa* (red), *Náussa* (white).
In bottles—*Santa Helena* (white), *Doméstica* (white-red), *Boutári* and most Pátras district wines.
White is always better than red though a palatable rosé, called *kokkinelli*, comes from Attica.
Retsina can be bought everywhere in Attica.

Other drinks

Ouzo is the local spirit. Together with the local brandy and vermouth it is best and cheapest bought draft.
Beer is now obtainable in many varieties.
Orange and lemon squash are both excellent.
Turkish coffee ashore—*sketo*, without sugar; *metrio*, with some sugar; *vari glyko* and *glyko vrasto*, very sweet.

Health. The incidence of typhoid and tetanus varies from year to year in Greece, but there is always some, and it is sensible to be inoculated. Practically all the well-known medicines and drugs can be bought in Athens and possibly in the few big towns, but nowhere else, so it is advisable to have a well-stocked medicine chest. The *Yachting World* diary gives an excellent and comprehensive list which covers most eventualities. Two useful additions are Sulphamezathine and Entero-vioform, as, inoculated or not, many people in the Mediterranean become afflicted with some form of colic, particularly if eating ashore.

Malaria appears to be completely stamped out.

Nowadays in Greece there is no trouble in finding a doctor on the larger islands and even in the smaller places there is generally a qualified medical practitioner, a chemist and, at the worst, probably a midwife.

In Turkey medical facilities outside the large towns fall short of the Greek standard. Although three-quarters of the Turkish population live in the country towns and villages, the great majority of the doctors and dentists practise in the three cities of Istanbul, Izmir and Ankara.

Shooting. Shooting cruises in Greece, usually in British yachts, continued until nearly the beginning of the First World War. Large schooners sailed from England in January or February, collected the owner and guests in Italy or Malta and then mostly proceeded to the Albanian coast and North Greece. There they found an abundance of duck, partridge, quail and woodcock. Those who entered the Aegean were limited to red-legged partridges,* hares and rabbits on the Islands, wild goat at Anti-Milos, and duck shooting on the Vardar marshes near Salonika. With the exception of the wild goat, all these still exist.

A special permit for shooting is required. The season varies each year.

On the Anatolian coast of Turkey a number of British and French residents from Istanbul and Smyrna used at one time to take advantage of the good shooting.

Fishing. At sea a variety of fish (listed on page xvii) are caught by day and, during the dark of the moon, by night.

Night Fishing. Five 'ducklings' (*Grigria*) are each manned by one man and fitted with enormous gas-lamps over the stern. They are towed out of harbour to the fishing ground by the mother-ship, a *trehandiri*, fitted with winches and line-reels, followed by the net-boat, astern of which come the five little 'duck-lings'. They usually have a long night on the fishing grounds and are seldom back in harbour until well after sunrise. The Turks occasionally use the same method of fishing, their craft being called *gugurru*.

The waters off the Anatolian coast, which receive the flow from a number of

* Being non-migratory they are always to be found on most islands; woodcock, snipe, quail, geese and duck only come in spring and autumn.

small rivers, yield the most fish, and are frequently poached by the Greek fishermen.

By far the best fishing is in the Bosporus. At Istanbul the bulk of Turkey's sea produce is sold, consisting chiefly of anchovy, mackerel, sardine, turbot and tunny.

Pollution in Greek waters still appears to be less than in other parts of the Mediterranean. The effects of untreated sewage and oil pollution may be considered to have the most harmful effect in three main areas: the Saronic Gulf, Gulf of Salonika and in Turkey the area around Izmir. There is also the Sea of Marmara where on the southern shores pollution has an an ill effect especially on the reproduction of bonito and mackerel.

Fish caught in the above areas should not be eaten.

The diminishing supply of fish is also due to overfishing, and this has compelled the Greek government to build some large fishing vessels to work in Atlantic waters.

Aegean Communications. There is a regular local steamer and car-ferry service from Piraeus to almost all the Greek islands, detailed schedules being obtainable from travel agencies. Air communication has been established between Athens and many of the islands.

There is almost no communication between Greek and Turkish ports.

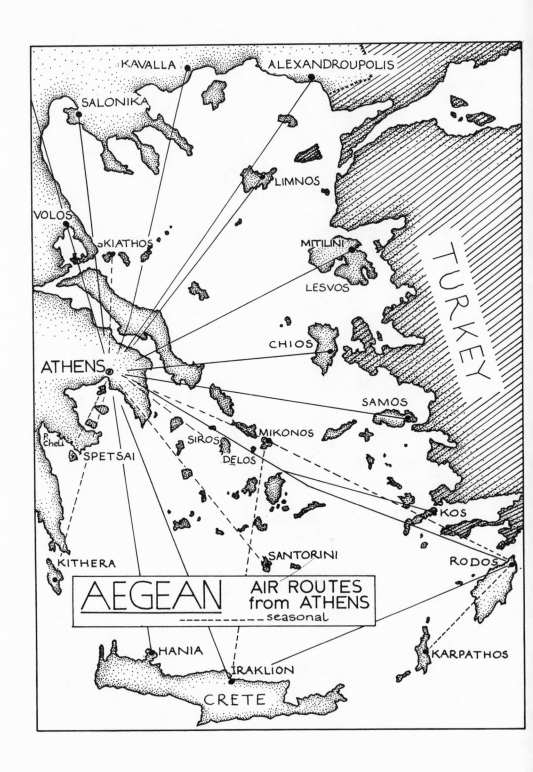

KAVALLA

ALEXANDROUPOLIS

SALONIKA

TURKEY

LIMNOS

VOLOS

SKIATHOS

MITILINI

LESVOS

ATHENS

CHIOS

SAMOS

P.Cheli

SPETSAI

SIROS

MIKONOS

DELOS

KITHERA

SANTORINI

KOS

RODOS

AEGEAN   AIR ROUTES
from ATHENS
----------- seasonal

KARPATHOS

HANIA

IRAKLION

CRETE

PILOTAGE

Calm as a slumbering babe
Tremendous Ocean lies
ODYSSEY V.256

The vagaries of the winds prevent the Aegean being classed as an ideal sailing ground; yet the appeal of the small sheltered ports and anchorages together with scenery of bold and striking contrasts more than compensate, and make the Aegean the most attractive part of the Mediterranean.

The winds, described on page xxiii, though largely predictable may also come up suddenly and without warning; but as the Aegean Sea is relatively small and well spaced with islands shelter is reasonably close at hand.

The coast, both of the mainland and the islands, is mostly hilly or mountainous, and with the exception of the islands lying a long way from the mainland and of part of Anatolia, the country is green and often wooded. The entertaining small ports, full of local colour, are often tucked round secluded corners, and reveal themselves quite unexpectedly.

When making an extensive cruise it is prudent to make use of the prevailing north wind and plan accordingly: i.e., during the Variables of May and June, it is recommended to make as far north as possible, and then, with the beginning of the Meltemi in early July, start cruising southwards with a fresh to strong fair wind behind one by day, and a calm at night. Similarly a yacht may expect to have a fair wind when coasting along the northern shore of Crete in an easterly direction.

The Mediterranean Pilot, Vol. IV (*Sailing Directions*), is the volume often referred to in this work. It is a mine of accurate information, and when further details of a place are required if not in sufficient detail in this book, *Sailing Directions* should always be consulted.

In the last century a number of British yachts, large vessels by today's standards, visited the Aegean. The owners often published accounts of their cruises and even the guide books provided information for yachtsmen—giving details of ports and anchorages as well as advice on chartering local boats. The accounts of these early cruises are of limited value, since the yachts, being large and without auxiliary power, used to visit only the larger bays and anchorages which are of little interest for the smaller yachts of today.

The most valuable information both on pilotage and archaeological matter is to be gleaned from reports by Her Majesty's surveying vessels and from observations by early travellers. All chart numbers quoted throughout the book refer to British Admiralty Charts.*

Entering the Aegean. The Western Approaches (page 3), Eastern Gateway (page 171) and Corinth Canal (page 32) are the passages into the Aegean and unless a yacht has already entered Greece she must do so at one of the following **Ports of Entry**: Piraeus (Passalimani), Vouliagmeni, Nauplion, Lavrion, Volos, Thessaloniki, Kavalla, Alexandroupolis; the island ports of Limnos (Kastro Merini), Mytileni, Khios, Samos, Syros (Syra), Rhodes; the Cretan ports of Hania, Heraklion and St Nikolaos. [Turkish Ports of Entry are listed in 'Introduction to Turkish Waters', page 82.]

The Weather and its Implications. Few countries as small as Greece have such a variation in climate. In some years at the end of March you may find summer at Kalamata and Rhodes, yet it is still winter in Arcady, Epirus and Macedonia. However, throughout the Aegean the latter part of April, May and June are usually good months for cruising. By mid-June the temperature has begun to rise sharply and it can be oppressive in July and August. The latter part of September and October are usually also pleasant sailing months.

Weather Forecasts in Greek and Other Languages. Naval bulletin at 1530.

News programmes, on 729 kc/s (412 m) are transmitted in Greek at 0745, 1315 and 1945, followed on each occasion by news in English, German and French. At the end of each transmission is the short weather bulletin. As times of transmission are apt to change, enquiry should be made at the first port of call.

The coastal station Athenai Radio gives forecasts in English on 2590 kc/s at 0545, 1156, 1745 and 2345. (These are all local times.)

Glossary of Areas in forecasts

North Aegean	*Voreion Aegeon*
Central Aegean	*Kentrikon Aegeon*
South Aegean	*Notion Aegeon*
S.E. Aegean	*Notionanatolikon Aegeon* or *Ikarion*
Cretan Sea	*Kritikon kai Thalassa Kithyzon*
and Kithera Strait	
Gulf of Corinth	*Korinthiakos*
Saronic Gulf	*Saronikos*

* Recently the Hydrographer of the Royal Greek Navy has made surveys of a number of small ports and anchorages which are now published in Greece. Many of them are helpful to yachts cruising in Greek waters. Similar plans now published by the British Admiralty are becoming available through Admiralty chart agents. The Turkish Admiralty has also established a hydrographic office, but surveys are still awaited.

E. Wind

Winds. The early Greeks associated the eight winds with certain seasonal conditions, and this phenomenon may best be summarized by the symbols carved on the octagonal marble Tower of the Winds standing intact below the Acropolis in Athens. It once had a water clock and a sundial. Its eight sides still face the important points of the compass, each being portrayed by a carved figure symbolic of the eight winds:

N
Boreas
now called
Tramontána
or *Vórias*

the violent piercing north wind: a bearded old man well wrapped and booted, holding high the hood of his cloak.

N.E.
Kaika
now called
Grégo or
Vorio
Anatolikós

the north-east wind, so cold on the Attic coast. The olives falling from the old man's charger depict the unfriendly nature of this wind to the vital Athenian fruit crop.

E.
Ageliotes
now called
Levánte or
Anatolikós

the more kindly east wind is portrayed by a handsome youth carrying the various species of fruit favoured by this wind.

S.E.
Euros
now called
Souróko or
Nótio Anatolikós

the frequently stormy south-east wind represented by an old man.

S.
Notos
now called
Ostra or
Nótios

the south wind—an unhappy clouded head, implying heat and damp. The fact that the figure is emptying a water-jug implies that the wind brings heavy showers and sultry weather.

S.W.

Libs	the south-west wind so unfavourable to vessels leaving Athens. A strong
now called	severe-looking man is pushing before him the prow of a ship.
Garbís or	
Nótio Ditikós	

W.

Zephyros	the soft and kindly west wind, represented by a lightly-clad youth carrying
now called	flowers and blossom, and gliding along contentedly.
Pounénte or	
Ditikós	

N.W.

Schiron	the dry north-west wind: a robust bearded little man, wrapped and booted,
now called	pouring water from a vase to denote the occasional rain from that quarter.
Maístro or	
Vório Ditikós	

During the last few centuries evidence from ships' narratives reveals that the Greek pilots had almost no logical understanding of changes in weather. Their predictions were invariably dictated by certain changes in shrubs, plants and other omens, e.g., certain pilots believed that the first appearance of the eggplant was followed by a north-easter of some continuance. If at sea when confronted with foul winds they would always seek shelter, having too great a deference for the elements to think of contending against them.

Not only do seafaring Greeks use the Italian names for most of their winds, nowadays they also box the compass in Italian; this is a legacy from the Venetians.

The Prevailing Summer Wind, so often referred to in this book, is the Meltemi ('Etesian' wind in British *Sailing Directions*). According to Herodotus it begins with the 'Rising of the Dog Star' and continues until the end of the summer. It may be expected to begin therefore, in early July and to continue sometimes until the middle of September. Caused by the low-pressure area over Cyprus and the Middle East, this wind has a mean direction between N.W. and north, except in the Turkish Gulfs, Kithera Channels and towards Rhodes where it blows almost west. It may be expected to start each day towards noon, reaching a velocity of force 5 to 6 and sometimes 7 by afternoon, and falling off towards evening. Quite often, without warning, it blows all night without diminishing in strength. When these conditions obtain, the wind on the Anatolian coast suddenly veers to N.N.E. during the hours of darkness. The Meltemi blows with the greatest strength from the middle of the Aegean towards the south. In the extreme north this wind is light, and in some northern areas a light sea-breeze is drawn in from the south.

The tall islands, which might be expected to form a lee for a sailing yacht working to windward, do not help, for the wind is always more violent under the mountainous coast than it is a few miles off. Certain islands, Andros and Amorgos for example, develop a heavy cloud formation over the mountains, an indication of strong north winds.

Summer Anchorages, July to early September, are therefore on the southern or south-eastern side of the islands, and though often open to the south, there is small risk during these months of the wind suddenly shifting in that direction. Vessels with power, wishing to work northwards, often start at night or early morning when the sea has gone down, and continue their passage until the Meltemi begins to impede their progress the following afternoon.

Other Seasons. In May and June there are usually light variable winds, also after the Meltemi season in the latter part of September and early October, when there are often pleasant sailing breezes. After the Autumn months, gales from N.E. and from S. and S.E. in December, January and February. Though nowadays many of the caiques take their chance of putting to sea during this period they formerly laid up, and in Venetian times vessels were actually fined for attempting to return home during the winter season.

Tides and Seiches. Admiralty predictions indicate a maximum rise of a few inches at some places to $2\frac{1}{2}$ ft at others. The level of the water is far more in-fluenced by wind and seasonal conditions than by tide and, therefore, for practical purposes tide need not be considered.

It is necessary to watch the sea level during a strong wind of long duration, and to bear in mind that in certain gulfs in the Northern Aegean the sea level during winter months may drop at least $2\frac{1}{2}$ ft and remain at this level for many weeks.

In places where violent squalls sweep down from the mountains miniature 'tidal waves' or Seiches may be formed; the surge from this is apt to sweep round the quay and call for some attention to a yacht's stern warps.

Currents. There is a general trend of current from north to south; in light settled weather it is very slight, but with strong sustained northerly winds it may start running with a maximum velocity up to 5 or 6 knots in certain channels—especially Doro and Kea, and between Andros and Tinos.

Only in the rare event of a strong southerly wind in the Autumn is this current likely to be reversed.

There is a gentle north-going stream setting up the southern part of the

Turkish Anatolian coast. This meets the general southgoing stream in the area north of Kos and the junction of the two currents is believed to have deposited the sand which has gradually raised the fringes of the Turkish coast and silted Kos harbour.

Taxation in Greek Waters. There are two long-standing laws imposing tax on·yachts under foreign flag based in Greek waters. So far these taxes have never been imposed. A communication from the Director of the National Tourist Organization dated 11 March 1974, reference No. 509945, addressed to the Author stated that the Greek government was 'seriously considering' suspending these laws. Owners of foreign-registered yachts intending to make their base in Greek waters should write to their own Consulate at the Piraeus to ascertain what the current position is.

Laying-up Ports and Repairs. Yachts normally stay afloat during the winter months and may be moored by arrangement with the local authority.

Near Piraeus are the two large marinas: Zea 350 yachts, and Vouliagmeni, 9 miles southward, 110 yachts. There are, however, possibilities of wintering in safety at certain inlets elsewhere, e.g., at the islands of Spetsai, Poros and Rhodes; also at Volos and Porto Cheli, but at some of these places facilities for repair work can be very limited.

At the Piraeus ports refitting and slipping facilities are close at hand at Perama; but most foreigners being unable to speak Greek have to employ the services of an agent. Arrangements may also be made for receiving yacht stores from England without paying duty. A modern repair yard, 'Olympic Yachts S.A.' has been established at the northern end of Gaidaromandri (Postal address, Lavrion). They are also yacht charterers. Their head office is at Zea Marina (Tel. 45/0211), General Manager, an American, many of whose staff speak English. Yachts and ships' boats are constructed in GRP; repairs, hauling out and winter-storage of yachts is undertaken, both ashore and afloat. (See details under individual ports listed.)

Running Repairs. During a cruise it may be necessary to make good some misfortune which is beyond the scope of ship's resources. It is then a matter of chance whether or not outside help can be obtained. At many islands and small ports there is a boatbuilder, or a joiner's shop, or a mechanic in the village willing to help.

Ships' Mails. It is usually quite safe for a yacht to arrange for mails to be directed care of the Harbour Master at any major port of call.

Berthing in Greek Ports. Normally yachts berth with an anchor laid out to seaward and stern to the quay. Some form of gang-plank is desirable, and a dinghy slung in stern davits can be a hindrance.

This method of securing has certain advantages: the yacht's side does not get rubbed by the quay; one has some privacy from the gaze of onlookers; but perhaps more important still, one is less likely to be invaded by cockroaches or other vermin which sometimes frequent the quayside. In this unfortunate eventuality, the only successful way to eliminate the pest is to purchase 'Fumite' tablets made by Waeco Ltd, of Salisbury, Wilts. Seal all apertures, ignite the tablets as directed and leave the yacht for 24 hours.

Cockpit awnings and side-curtains are essential, not only to protect the crew from the burning rays of the sun, but also to shield them from the gaze of the idlers on the quayside.

Greek Nautical Terms: almost all of Italian origin.

Karína	Keel	Lagouthéra	Tiller
Plóri	Bow	Lásca	Pay out
Prími	Stern	Víra	Haul in
Kouvérta	Deck	Flókos	Jib
Taboúkio	Coach roof	Mezzána	Mizzen
Albouro	Mast	Paní	Mainsail
Bastóuni	Bowsprit	Mandári	Halyard
Mátsa	Boom	Aristerá	Port
Timóni	Helm	Dexiá	Starboard

Turkish nautical terms are given in 'Introduction to Turkish Waters', p. 83.

Chartering. The Greek government has decided to enforce Law No. 469 of March 1969 which forbids yachts wearing foreign flags to charter or otherwise engage in trade in Greek territorial waters. Many charter firms are advertised, but Nauticlub of 6 Venezelou, Athens 134, who charter Dufour yachts, has been recommended (1973). There is also Olympic Yachts, who build 'Carter 32s'. The Greek Tourist Organisation recommends Captain Louis, 4 Valaoritou Street, Athens 134.

Cost of Living. The cost of repairs, laying up, food, etc., comes no longer within the term modest, for Greece like other west European countries has been caught by inflation. At the end of 1973 prices of many commodities had more than doubled within a few months.

I

Western Approaches to the Aegean

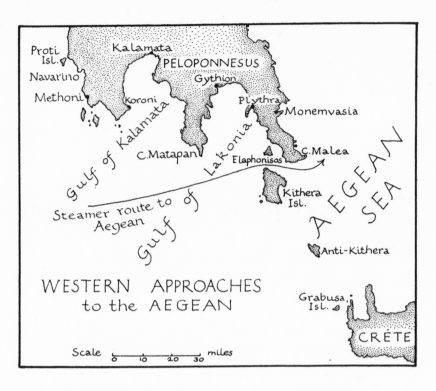

WESTERN APPROACHES
to the AEGEAN

Scale 0 10 20 30 miles

NAVARINO TO KALAMATA

Navarino Bay (Navarin)
Pylos
Methoni
Island of Sapienza

GULF OF KALAMATA or MESSINIAKOS

Koroni
Kalamata

THE MANI

Limeni
Mezapo
Gerolimena

GULF OF LAKONIA

Asamato Cove
Vathi
Port Kaio

Kolokithia Bay
Meligani
Solitare
Nymphi
Kotronas
Skutari Bay
Gythion
Xyli Bay
Plythra
Island of Elaphonisos
Poriki Lagoon
Vatica Bay
Vrakhonisos Petri

Island of Kithera
    St Nikolo
    Kapsali Bay
    Makri Cove
    Panaghia

Island of Anti-Kithera
    Port Potamo

I

Western Approaches to the Aegean

From the southern shores of the Peloponnesus protrude three peninsulas forming the Gulfs of Messenia (or Kalamata) and Lakonia. Each gulf is of interest both for places of antiquity and for the few sheltered anchorages from which a shore excursion can be made.

This region is apt to be afflicted with boisterous weather and, especially in the case of a sailing yacht, it may therefore be useful to have full information on available shelter in the event of an emergency. Though north-westerly weather is usually associated with this area during the summer months, easterly or south-easterly gales sometimes occur in the spring, and it is then that a good port of refuge should be kept in mind.

NAVARINO TO KALAMATA

A vessel approaching from the west and suddenly encountering adverse weather when south of the Pelopponesus would be well advised to make for Navarino if possible. This large bay is easy of access in bad weather and its sheltered small port of Pylos is of great historical interest.

Navarino Bay is sometimes used by British liners embarking Greek emigrants for Australia; they are brought to Pylos by road from Athens.

Pylos. Chart 211

Approach and Berth. On entering the bay, head for the extremity of Pylos breakwater—no difficulty day or night. Now turn into the port and lay out anchor to S.E. hauling in the stern to the mole. With easterly gales strong gusts sweep down the hilly slopes but the holding is good and the sea undisturbed. Only with S.W. gales is there a swell.

Facilities. There is a fresh water tap near the extremity of the mole, a number of fresh provision shops, one or two bars and restaurants and an attractive small modern hotel. Bus communications with Athens.

Earlier History. The earliest event recorded by Thucydides in his history of the Peloponnesian War was the 'Sphacteria Incident' in 425 B.C., when a small Athenian naval contingent under Demosthenes was left at Navarino as a thorn in the flesh of Sparta. But Spartan soldiers soon occupied the land around and besieged Demosthenes for some months in the heights of

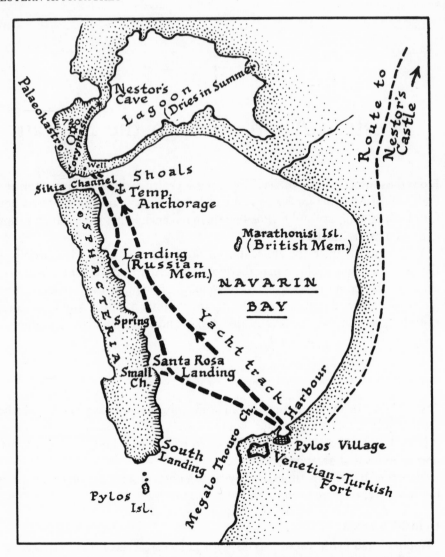

the Coryphasium peninsula. With the arrival of the main Athenian expedition, the besieging Spartans were themselves overwhelmed and a victorious fleet returned to Athens.

To investigate the scene of this early operation, one must proceed with the yacht to the sandy shore close to the shallow Sikia Channel, and anchor off the ancient port of Coryphasium, whose mole can still be discerned disappearing among the rushes into the sand. From here a mule track ascends the 700-ft hill to the fortress on Palaeokastro. This was where Demosthenes detached himself from the Athenian expeditionary force bound for Syracuse and, having seized this peninsula with half a dozen triremes, set himself up for the summer months to defy the besieging Spartans. Standing on the top today one looks down on the shallow channel where Demosthenes once sheltered his small squadron.

The existing fortress is of medieval construction, with battlemented walls in good preservation. From here there is also a magnificent view across the large semicircular bay of Navarino towards the green undulating country beyond.

Descending the steep northern slope, one soon comes to the stalactite cave where Hermes was reputed to have hidden the cattle he had stolen from Apollo. Inside the cave, when the cloud of bats has scattered, the glistening sides become visible, lit by a shaft of light from a hole high up in a domed roof giving a cathedral-like effect. By going on down from the cave and proceeding along the shore by the dried-up lagoon one soon reaches the starting point.

It is impossible to anchor off the steep cliffs of Sphacteria, and one can only land by dinghy at 'Russian Cove' while the yacht is anchored elsewhere. From here a track ascends to the northern one of the three peaks. This had been the Spartan stronghold until the return of the Athenian fleet from Syracuse when the tables were turned and the besiegers became the besieged. Demosthenes effected a landing, cut off Spartan supplies and eventually forced the surviving garrison to surrender. This dramatic and decisive conclusion to the campaign was never forgotten by the Athenians and for six centuries the Spartan shields were exhibited at Athens. On the hilltop today is the ruin of a small fort, but it is the setting itself which brings to life the events of the narrative so vividly told by Thucydides.

In 1827 an equally dramatic event took place which led to Greece obtaining her independence. The Turkish–Egyptian army was occupying the Peloponnesus and their fleet of 82 warships was at anchor in Navarin Bay. On 20 October an allied fleet of 27 warships including French and Russian ships, all commanded by Admiral Codrington, sailed into the bay. Owing to some trigger-happy Turkish ships firing at the boats of the allied fleet, Codrington's ships opened fire and, fighting fiercely throughout the day and most of the night, sank all but 29 of the enemy.

In the square at Pylos is the memorial, with busts of Codrington and his allied admirals, and on the island of Sphacteria, at Panagoulas, and on the islet of Chelonaki (Marathonisi) are small obelisks or modern plaques to commemorate the dead sailors of the French, Russian and British fleets respectively.

Treasure-seekers have made repeated attempts to work on these wrecks, and in 1913 a salvage operation having located some of the remains of 43 ships achieved no results. They had hoped to recover a portion of the 2,000 guns (half of them bronze) and some of the gold and jewellery from the Turkish and Egyptian flagships. Nowadays skin-divers report that the wrecks are largely buried in mud. Peter Throckmorton, an American marine archaeologist and diver, examined the bottom in 1961 and reported finding only 8 wrecks, all at depths of about 165 ft; their frames were all that protruded above the soft mud and the remainder of the Turkish fleet appeared to be completely buried.

> Wedges of gold, great anchors, heaps of pearl,
> Inestimable stones, unvalued jewels,
> All scatter'd in the bottom of the sea;
> Shakespeare, King Richard III.

Apart from a well-preserved Turkish fort at the entrance to the bay, there is one further ancient site that should not be missed. This is Nestor's palace of about 1200 B.C., the foundations of which have only recently been excavated by Professor Blegen; it was here that many of the famous Linear B tablets were discovered. The museum at the Khora has many objects from the palace and other sites near by.

Eight miles southward from Navarino is the south-westerly point of the Peloponnesus with the remains of a Venetian port, Methoni, behind it.

Methoni lies in a shallow bay, inadequately protected by a breakwater, with a modern village close by. A massive Venetian fortress jutting into the sea dominates the port. (See photograph, fac. p. 8.)

The ancient walls of Methoni and Sapienza Island beyond

Approach and Berth. Charts 719 and 682 show there are no difficulties day or night. After rounding the extremity of the breakwater the sea-bed rises very quickly. The most conspicuous object by day, not clearly shown on the chart, is the large Turkish tower on the southern point of the fortress. In fair weather only, a yacht may berth stern to the small quay 20 yds inside the mole with anchor laid out to the northward; the depths here are 10 ft— it may be preferable to anchor off, with the same shelter, in 2½ fathoms where there is good holding and sufficient swinging room. Bottom is thin weed on sand and there are a few stones. A swell works round the end of the mole and in bad weather from the south the place would be untenable.

In order to land at the castle or approach the village, one has to walk along the very rough 150-yd mole or land by dinghy at a small mole to the N.E., used by fishing craft.

Port Facilities. Fresh water and fuel laid on to a small quay near the mole-head were reported as being unserviceable in 1975. The village, rather dull and without character, now has a small tourist hotel and two cafés on the seafront where a fine sandy beach attracts a number of tourists in the summer months. They usually arrive by car via Pylos.

The vast Venetian fortress is worth a visit. Although within the walls today no building of interest remains, in 1770, when it was manned by 6,000 Turks, it played its last active role by cutting off the supply route to a Russian fleet which had based itself at Navarino. Sorties against the fortress by Russian sailors supported by Greek troops were unsuccessful and eventually the Russians were compelled to abandon their base.

In Venetian days this was one of the 'Eyes of the Republic' and because of its strategic position it became a relatively large port.

From the top of the Adriatic where 'Venice sat in state, throned on her hundred isles' the Pilgrim galleys under naval escort made voyages every year to the Holy Land. Methoni, which lay across their route, was invariably a port of call where oarsmen were rested and the vessels replenished with food and water before continuing the voyage via Hania, in Crete, on their passage to the Levant.

Island of Sapienza. Port Longo is a suitable anchorage in S. and W. winds, and should be approached by the S. Channel. The southern part of the port is sandy and affords the best holding near a beach where the lighthouse keepers haul up their boats, and where a path leads to a fresh water spring. The island is uninhabited. Four wrecks, one an Austrian brig, were recently discovered at the side of the cove by American divers. The wrecks are well clear of the anchorage.

In the 17th century, sailing ships from England sometimes called here, and anchoring under the lee of Sapienza Island refilled their water casks at Methoni. A warning in John Seller's *English Pilot* of 1677 states: 'Those that ride there must be sure to keep good watching lest your rigging and ropes be cut, for the Inhabitants of the place are very Thieves.'

It now seems unbelievable that in the middle of the last century the British Government seriously contested the rightful ownership of this insignificant island. They maintained that Sapienza, having been a former Venetian possession, must be surrendered to Britain. Largely due to the determined efforts of Colonel Leake, a distinguished traveller and Hellenophile, this claim was eventually dropped.

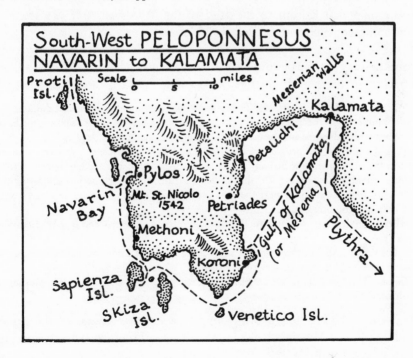

GULF OF KALAMATA (MESSINIAKOS)

Proceeding eastwards and passing beyond Venetico Island one enters the wide Gulf of Kalamata or Messiniakos. To the north-east and round the next headland is the other 'Eye of the Republic': **Koroni**—an elevated, walled city overlooking the port with a reasonably sheltered anchorage behind a mole.

> **Approach and Berth.** Chart 719, with a small inset of the anchorage, shows the approach quite clearly by day or night. The fortress walls and bastions are visible a great distance off. 100 yds off the southern shore and up to 70 yds from the breakwater the bottom is short weed and sand. Farther out, and west of the extremity of the mole, there are some rock slabs.
>
> The anchorage is slightly exposed to the afternoon day breeze from the north-west which may make boat landing rather a wet undertaking.
>
> **Port Facilities.** These are few, there being only one or two shops for provisions and a good taverna on the water-front. Ice available in the main street.

The Venetian fortress, standing on the hill overlooking the village and port, is interesting to explore. The convent occupying part of the summit is inhabited by some nuns, who take great interest in maintaining a colourful flower garden.

An interesting excursion is a 20-minute drive through beautiful country to Petriades village. This is almost the only place in Greece where in the summer months the large 'Ali Baba' jars (amphorae) are made by hand without the aid of a potter's wheel.

Continuing past Koroni to the head of the Messenian Gulf you reach the largest commercial port of the Peloponnesus.

Kalamata is a very busy place in the Autumn months, when nearly three hundred steamers call to carry away the figs and currants.

> **Approach and Berth.** Chart 719. The town is easily distinguishable against the hinterland by day; but at night the harbour lights can be seen at only half the distance claimed. The port has recently been dredged and the quays improved. The inner basin is clean and well-sheltered, and the town of 50,000 people, reached by a frequent bus service, is a quarter of an hour distant. It has an interesting artisan quarter, some good shops and a small modern hotel.
>
> After entering the port, a yacht should make for the north-west corner and berth in the basin with stern to the quay near the port office. Mud bottom, and depths of 28 ft nearly everywhere—good shelter.
>
> **Facilities.** Fresh water, which is good, is laid on to the quay. Petrol and fuel oil are available close by.
>
> A bus runs to Athens, three times a day, taking 10 hrs. A fast train takes about the same time. There is also a daily air service to Athens.
>
> **Officials.** This is a Port of Entry. Harbour Authority, Customs, Police, Immigration and Health.

A 40-minute drive inland brings one to a lengthy section of the massive walled defences of Messene. Raised against invasion by their hereditary enemy,

1   The tower at Methoni, Peloponnesus. *See p. 6*

2   The harbour, Idra. *See p. 27*

3 The Corinth Canal. *See p.* 32

4 Zea Marina, Piraeus. *See p.* 34

the Spartans, in the middle of the 4th century B.C., these battlements, with their towers and gates still erect, can be followed on foot for a considerable distance over the hills. Despite earthquakes, these huge pieces of stone, neatly pieced together, mostly retain their perfect bonding today.

THE MANI

On the eastern shores of the Messenian Gulf is the rugged and largely barren coast of the tall Mani Peninsula. Its mountain ranges ascend to nearly 8,000 ft and exert a dominating influence on the winds inside these two gulfs. At the southern tip of the peninsula is the insignificant Cape Matapan (Ténaron to the Greeks). The eastern shores are inhospitable, and though Limeni is claimed to be a port for yachts, it is impossible to lie there comfortably in westerly winds. (See map page 11.)

From Limeni southwards a number of unusual villages with prominent square towers can sometimes be seen from seaward on the hill slopes. This is the country of the Deep Mani and these Nyklian towers were built from about 1600 onwards until the close of the 18th century. They were feudal strongholds built by the descendants of the former Nyklian families who came to the under-populated Mani country on the destruction of their own city, Nykli, in Arcadia, in 1295.

The towers, it seems, first grew up after the new settlers had occupied this lean and partially arable land. Refugees frequently entering, naturally sought land for themselves, and since it became largely a question of survival, the original settlers built these novel defences to deny further incursions on the land and into the villages. Usually of three stories, these towers may be seen both as a protection for the soil in the open country and for guarding the peri-meters of villages. Because of the local vendettas, the village towers subsequently increased in number, each becoming a family stronghold. Some of them are still lived in, though in other places the whole village is largely deserted. Their appearance is more interesting than attractive. There are also a few remaining small Byzantine churches with frescoes.

The people nowadays are pleasant enough; but the traveller Wheler writing in 1675 calls them 'famous Pirates by sea, and Pestilent Robbers by land'; and Captain Beaufort a hundred and fifty years later remarks:

'In the district of Maina, the Southern province of the Morea, there is a regularly organized system of absolute and general piracy. The number of their vessels or armed row-boats fluctuates between twenty and thirty; they lurk behind the headlands and innumerable rocks of the archipelago; all flags are equally their prey, and the life or death of the captured crew is merely a matter of convenience.'

9

A few miles southward of Limeni is Pirgos with its spectacular stalactite Caves of Diros. Recently adapted for sightseers, boatmen are now provided and the caves are electrically illuminated. It is best reached by road from Gythion.

Mezapo, southward of the caves, is a small place lying in an open bay with a largely deserted village; and after rounding Cape Grosso with its impressive steep-to cliffs there is

Gerolimena, a small hamlet at the head of a little cove. Distinguished by a couple of small churches and a large yellow house, the place is provided with a quay where the mail steamer berths.

> **Berth.** In settled weather a yacht should approach the quay (5 fathoms), anchor to S.W. Secure stern to the shore.
> **Facilities** are very limited. A weekly steamer. A new road was recently completed to Gythion.

Except for Koroni and the modernized port of Kalamata, the Gulf of Kalamata is hardly worth a visit.

GULF OF LAKONIA

Rounding the uninspiring Cape Matapan one enters the Gulf of Lakonia.

To the British the name Matapan recalls the victorious battle in World War II at a time when England's strength was seriously threatened. Admiral Lord Cunningham's fleet brought the Italians to battle in a night action about 100 miles S.W. of Cape Matapan, successfully disabling one modern battleship, sinking 3 armoured cruisers and 2 destroyers for the loss of one aircraft.

There are some attractive places on the mountainous steep-to Mani shores, but apart from one or two coves shown in the plans on Chart 712 there are hardly any safe places to leave a sailing yacht for more than an hour or two. This is largely on account of the squalls which may at any time descend with violence from the steep Mani ranges above. Off this shore during spring and early summer the wind normally sets in from W. to S.W. at about 1100 with considerable strength, and falls off in the evening.

Asamato Cove is comfortable in settled weather, when a yacht should anchor in the north-west corner of the bay with a warp to the shore. The bottom here is inconveniently deep and shelves quickly. There is only a fisherman's hut at the head of the creek. This cove is less subject to squalls than other places in this area.

Vathi is a deep-cut inlet often claimed to be better than Asamato, though subject to violent squalls in westerly winds.

Port Kaio. Chart 712, plan. This is the best shelter near Matapan. Usually a yacht anchors in the southern creek in 5 fathoms on a sandy bottom, where there is plenty of room to swing and the holding appears good; but being open to N.E. it is sometimes advisable during adverse conditions to shelter in the northern creek close under the conspicuous monastery on the hillside.

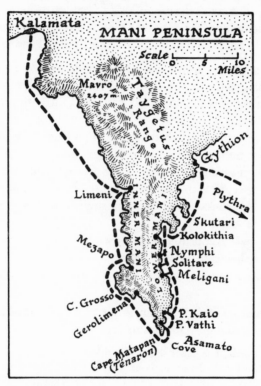

A short quay and a still shorter mole have recently been built in the S.E. corner; the 4-ft depths at the mole-head enable a yacht to run out a stern warp when anchored off, and to make use of a little shelter when landing in the dinghy.

The 'towered' village, some 20 minutes' walk up the hill, is hardly worth the ascent, for most of the houses are deserted and what remains is indescribably poor. The monastery on the opposite shore is also deserted. Half an hour's walk takes one to the village of Marmari; here is a very small chapel with 17th-century frescoes. The walk to the lighthouse takes an hour: the famous cave—the entrance to Hades—nearby is reached by following a goat-track passing through the low scrub which covers most of the hillside.

In this wild, open country thousands of quail may sometimes be seen. In April they are northbound, often calling at Aegean islands. In September they may be seen taking off for Africa, preferring to make the 200-mile sea-flight at night.

Continuing northwards and following the high rugged coast one soon reaches

Kolokithia Bay. One notices some delightful green slopes and attractive valleys, yet there are no places, with the exception of Gythion, where one would dare to leave a sailing yacht at anchor for more than an hour or two unless the weather was very settled. The following places are mostly small and rather exposed:

Meligani—a small bay, with a few houses, open to the east.

Solitare—similar to the above, but more used by small caiques.

Nymphi—a narrow rocky inlet 150 yds long and with an open beach, and open only to the east.

Kotronas lies in a most delightful setting in a small bay with a quay (6 ft); anchorage is in 5 fathoms; close in there are stones on the bottom. Ashore there are a few houses and a taverna—a few fishing boats use the place. As this anchorage is so susceptible to the violent gusts from the hills, a small quay has been built into the rocks about 400 yds southwards, where caiques usually anchor for better shelter.

Skutari Bay (Chart 712, plan) has lovely scenery, but there is no safe anchorage for a yacht—it is liable to strong mountain gusts, especially from the west. Fisherman's Cove is the only anchorage, in 3 fathoms, on a sandy bottom.

Gythion (Gyithion). Chart 712, plan. A pleasant deserted old port with a small town—useful for making excursions to Sparta and Mistra.

> **Approach and Berth.** The Chart shows that there are no difficulties day or night, and a yacht should make for the Inner Harbour. Secure stern to the mole with anchor to the westward in depths of 2 fathoms—bottom is firm clay. Though the harbour appears to be reasonably sheltered it can in fact be dangerous for a vessel to lie here during strong northwest winds on account of the violent gusts from the Taygetus Mountains. Easterly winds bring in a swell.
>
> **Port Facilities.** Fresh water of poor quality is available by hydrant from the quay. Diesel fuel is also obtainable from the quay and petrol from Shell on the quayside. There are ample provision shops with fruit and vegetables; two or three old-fashioned hotels and two restaurants. The Piraeus steamer calls twice a week; there is a daily bus to Athens (8 hrs) and two or three buses a day to Sparta.

Although the principal port of the province, the population of Gythion (about 7,000) is still declining, there being little employment here and in the neighbourhood. Many Greek tourists come for the bathing in the summer months.

The sea walls of the ancient port may be seen underwater off the outflow of the stream north of the town.

A newly constructed road, passing over the mountains and through attractive green cultivated country, enables buses to reach Sparta in an hour. This is a modern town of little interest; but Mistra, 15 minutes further, is a most interesting Byzantine city standing under the Taygetus ranges, with many churches and convents still in good order. It is well worth a whole day's visit.

Plythra, the port of Xyli Bay, is shown on Chart 712. Protected by a long breakwater it is a dreary, barren little place. (See map page 15.)

Approach and Berth. The depth off the breakwater in the approach channel is 12 ft and the bottom uneven rocks. By night a hand lantern is exhibited on the mole-head. Berth not more than 30 yds inside the mole-head with stern to quay, bows northward. Bottom is uneven rock, boulders and gravel. Above- and below-water rocks lie only 60 yds north of the mole. It is not a safe harbour.

Facilities. Very limited provisions to be bought at the hamlet. A 4-ton crane is available. No good fresh water close by. There is the Government Pavilion for a few tourists in summer. Buses run daily to Sparta.

The port was constructed for the shipment of figs from the hinterland and is used in the autumn months. The ancient town lies submerged near the root of the mole.

Island of Elaphonisos, only 12 miles farther south, has its village on the eastern end of the boat channel. A fine lagoon is formed on the island's western side by a low line of rocks (Poriki) sheltering the anchorage from all weather except strong westerly winds, but there is nothing of interest ashore.

Vatica Bay, throughout history, has provided shelter during hostilities for the warships of every nation endeavouring to control the western approaches to the Aegean; in early days Roman and Venetian galleys were stationed here, and in each of the recent World Wars both British and German patrol vessels. Neapolis, a large village on the north-eastern corner, is a calling place for the steamer; it affords but little shelter for a yacht although recently a pier has been built. In fact, except for an excellent lee close under its shores, especially in Vrakhonisos Petri (N.W. corner), this bay is not recommended for a yacht under normal conditions. (This anchorage is described in *The Ionian Islands to Rhodes* supplement.)

South of Elaphonisos Island is the 4½-mile wide Elaphonisos Channel separating it from Kithera Island. This channel provides the main route for vessels entering the Aegean from the west.

> *Forsaken isle! around thy barren shore*
> *Wild tempests howl and wintry surges roar.*
> WRIGHT (*Horae Ionicae*, 1807)

Island of Kithera

is mountainous and steep-to with a barren-looking coast. There are two sheltered bays: St Nikolo (Avlemona) on the south-eastern corner of the island, and Kapsali Bay with the Chora (capital or main village) on the south coast. Plans are given on Chart 712.

There are also two places of shelter on the north-east coast, suitable only under favourable conditions: Panaghia with its 100-yd breakwater and the sandy lagoon of Makri sheltered by an islet. (Details—see *The Ionian Islands to Rhodes*.)

St Nikolo (Ayios Nikolaos) is a name unknown to local Greeks, who call the place **Avlemona.** This is the safest harbour in the island, sheltered in all weather, though open to southerly swell.

> **Berth.** A small quay with depths of 3 fathoms is sometimes occupied by caiques, otherwise it is the most suitable place for securing a yacht's sternfast, with her anchor laid out to the southward. The basins are small, there is swinging room if desiring to anchor in the outer basin in depths of 3 or 4 fathoms.

Though the configuration of the port is attractive, the barrenness of the surrounding country and the poor decaying hamlet make no appeal for a visiting yacht.

There was an occasion, however, in Nelson's day when the approach to this little harbour was causing much concern:

> On 17 September 1802 the small brig *Mentor* conveying 17 cases of the famous Parthenon frieze was on passage to Malta; seeking shelter from a westerly gale she put in at St Nikolo Bay. Her two anchors began to drag, and in trying to make sail she cut her cables but drifted on the rocks and was holed; she sank in 60 ft close off shore, the crew managing to reach the rocky coast, all being saved. It was two years before divers from Kalimnos and Symi (whose sailors continue this vocation today) were able to complete their task, and retrieve all these cases from the wreck. Finally on 16 February 1805 the transport *Lady Shaw Stewart*, under orders of Lord Nelson, called at St Nikolo, loaded the cases and conveyed them to England.

As well as the Elgin marbles, this stormy sea had formerly taken a toll of Greek sculptures conveyed in Roman ships, many of which had been wrecked on their way to Italy. Thanks to the efforts of Greek sponge-divers in recent years a few of the Athens Museum's greatest treasures have been recovered from the sea-bed off Kithera.

Kapsali Bay. Shown in a plan on Chart 712, it lies in a mountainous setting with an anchorage open to the south; it is dominated by a massive Venetian castle. The Chora (capital of the island), lies 600 ft up and is one of the most attractive little towns in Greece.

Approach and Berth. A yacht can anchor in the bay or berth behind a short breakwater extending from a rocky spur where the lighthouse stands, and where shelter is better. The new quay has a depth of only 8 ft, but is useful for securing a sternfast when the yacht has laid out an anchor to the westward. The sea bottom in the anchorage is sand, but near the quay among patches of sand are loose rock and stones, giving uncertain holding. The bay is susceptible to swell, and untenable in Sirocco winds. In the summer months westerly winds predominate, with an occasional spell of north-easterly weather.

Port Facilities. Fresh water, which is good, is available from a tap and also from a hydrant at the quay. Here also is a pump for diesel fuel. Fuel can be bought in the port which consists only of a few houses; limited provisions can also be bought, but for greater demands one must go to the main village.

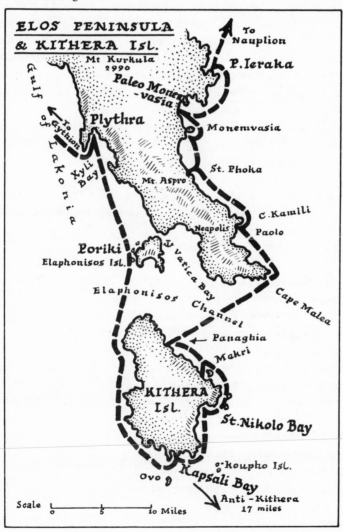

The Chora, a full half hour's walk up a steep hill, lies in a commanding position beyond the Venetian castle. Its winding, fascinating streets with well-stocked shops are remarkably clean and neat. Good fish, including crawfish, are often obtainable there and in the port; there is a modest hotel and restaurant. People are friendly everywhere and tourists unknown. There are one or two motor-drives to the other villages in the centre of the island.

The island continues to export some palatable retsina for which it was once famous.

The Piraeus steamer calls twice a week. For many years there has been a meteorological station here, and one may still obtain a useful forecast.

In earlier days this island was regarded as a watch-post for the Gateway to the Aegean. After the Napoleonic wars Kithera, together with the Ionian Islands, was ceded to Britain, and was garrisoned by a small detachment under a subaltern's command. The garrison was relieved every six months, it being considered 'a very lonely station'. Some English cannon, a bridge and a few graves are the only remains of this British occupation.

Though caiques and small mail-boats sometimes land passengers at Makri* Cove and at Panaghia (Pelayia) on the east coast, neither is recommended, the former having but little interest and the latter lacking shelter.

Island of Anti-Kithera lies between Kithera and Crete. The 10-mile wide navigable channels on either side of it are used by vessels proceeding in the direction of Crete.

Port Potamo with its small hamlet is shown on Chart 712, but few vessels call, partly because of the heavy swell created by fresh northerly winds. This small island, of no significance today, was much in the news about Easter 1900 when a sponge-boat returning to Symi discovered the wreck of a Roman vessel close S.S.E. of Potamos. This resulted in the National Museum of Athens acquiring some of their finest 4th-century B.C. bronze statues, marble figures, pottery and glass.

The sponge-boat, returning to her home port of Symi, had been driven off course and was sheltering under the lee of Anti-Kithera. The divers decided to examine the bottom in case there might be sponges. Instead of sponges they were astonished to find statuary, and had the good sense to get in touch with archaeologists in Athens. After some months' work, diving in depths of more than 30 fathoms, several statues and other relics were recovered. The site was then abandoned and was not re-examined until 1952 when Cousteau and his divers arrived. Meanwhile, the salved objects, now in Athens, were awaiting analysis

---

* Description and plan see *The Ionian Islands to Rhodes* by H. M. Denham.

by modern methods, which revealed interesting facts: though some of the statues were of the 4th century B.C., others proved to be copies. One of the more remarkable finds was parts of an astronomical clock which, by careful decipherment of the inscriptions, was partially reconstructed.

The vessel herself was judged to have been about 300 tons burden; her underwater planking was of elm, which by carbon analysis of the small piece recovered, dates the tree from which it was formed to be between 180 and 260 B.C.; she was copper fastened and lead sheathed. None of her lead anchor stocks, although recovered by divers, ever reached Athens.*

Five miles N.W. of Anti-Kithera are some rocky islets. One, named Nautilus Rock, is so called in memory of H.M.S. *Nautilus* wrecked during the dark hours on the morning of 3 January 1807. This frigate was carrying important despatches from the C-in-C to the Admiralty and, running before a strong N. wind, had in the darkness mistaken the silhouette of the islets for part of Anti-Kithera Island. She altered course to the west and so ran hard up upon the rocks. The ship soon began to break up and of her crew of 122 only 64 survived. The story of their great privations on the islet makes harrowing reading, and inspired Byron to write:

> . . . *and you might have seen*
> *The longings of the cannibal arise*
> *(although they spoke not) in their wolfish eyes.*

* See *Shipwrecks and Archaeology* by Peter Throckmorton, Boston, 1970.

CHAPTER TWO

Cape Malea

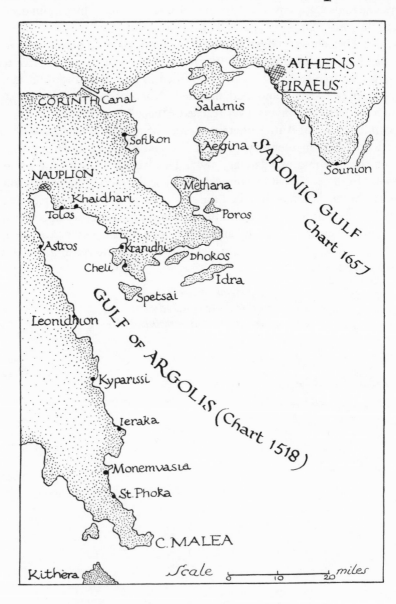

ATHENS
PIRAEUS

CORINTH Canal

Salamis

Sofikon

Aegina

SARONIC GULF
Chart 1657

Sounion

NAUPLION

Methana

Khaidhari

Poros

Tolos

Astros

Kranidhi

Dhokos

Cheli

Idra

Spetsai

Leonidhion

GULF OF ARGOLIS (Chart 1518)

Kyparissi

Ieraka

Monemvasia

St. Phoka

C. MALEA

Kithera

Scale   0   10   20 miles

to Sounion

2

Cape Malea to Sounion

CAPE MALEA TO THE GULF OF ARGOLIS

Slowly sinks more lovely ere his race be run
Along Morea's hills, the setting sun;
Not, as in Northern climes, obscurely bright,
But one unclouded blaze of living light.

BYRON

CAPE MALEA

This bold mountainous headland rising to nearly 2,000 ft forms the turning point into the Aegean. Completely isolated and standing on the hillside close westward a few hundred feet above the sea stands a low, white monastery now inhabited by half a dozen nuns.

With westerly winds the cape should be rounded at least a mile off, especially when turning northwards towards the Gulf of Argolis.

This noble headland makes a profound impression, and to the ancient Greek sailors on a long voyage to some distant colony it was perhaps the last they were to see of their own country for many months to come. 'Round Malea and forget your native country' was the saying attributed to these early sailors. Many centuries later, shortly after the hey-day of Venice, small vessels of the British Levant Company,* after a voyage of 6 or 7 weeks from England, used, in their turn, to round this Cape into the Aegean. Shipping cargoes mainly at Constantinople and Smyrna, they also visited the Port of Lions (Piraeus) and Monemvasia; but the Aegean islands, except perhaps Chios, were of no interest for trading purposes. Having entered the 'Arches' (a corruption of archipelago) they called at Milos for a pilot, and sometimes an armed naval escort, for the Aegean was then a hunting-ground for pirates.

Today the shipping activity off Cape Malea is nothing compared with that off such headlands as St Vincent and Europa Point.

---

* The French, more successful in the Levant, had as many as 700 vessels in this trade shortly before the Napoleonic Wars.

From Cape Malea northwards a 2,000-ft mountainous spur stands steeply above the coast; the foothills are partially cultivated. There are some small villages concealed in the valleys. Only indifferent shelter can be found before reaching Monemvasia and Ieraka.

Port Paolo lies 1½ miles W.S.W. from Cape Kamili. It is a very small fishing cove with 12-ft depths protected by a 50-yd mole extending in a southerly direction from the northern shore; a very small white church at the root of the mole makes an excellent sea mark. The cove should be used only in settled weather, and it is susceptible to an easterly swell. There is no habitation apart from a small farm and the hamlet 2 or 3 miles distant. Except for some cultivated valleys and noble mountains there is nothing of particular interest.

St Phoka is 5 miles south of Monemvasia, and consists of a very small inlet behind an islet. It can be recognized from seaward by the few houses of the hamlet, and the islet by its small church. The approach is in a north-westerly direction, leaving the islet with its protruding underwater rocks to starboard. The channel is narrow with 2-fathom depths, and on no account should a vessel attempt to enter in the event of an easterly swell, which can be seen breaking on the rocks. Within the inlet there is just room to swing in 2 fathoms.

Monemvasia. A small Gibraltar-like headland is joined to the mainland by a causeway. This acts as a breakwater and affords temporary anchorage either north or south according to the weather.

>**Anchorage.** Chart 712. Either side the holding is poor, but the most convenient place to anchor is 80 yds from the western shore and 80 yds from the bridge. The bottom here is flat rock with sandy patches and small boulders in a depth of 7 fathoms. In the event of unsettled weather it is advisable to anchor in the bay of Paleo Monemvasia 2½ miles northward.
>**Facilities.** The stone landing-pier at the eastern end of the Causeway leads to the new village of over a thousand people. Here there are shops with fresh provisions, wine, post office and ice store. Water is obtainable only from cisterns in the private houses. In the Venetian village on the Rock only a few of the old houses are inhabited; but there is a restaurant for tourists and a taverna.
>
>There is a regular steamer communication with Piraeus twice weekly (7 or 8 hrs), and a daily bus service to Athens. Cruise steamers often put in here for a few hours.

The peninsula with its walled Venetian town is worth visiting, and the Byzantine church of St Sophia on the summit even more so. From here the outer walls of the fortifications are impressive and lend support to the stories of the many sieges this stronghold has withstood.

Monemvasia was also a centre of commerce famous in medieval days for its

Malmsey* wines, which were of wide repute. Here the jars of wine were assembled from places on the Morea coast and from some of the islands to await onward shipment to Western Europe, including England.

Paleo Monemvasia. A small sheltered bay with depths of 3 to 5 fathoms over an irregular smooth rock and sandy bottom. This is a much better place for a yacht than Monemvasia in unsettled weather.

> **Anchorage.** Chart 1684. The two wrecks shown on the earlier chart have probably dispersed and it is now safe to anchor anywhere convenient on a sandy bottom.
> **Facilities.** There are half-a-dozen fishermen's cottages and a small taverna where basic provisions may be obtained. A road goes to Monemvasia—an hour's walk.

Port Ieraka (Yerakas). This is the best sheltered and most pleasant port between Cape Malea and Spetsai.

> **Anchorage.** Chart 712. This is well protected by the configuration of the steep coast; the only inconvenience is the occasional down-currents of wind under certain conditions. One should anchor in 5 fathoms rather than get into lesser depths, when the bottom becomes too hard for a plough anchor to be sure of holding.

A few cottages of the hamlet line the water-front at the foot of the steep sides of the anchorage. The steamer from Piraeus calls twice a week.

Port Kyparissi. An anchorage off a small village lying in a spacious bay at the foot of steep, wooded mountains. Though open to the east and subject to strong down-draughts during westerly winds, there are convenient depths for anchoring off a small quay. This place is suitable only in settled weather.

Port Phokianos. This is a large, deep inlet in the mountainous coast with a few deserted houses at its head. It is an unsuitable anchorage.

THE GULF OF ARGOLIS

Entering the Gulf between Cape Sambateki and Spetsai, some of the small ports and anchorages only a few miles apart are of interest to a yacht.

> **Local Winds.** Under fine weather conditions the day breeze blows from the S.E. up the gulf, starting before midday. There is a light breeze beginning before dawn and lasting until about 10 o'clock, blowing down the gulf from the N.W. With fresh westerly winds the mountainous shores of the gulf are subject to down-blasts, and the coast should be passed with an offing of about 3 miles. In some of the ports at the top of the Gulf the more violent squalls may set up a series of miniature tidal waves. With a rise and fall of 1 to 2 ft they may occur at few-minute intervals and can be embarrassing to yachts secured with stern warps to a quay.

* Corruption of Monemvasia.

West Side of Gulf

Scala Leonidhion. Chart 1518. This small port for Leonidhion village has a short mole affording poor shelter. Though of no interest to yachts, the Piraeus steamer and caiques call here to collect passengers and produce from the hinterland.

Astros. A pleasant, small fishing port protected by an 80-yd mole—a good summer anchorage—and only untenable during S.E. gales.

> **Berth.** Nearly 2-fathom depths extend towards the extremity of the mole but along the water-front the harbour has largely silted. A yacht can berth stern to the quay, anchor towards the village.
> **Facilities.** Excellent water from a tap on the quay. Limited provisions.

Though only a poor little village it has a small restaurant, and a modest hotel was recently built. Daily bus service to Nauplia and Athens, and southward to Leonidhion.

A delightful half hour's drive takes one to the Byzantine monastery of Moni Loukas on the mountainside.

Nauplion lies at the head of the gulf and is a pleasant town with much of historical interest close by. Formerly a small commercial port, this place has recently become a tourist centre. The town is clean and interesting, and the port reasonably well-sheltered in the summer months. It merits a stay of two or three days.

> **Approach and Berth.** Chart 1518. The harbour is spacious and easy of access. The 'day breeze', setting in about noon, blows up the Gulf from the S.S.E. and is inclined to be gusty from the high land off the port. At night there is often a land breeze.
> During settled conditions it is convenient to berth in the eastern corner of the western basin opposite the Hotel Grand Bretagne, with stern to quay and bows N.N.W. In the event of N.W. squalls from the Arcadian Mountains it is advisable to move into the inner basin, which has recently been dredged.
> These squalls sometimes cause a surge in the port abreast the quays, when it is necessary to slacken off the stern warps.
> **Facilities.** Everything can be bought locally and the shops are close at hand. The town has recently acquired a water supply piped from the mountains. Fuel at the quay.
> The old Venetian port, Bourdzi, is no longer a smart hotel-restaurant. Modern hotels have been built, one lying on the saddle with splendid views. In the town are several other hotels and restaurants of varying category.
> **Officials.** Nauplion is a Port of Entry and consequently has the full quota of officials.

The Venetian citadel on the summit of Palamidi, approached by 857 steps, is worth the ascent, especially on a clear day when the views across the Argos

Plain are magnificent. In the town there are many houses in Venetian style and a museum of limited interest.

There are interesting day excursions by car or bus to Tiryns, Argos, Mycenae and Epidaurus; also communication by bus with Athens—a 3 hr journey.

When Greece first obtained her independence in 1832 Nauplion became for a short while the first capital of the country, Athens at this time being a village of little significance. At St Spyridon church, Capodistria, the first governor of modern Greece, was assassinated; bullet holes can still be seen by the door.

East Side of Gulf

Tolos (or Tolon). A partially sheltered anchorage protected by an island off the 'seaside' village of Tolos (Tolon).

> **Anchorage.** Many fishing boats moor off, there being no harbour; with northerly winds the anchorage is susceptible to strong gusts off the hills. There are convenient depths of about 3 fathoms with good holding about 100 yds offshore.

This village, only 12 kilometres from Nauplion, has become a minor resort with some small hotels, modest restaurants and shops.

East of the village are some ruins on the promontory. This is ancient Asine whose harbour is now silted and filled with sand; from here Agamemnon's expedition set off for Troy.

Khaidhari. A sheltered inlet near the ruins of Mezes. The sea-bed rises sharply at the head of the bay to 2 fathoms. No village—rather bleak and steep hills either side of the inlet, causing strong gusts with N.W. winds.

> **Anchorage** is off the beach, west of the houses, in 3 fathoms, sandy bottom.

Koiladhi, the port for the large village of Kranidhi, lies in a sheltered bay whose entrance is difficult to discern. Here is a small primitive village, mostly inhabited by fishermen who, after their night's fishing off the coast, land their catch at Porto Cheli, for conveyance to Athens.

> **Approach.** Kranidhi village with its white houses stands out in the distance. The small light structure, painted white and standing on the S. shore, is also conspicuous.
> **Anchorage.** The best anchorage is off the S.E. point of the village in 2 fathoms. With northerly winds a slight swell enters the port; but in his shallow anchorage holding is good and the sea breeze steady.

Port Cheli (or Kheli) is a large but shallow enclosed bay with perfect shelter. During recent years much building has taken place, new hotels and villas having spread themselves along the shores of this former unspoilt natural harbour.

Anchorage. Anchor N.E. of the village quay and swing or lay out the anchor northwards and haul in the stern. There is 10 ft depth at the quay and 2 fathoms in the middle. Fresh water is available from a tap at this quay and at the 'Fish Quay', but it is inclined to be brackish at both places. This is a safe, but remote, place to lay-up in winter.

Facilities. Local fresh water being of poor quality it is advisable to replenish from a tanker lorry. Provisions are sometimes in short supply but can be obtained from Spetsai by the ferry. Hotels and restaurants have recently grown up. A bus service operates between here and Nauplion, connecting with Epidaurus. An airport was under construction in 1973.

Archaeologists from Pennsylvania University have recently examined part of the harbour and discovered under the mud the wall defences of the 5th-century B.C. town of Halieis. By means of an ingenious device of flying a balloon with a camera triggered by a diver they were able to complete the excavation of a fortified tower.

Kosta. An open sandy bay with short jetty, it is the mainland terminal for Spetsai. People leave their motor-cars here and cross the strait ($1\frac{1}{2}$ miles) by caique to Spetsai. There is a taverna on the shore by the jetty. Excellent for bathing, and in summer a fair temporary anchorage, though the bay is entirely open to the south-east.

Island of Spetsai

is a hilly island, wooded on the north, well known to Athenians as a summer resort. There are two harbours: the Boat Harbour off the village centre where the Piraeus ferry calls, and **Balza** (a creek at the N.E. end of the island) which is suitable for yachts, berthing, servicing and laying-up.

Approach and anchorage for Balza. Chart 1518. The lighthouse stands out fairly well and the port may be approached by day or night—see plan on page 26.

Yachts usually anchor to the S.W. of the lighthouse off a small stone pier in depths of $2\frac{1}{2}$ fathoms. This is open to N.W. and a swell sometimes rolls in, but the holding is good. Land at stone pier in dinghy—8 minutes' walk to the village.

Berth in the Inner Harbour. There is a quay (with shallow depths close in) where caiques berth and work their cargoes. Towards the head of the creek there is usually more room, though it is necessary to berth well away from the quay. Here are a few suitable berths for small yachts (up to 20 tons) to lay-up for the winter, where shelter is better than at most Aegean ports.

Port Facilities. Provisions may be bought nearby from a caique that brings them across from the mainland. The large hotel 'Poseidonion' and several smaller ones, also restaurants, are all 10 minutes' walk from Balza and close by the Boat Harbour. Water can be obtained from the quay: also diesel fuel, petrol and paraffin.

There are two small shipyards where local caiques are built and small yacht repairs can be undertaken, including the slipping of a yacht up to 7 ft draft. The technical resources on the island are limited.

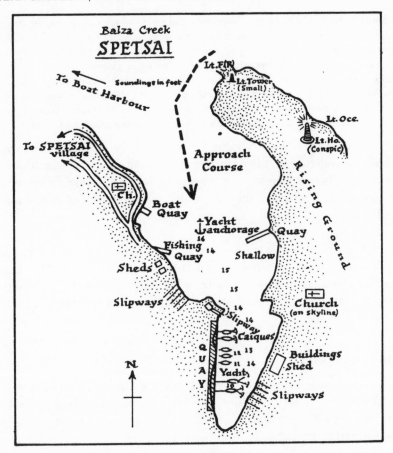

When laying-up a yacht here it is essential to realize that during the winter months the sea level drops about 2½ ft.

A large finishing school for boys lies to the westward of the hotel, both buildings being conspicuous when approaching from the west. Most of the villas are empty in the winter months, and only the small local population remains.

There are no motor-cars, but a few horse-drawn gharries.

Island of Spetsopoula, lying close S.E. of Spetsai with a yacht harbour, is privately owned by Mr Stavros Niarchos, the Greek ship-owner.

IDRA AND THE SARONIC GULF

Both the mainland and the island ports are within 50 miles of Piraeus and can be reached by ferry steamers within 3 or 4 hrs, or in summer by hydrofoil far more quickly. Chart 1518 shows Idra and the mainland coast (with the island of Poros) beyond the Methana Peninsula.

Before entering the Idra Strait there is the uninhabited and largely barren island of **Dhokos** with two partially sheltered coves on the northern side, suitable as a temporary yacht anchorage. There is also on the mainland the shallow little port of **Ermioni** with its adjoining hamlet connected to the main road system. Though pleasant for a night anchorage, none of these places is recommended for a special visit.

Island of Idra (Hydra)

is a long barren island with a central spur rising to 2,000 ft. Its interest lies in the picturesque small port, where almost the whole of the island's 3,000 population live. The attractively built houses of early Idriot families rising one above the other forms an amphitheatre round the three sides of the harbour. (Chart 1825.)

Approach and Berth. The entry is straightforward day or night, and a yacht should berth off the main quay near the church, or if this is congested with caiques (as it sometimes is in summer) berth stern to the breakwater. Though appearing to be a well-sheltered port it can, in fact, be very disturbed in N.W. winds, and Idra is certainly not such a safe harbour as Spetsai. (See photograph, fac. p. 8.)

Facilities. Except during the height of the tourist season it is easy to step ashore on the clean broad quay where all the shops are, and to find a wide choice of fresh provisions (brought across from the mainland). Fresh water is very scarce. There are a number of restaurants on the quay, some modest hotels and a bathing place on the rocks outside the harbour. Small repairs can be done by a yard that builds local motor-boats. A school of navigation stands above the steamer quay where the Piraeus steamer calls 3 or 4 times daily in summer—a 3-hr passage; also a hydrofoil boat calls. Also ferry connections with Spetsai and Epidavros.

Apart from the little church of Ayios Ioannis (with original frescoes) close above the town, the only excursion is an hour's climb to the monastery of Prophitis Ilias. It stands high on the mountain, and a mule can be hired.

Though the monastery is uninhabited and without interest except for its bell-tower, the neighbouring convent is attractive and well maintained by a few nuns. It affords a magnificent view.

Though crowded with tourists in summer during the day, Idra is a colourful little port much animated by the gaily-painted caiques unloading their produce, and by the arrival of the fast ferry-boats from Piraeus embarking and disembarking passengers many times in a day. By night the place quietens down, for the tourists have left, and only those with summer villas and the local people remain.

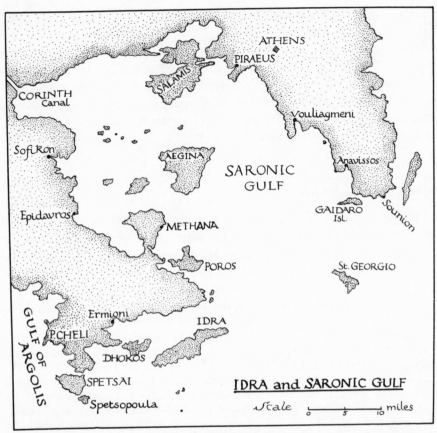

Earlier History. From the harbour looking up at the houses it is at once apparent that many of them were built for people of wealth and, except for Spetsai, have nothing in common with the humble dwellings on other islands. Relatively large and constructed of a grey stone now weathered, they are usually approached by a small garden with shrubs through which can be seen a panelled door with a richly moulded knocker. On the seaward side is a loggia standing on the steep parapet with a commanding view over the port.

They were built in the 18th century by Albanian-speaking families, who migrated here at the time of Turkish suppression, and by the latter part of that century had developed a maritime trade with many parts of the Mediterranean. A large number of sailing craft were built here; schooners and brigs were soon earning big profits.

When the War of Independence broke out in the early twenties of the next century, these families together with those from the islands of Spetsai and Psara put their ships at the disposal of the newly-formed Greek Navy. At that time there were 4,000 seamen on the island, and about 150 ships of which no fewer than 80 were of 300 tons burden or more; most of them well manned and armed.

History has handed down accounts of spirited actions against Turkish warships. On one occasion they captured a Turkish corvette and decided to name her after the island; she thus became the first *Idra* of the Greek Navy.

Some Idriot leaders have been highly praised for their part in the War, especially Admiral Miaoulis whose statue now stands outside the church, the other Greek patriots such as Thombazi and Condouriotis, whose descendants still own their original family houses.

Commerce recovered after the War and thrived well into the latter part of the last century. The presence of bollards and mooring facilities in the more sheltered coves of Idra and Spetsai reveal where these schooners and brigs were laid up in the winter months.

Island of Poros

has an attractive, landlocked bay sometimes used as a Fleet anchorage. It is a pleasant place to visit in a yacht, with its green shores and one or two coves; the small town is pleasant.

Approach. Chart 1657. The northern entrance can take unlimited draft; but the tortuous eastern channel, which is used by the Piraeus ferry-steamers, must be treated with caution. Here the northern shore must be followed within 100 ft in certain places—see sketch.

Anchorage. It will be noted that the 10-fathom sea-bed rises sharply at the sides to 3 fathoms or less. Yachts are now required to berth with stern to the new West Quay—midway between the ferry landing and the naval hospital. One should avoid mooring close off the yacht station for here the water is shallow and exposed to the north.

Note. The Inner Harbour, which according to the British chart is being dredged to 12 ft, has in fact barely 6 ft and is used exclusively by naval boats. It is, however, possible to anchor in the small coves on the north side of Poros Bay, which, though somewhat far from the town, are claimed to be fairly sheltered and afford pleasant anchorage.

Port Facilities. Fuel and water at Yacht Station, but beware of shallow water.

View from the eastern entrance to Poros looking towards N.W.

There is an ice factory at Galata, where petrol and diesel fuel may be bought, as well as on the island itself.

Summer hotels and some reasonably attractive restaurants are close to the steamer landing place. A tourist hotel with bathing place has been built outside the town, being approached by the one and only road, a couple of miles distant from the main quay.

A steamer service during the summer months connects with Piraeus via Aegina, taking about 3 hrs. There is also a less frequent service to Idra and Spetsai.

A small naval hospital will always help in an emergency.

The monastery and the ruins of the temple of Poseidon are worth a visit. The monastery can be reached by bus or taxi in 15 minutes and also by motor-boat, and the ruins of the temple are an hour's walk above the monastery—mostly through pinewoods.

An interesting visit can be made to Troezen where in 1827 the first meeting of the Greek National Assembly was held, and Cabo D'Istria was elected president. Troezen can be reached either by bus from Galata, or by 40 minutes' easy going on foot from Vidhi, a poor anchorage at the western end of Poros Bay. Though the ruins of the temple of Hippolyte and the Byzantine church are fragmentary, the mountain views across the fertile plain are magnificent.

Proceeding from Poros to the island of Aegina one passes the tall, massive **Methana Peninsula.** There is anchorage at the head of the isthmus on either side and also at the small port of Methana on the east side where all the Piraeus ferries call. Few yachts make use of these places, preferring the more convenient ports and anchorages of nearby Poros and Aegina. The peninsula, however, with its steep, green slopes rising abruptly from the sea is most impressive from the deck of a yacht.

Island of Aegina
(Spelt 'Aiyina' on Admiralty charts and 'Egina' on Greek charts.)

This is a hilly island, cultivated in places, with a well-sheltered though shallow little port—a seaside resort for Athenians.

Approach and Berth. Chart 1657, plan. The approaches to the port have recently been dredged and the shoals removed. Now the one obstruction remaining is marked by a buoy. The shoals were caused originally by concrete and stone blocks believed to have been set in the sea-bed by the early Greeks to form a protective zeriba round the mouth of their original harbour. Inside the port has also been dredged, and yachts now berth off the yacht station, stern to the quay, at the southern breakwater in 2-fathom depths. It is usually crowded.

Port Facilities. There are provision shops and a fish market close by. Petrol and fuel may be obtained from a pump, and ice is available. Water is not easily come by; but it can be obtained by water-cart rather expensively. Taxis are available. There are one or two modest hotels; a palatable white wine may be bought locally.

The small town of Aegina is unattractive; the island, though green in early summer, and partly wooded, dries up in the hot weather.

There is ferry communication with Piraeus several times a day, and also with Poros, Idra, Spetsai and Leonidhion.

Though the local museum is hardly worth a visit, the drive to the Doric temple of Aphaia is picturesque and the temple very fine. For a yacht, this may be visited best from **Ayia Marina Bay.** Though open and entirely exposed to the S.E. quadrant, this bay is much frequented by yachts from Piraeus. From the modern hamlet, now become a sea resort, and visited by many day-tourists, a path leads up to the temple of Aphaia.

On the north side of the island at Planaco is a boatyard (Tessos of Mailles) which has been recommended for hauling out and repairing small yachts.

Historical. In the middle of the 5th century B.C. when Aegina had grown strong enough, both militarily and commercially, to be a rival to Athens, the Athenians attacked it, but only after a four years' siege by their fleet was the island captured and its population deported. Nearly 2,000 years later Aegina suffered a worse catastrophe when the pirate Barbarossa overran the Aegean islands. In Aegina he butchered the men and carried off 6,000 women and children. When the French fleet put in here soon afterwards their admiral reported he could find no people living on the island.

Palaia Epidavros is a charming anchorage at the foot of the Peloponnese mountains with an interesting approach.

Approach and Berth. Chart 1657. The leading marks through the narrow approach channel are still described in *Sailing Directions*, the passage through the Narrows now being facilitated by prominent port and starboard beacons with lights Qk. Fl. (R) and (G).

Either anchor in 2–3 fathoms in the middle of the bay or berth off the quay. The yacht station, with fuel supply tanks on the quay, has a mooring buoy in 12-ft depths. The bottom shelves to under 10 ft by the quay. By night a light is now established at the corner of the quay.

Facilities. The village of 500 people has little to offer apart from fruit and vegetable shops. There is an hotel and restaurants; a bus runs daily to Nauplion; the ferry calls.

One should hire a taxi and drive to the theatre at Epidaurus—the finest in all Greece, less than an hour along a good road.

Continuing in a N.N.W. direction, close under the tall mountainous coast is a well-sheltered bay with a hamlet on the water-front:

Sofikon, an attractive, spacious anchorage in mountainous surroundings.

Approach and Anchorage. Chart 1657. After avoiding obstructions both outside and at the entrance, anchor in the N.E. corner of the bay, off the eastern end of the village, in 3 or 4 fathoms. Shelter is all-round.

The hamlet has only three shops, but modern villas are now springing up round the bay. A new road leads to Poros.

Towards the N.W. corner of the Saronic Gulf lies the undiscernible entrance to the Corinth Canal at Kalamaki. Before reaching this, however, is the small cove of Kenchraié, the ancient Aegean port of Roman Corinth. Recent excavations have enabled some interesting mosaics and glass panels to be recovered. As the Gulf narrows, a mountain with medieval fortifications stands out prominently in the distance. This is Acro-Corinth and, though it lies on the west side of

the Corinth Canal, it is the best distant mark for the Canal approach; the Canal
entrance cannot be discerned until one is almost there.

Corinth Canal

This 3-mile cut much used by local steamers and caiques saves a distance of 140
miles on the sea route round the Peloponnesus. The canal is 80 ft wide and 25 ft
deep in the middle. (See photograph, fac. p. 9.)

The canal office is at the Aegean end of the canal. A yacht wishing to pass
through should go alongside a quay at the entrance, when an official will come
aboard to calculate the dues. When the canal is clear, the red flag is hauled down
and a blue one hoisted; the yacht then proceeds without a pilot, passing between
vertical limestone cliffs 250 ft high.

In 1974 the charge for a 20-ton yacht was something under £10 for her first
passage, and is payable in Greek currency. The fees are calculated on a vessel's
net tonnage and there is no longer a reduction for the return voyage. In 1974 the
canal closed to traffic on Tuesdays from 0600 to 2000.

Though originally it was feared that there might be an inconvenient current,
there is, in fact, seldom any flow of consequence, and only on rare occasions does
it reach 2 knots due to strong winds. The sides of the canal are continually
breaking away and have to be repaired; this operation, which is performed on
Tuesdays, involves closing the canal, vessels being advised by 'loud hailer' as
they approach the entrance.

Early History. This waterway was not cut until the 'eighties of the last century. The project
was, however, seriously considered by both Caligula and Nero; the latter ordered a survey,
and appeared in person to inaugurate the digging, lifting the first clod of earth with a golden
shovel. Pausanias states that work started in A.D. 67 with a labour force of 6,000 Jews, but
owing to the troublesome times which followed the undertaking had to be abandoned,
and thus the custom of hauling the galleys across the isthmus 'on rollers' continued throughout the centuries. The serious need for a canal did not again arise until the Austro-Lloyd
Steamship Company secured the monopoly of the Levant trade during the last century.
They found it necessary, though inconvenient, to build a good carriage road across the
isthmus to convey the passengers arriving by sea at Loutraki to the steamer awaiting them
at the other side.

During the 16th century British sailing vessels came to the roadstead W. of Corinth, to
load the small dried grapes known to the French as 'Raisins de Corinth'. The English adopted
the word currant—a corruption of their port of origin, Corinth.

Eighteen centuries had now passed since the Romans abandoned their work;
and when the French engineer, Gerster, came to construct the canal in 1881 he
found two sections of Nero's excavations at the western side of the isthmus—
one of 2,200 yds and another 1,700 yds in length, and each about 50 yds wide.

The French took about twelve years to complete the task, and the canal was opened in 1893.

> . . . Salamis—where fame
> In noontide splendour shone,
> and blazed on Greece the deathless name
> That dawn'd at Marathon.
>
> CARLYLE

Island of Salamis

is a hilly island with clusters of trees and partial cultivation with small villages. Its interest to a yacht lies in the winding channels at either end (Chart 1513) and the partly sheltered anchorages used mainly by Piraeus yachts when out for a day's sail.

At the eastern end of the island lies the strait where in 492 B.C. the decisive battle against the invading Persian fleet was fought. Today this area is mostly taken up by the Greek Navy and repair yards. The ledge where Xerxes is said to have sat watching the destruction of his 2,100 galleys by the 480 vessels of Themistocles is marked on the chart.

Cape Konkhi on the southern tip of the island provides for a small yacht an unusual summer anchorage among some rocky islets.

Approach and Anchorage. Approaching the lighthouse on a northerly course, turn eastwards passing between the islet and the shore. The depths shoal to 9 ft, but later deepen to 3 fathoms where, on a sandy bottom, one may anchor. Shelter is good except from E., but only small yachts not exceeding 7-ft draft should attempt it even in fine weather.

PORTS OF PIRAEUS (PIREEFS)

Close eastward of Salamis is the great commercial port of Piraeus which since earliest days has served the city of Athens. Beyond it is the small but ancient port of Zea, which during recent years has been enlarged and dredged to become a modern yacht marina within less than an hour by road from Athens. Another marina, Vouliagmeni, one-third the size of Zea and 10 miles south of it, has also been completed. Many visiting yachts crowd into these marinas during the summer months and many lay-up here in winter; but there are other possibilities for laying-up in safety at more remote places such as Spetsai, Porto Cheli, Rhadoes, and near Volos, all of which are described under the port headings. Nearer to Piraeus is also the new laying-up yard of Olympic Yachts S.A. at Lavrion. (See photograph, fac. p. 9.)

Zea was planned as a yacht harbour about 1960. Breakwaters were constructed to form a deep outer basin known as Freatida, and the ancient inner port, Passalimani, was dredged. Quays have been built in the outer port (4-fathom depths) to enable the larger yachts to berth stern-to, and in the inner port ($1\frac{1}{2}$ to $2\frac{1}{2}$ fathoms) stone piers have been completed to moor the smaller yachts in a similar manner. Altogether about 320 yachts can be accommodated; facilities are being arranged to provide convenient service in summer and when laying-up for the winter. The resources of the town of Piraeus are close at hand.

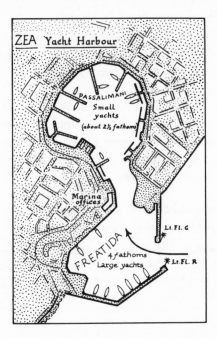

Approach and Berth. The entrance is well lit and there is no difficulty day or night. A harbour boatman may be there to direct the newly arrived yacht to where she should berth.
Officials. A Port of Entry: Harbour office is on W. side of the Narrows, together with National Tourist Office.
Facilities. Water, fuel and electricity are to be laid on at the outer berths. Provision shops and restaurants are close by. The Piraeus bus passes close to yacht berths with connections to Athens (see under Athens, page 37). Yacht Chandlers on the seafront near the Underground station (Piraeus). Sailmaker: Manolis Pantelis, 55 King Paul Avenue, *Piraeus 17*, is the agent of Bruce Banks Sails Ltd, and can effect all normal repairs. One should realize that British paints, cordage, fittings etc., are 80 per cent more expensive here than at home; but all are obtainable out of bond though only in large quantities. Stores, however, can be sent by sea from England, consigned direct to the yacht via a Customs agent in Piraeus. In 1974 it was possible for a yacht to obtain duty free wines and spirit from one of the ship chandlers in the port.

Harbour Dues. A tariff of charges for yachts berthing at Zea and Vouliagmeni is based on the vessel's gross tonnage, and the charge is made for a minimum period of 3 days' stay. At Vouliagmeni the charges are about 20 per cent more. One should examine the brochure on tariff charges, printed in English and handed to the yacht on arrival; there are certain clauses which might be of benefit to a yacht when deciding upon her length of stay in the port. A deposit is required to be paid on arrival.

With southerly gales a reflected swell enters the outer port. In winter, gales occasionally cause seas to surmount the breakwater and cascade on to the quay, endangering the yachts within. The inner harbour is inclined to be dirty and smelly but, with the sewage pipes being diverted, there should be an improvement. Its great advantage is that it is safe in all weathers.

Hauling-out and slipping cannot be done locally; a yacht must go to Perama—about 3 miles in the direction of Salamis—and arrange with one of the many yards whose resources are very limited. While waiting to slip, a convenient anchorage with all-round shelter can be found at Paloukia, Salamis. Individual arrangements must be made if desiring the services of a painter, plumber, engineer, metal-worker etc. Most of these artisans are to be found in Perama or Piraeus. For those who speak no Greek there are a few agencies who can arrange these services, but very few yacht-owners report favourably on this indirect way of approach. When laying-up afloat it is essential to leave a caretaker on board, or alternatively and less satisfactorily, make arrangements with an agent. An English agent who can be helpful is Mr Roger Stafford of Odos Aintos Palaon Falcron, Attica. See also p. 33.

Tourkolimano, the small harbour for Greek yachts and Class boats only, is always crowded. Foreign yachts may not enter without permission from the Royal Hellenic Yacht Club whose palatial white building stands on a promontory overlooking the port. The Club secretary is always willing to give helpful advice to a visiting yacht.

The sides of the port are lined with expensive restaurants and one or two yacht agencies. On summer nights the scene is animated by crowds of Athenians dining at the waterside in the cool of the evening.

Southerly gales during winter make the place uncomfortable. Except for the modern quays this little port has survived practically unchanged since the days of Themistocles.

The Commercial Port of Piraeus (Chart 1520) has been greatly extended during the recent centuries, and today presents a scene of much activity, for not only does it accommodate the large liners and freighters, but all the local ferry services to Aegean ports. It is dirty and quite impossible for a yacht to berth here, all wharves being occupied by steamers, loading and unloading usually in the proportion of one to three respectively.

St George, the small commercial harbour lying partly under the shelter of the

E. tip of Salamis, has very recently been rebuilt to handle larger ships; but this port is forbidden to yachts. Caiques, trawlers and small coasters from the islands still land their cargoes here. One used to see many wine schooners from Rhodes, Kos and Chios; corn came from Macedonia; marble from Tinos, Naxos and Paros, olives from Mytilene and Itea, goats and cattle from many islands. For the return voyage caiques loaded largely with imported goods, machinery, tinned food—even Yarmouth bloaters.

The whole area between Perama and the eastern shores of Salamis is crowded with antiquated merchant ships awaiting their turn at the shipbreakers' yards nearby. Considerable development including the construction of breakwaters and wharves continues to progress, but the water being filthy yachts are advised to avoid the area.

Brief history of the harbours. With the exception of St George, the harbours were originally laid out in 493 B.C. when, in consequence of the Persian danger, Themistocles persuaded the Athenians to build stone breakwaters. These were largely of 10-ft square stone blocks on rubble foundations fastened with iron cramps run in with molten lead. The harbour approaches were then fortified and the two long walls leading to Athens were provided with adequate protection against enemy attack. Throughout the Venetian era the commercial harbour of Piraeus was known as Porto Leone, and although the marble lion was removed to Venice by Morosini in 1687, the port continued to be known by this name for at least another century. The lion now resides outside the Arsenal at Venice.

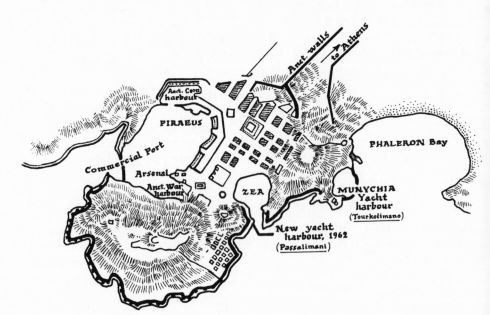

Piraeus, Zea and Munychia. Early Greek harbours and their adaptation to modern use.

Athens can be reached from Passalimani by taking a bus to Piraeus Station whence the electric trains (every 6 minutes) reach Omonia Suare in 20 minutes. Green buses (every 15 minutes) reach Syntagma (Constitution Square) in 35 minutes. Alternatively, blue buses pass the Stadium (Athens) and go on to Kifissia. Both may be boarded in Korai Square by the Demotic Theatre, Piraeus. A taxi takes 20 minutes.

The guide-book gives details of all that is of interest in Athens. No one should miss seeing at least the Acropolis and the National Archaeological Museum. (All museums are free on Thursdays and Sundays.)

There is air and train communication with England: the aircraft in $3\frac{1}{4}$ hours, and the Direct Orient and the Akropolis Express in $2\frac{1}{2}$ days. Local Greek airlines fly to some twenty Aegean islands or mainland ports—see p. xxii.

On the Attic coast just south of the airport is the residential coastal area of Glifadha. Here a marina has been built, but it is somewhat exposed to southerly gales and is very noisy because of its proximity to the airport.

Vouliagmeni, the first yacht marina to be constructed in Greece, lies on the Attic coast 10 miles from Piraeus, and provides accommodation for 100 yachts; here are also many facilities both in summer and when laying-up in winter. The limited space available is usually fully booked; in the sailing season a visitor may be allowed to use the berth of a resident away cruising, but for lay-up it is prudent to make arrangements in advance.

Approach and Berth. The plan illustrates that entry is easy by day or night, but in the summer months a visiting yacht may often find the harbour full and consequently may have to anchor outside.

On arrival one must be ready to pick up a buoy tailed to a chain bow mooring—the club boat assists. The yacht's stern is then hauled into the quay. Anchoring inside the port is forbidden. A copy of Port Regulations, printed in English, is handed to the yacht on arrival.

Shelter is normally good; only during winter strong southerly gales send in a reflected swell which necessitates yachts easing out stern warps and working fenders.

Officials. A Port of Entry, Harbour Master and Customs.

Facilities. Fresh water, telephone and electricity are laid on at each berth as well as at the pier. Fuel is available at the S.W. quay as well as at this pier. Laundry on the quay. Bread, vegetables, fruit and ice vans call at the Club house. Vouliagmeni village is a mile distant with good restaurants and shops: from here there is a half-hourly bus service to Athens (40 minutes) —there are also occasional buses from the Marina to Athens. One or two smart hotels are near the Marina. The airport is 20 minutes by taxi. Only small motor-yachts and dinghies can be hauled out for refitting. Vouliagmeni's facilities however are expensive, and to lay up here is more costly than at Zea, and certainly more expensive than at Malta in 1974. One reason for high charges is that the services of technicians, artisans etc. can be obtained only from Athens; cost of transport by taxi is no small matter. For laying-up and repairs, see also Gaidaromandri on the Attic coast, page xxviii and 44.

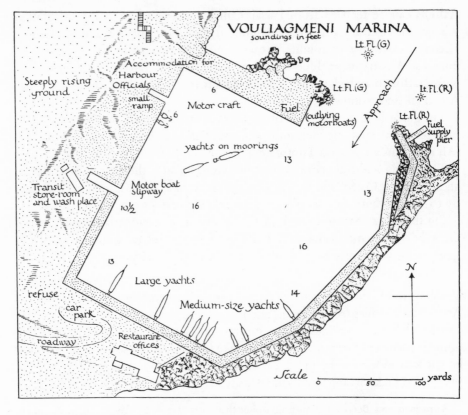

It is possible to bathe from the rocks on the far side of the offices and restaurant, which is one of the attractions in hot weather, compared with Zea.

Sailing south-eastwards along the Attic coast towards Cape Sounion a yacht may pass between Gaidaro Island and the shore. During Meltemi conditions violent gusts sweep down from the hills, and sailing yachts are advised to follow the custom of local craft by shortening sail when passing through this passage.

> *Here in the dead of night by Lonna* steep*
> *The seaman's cry was heard along the deep*
> FALCONER—After his shipwreck in *Britannia* on
> this Cape in 1762. He was one of the three saved.

Sounion. One can see Cape Sounion in the distance and, against the blue sky, the temple of Poseidon whose columns of Attic marble now appear quite white, and are in fact crystallized and glazed with the salt spray of twenty-four centuries.

* Lonna, a corruption of Colonna, the Venetian name for Sounion.

To the early Greek seamen this headland with its historic temple was the last they saw of the mother country as they sailed out to the Ionian colonies and the distant domains that were once the glory of the Greek Empire.

'Place me on Sounion's marbled steep', wrote Byron; and here the poet, in common with many others, has chiselled his name at the base of one of the columns.

The view from the cape is magnificent. In the north are the peaks of Hymettus, once 'the happy hunting ground of bees', and sweeping towards the west lie the islands of Aegina, Poros and Idra; farther to the south and the east can be seen the dark silhouettes of the mountainous Cyclades with Kithnos and Kea, and the nearby Makronisi. Much of this has been spoilt by an enormous hotel on the beach and a motel close by the temple.

The Anchorage is frequently used by yachts throughout the summer and by caiques and small coasters during N. to N.E. gales when the anchorage may be crowded. The bottom is largely sand, but there are stones and rocks causing the holding to be very uncertain. Open only to south, shelter from other directions is good. A short stone pier facilitates the landing by dinghy.

Note. The nearby anchorage at Legraina is claimed to be better holding than Sounion.

By day there is a constant stream of motor coaches bringing tourists from Athens to see the temple, but by the evening the place is relatively quiet.

'A range of columns long by time defaced'

CHAPTER THREE

Cape Sounion

to Salonika

GULF OF PAGASITIKOS (VOLOS)

Trikeri
Palaio Trikeri
Vathudi
Port Pteleos
Mitzellas
Fearless Cove
Port Volos
Trikeri Channel
    Andriami
    Platania
    Pondiko Islet

NORTHERN SPORADES

Island of Skiathos
    The Harbour

Island of Skopelos
    Port Skopelos
    Glossa (Klima)
    Panormos Bay
    Agnonda
    Staphilis

Island of Alonissos
    Murtia Bay

    Patateri
    Stenivalla

Island of Peristera
    Vasiliko

Island of Pelagos
    Ayios Petros
    Port Planedhi

Island of Skantzoura
    Parausa
    Ormos Skantzoura

Island of Skyros
    The Port of Linaria
    Linaria Cove
    Port Trebuki, with Akladi Cove
    Renes Bay
    Glifadha Cove

COAST FROM NORTHERN SPORADES TO GULF OF SALONIKA

Salonika
    Mount Olympus

3

Cape Sounion to Salonika

CAPE SOUNION NORTHWARD

There are two routes:

(a) Leave Evvia to the westward and, sailing in more open water, a yacht passes through Doro Channel (Stenon Kafirevs) northwards. A similar choice was made by Odysseus when returning from Troy: 'In this dilemma we prayed for a sign, and heaven made it clear that we should cut straight across the open sea to Evvia.'

(b) Pass through the narrow inner passage between the long island of Evvia and the Attic–Boeotian shore.

Island of Evvia

with tall rugged mountains, fertile plains, forests and mines is, after Crete, the largest island in the Aegean. The more interesting places and anchorages lie on the S.W. shores, and are described when considering the Inner Passage between Evvia and the mainland.

Evvia has its principal port of Halkis in the narrow Euripo Strait (described later). Karistos lying in a bay the southern end of the island is a small town standing beneath Mount Ochi with a small port. Yet a third small port, Kimi, lies on the east coast; protected by two breakwaters, Kimi is the supply port for the island of Skyros, and much used by caiques.

The Open-Water Route

Until after the First World War when caiques still had no motors, they always chose the open-water route to make their northing. When bound for Salonika they took advantage of the fact that the N.W. wind blowing from the Attic shores in the summer, changes its direction as one moves farther eastward. Thus sailing vessels, having stood across, were often favoured with an easterly slant enabling to fetch right up the Salonika Gulf.

The open-water route takes a sailing vessel to the north-eastward, passing S. of Evvia and through the Kea and Doro Channels, where anchorages on Andros Island are described in Chapter 7. A yacht can also put in at

Karistos, a pleasant growing village by a small port lying in an attractive mountainous setting.

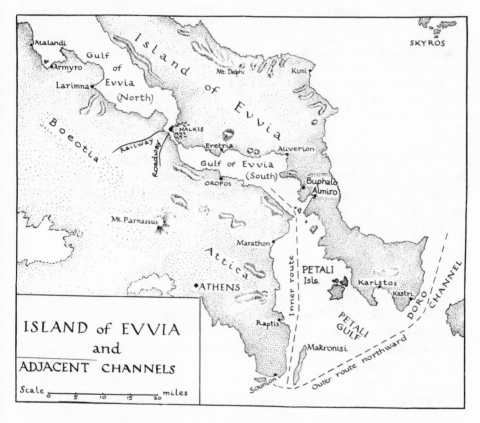

ISLAND of EVVIA
and
ADJACENT CHANNELS

Scale |0 5 10 15 20| miles

Approach and Berth. Plan on Chart 1597. Enter the harbour and proceed to inner basin, berthing stern to the quay by the village square and Harbour Office. Deep water until close to the quay (10 ft). Harbour lights. Shelter is good in all weather, except for very strong Meltemi gusts from the mountains.

Facilities. Excellent fruit, vegetables and fish; tavernas close by. A new 'B class' hotel with bathing beach E. of village. Communication by bus with Halkis and other villages. Daily steamer service Rafina–Andros calls here. Water-tap in N.W. corner of town square; water is excellent.

The modern village lies at the foot of a Venetian fort built on the site of an ancient Greek acropolis; west of the village is a cultivated plain; the whole district is partially wooded with plenty of vegetation. A number of mineral springs well up from the sand at the E. corner of the bay.

In Roman days the port was used for the export of green marble which is still quarried in the hinterland.

Pilotage Notes for this route. Both the Kea Channel and the Doro Channel (Stenon Kafirevs) are notorious for the strong winds which funnel through them, and for the short steep seas and the strong currents which a strong Meltemi causes, particularly in the Doro Channel where it can reach 5 or 6 knots. If desiring to await better conditions, there is good anchorage in Gavrion Bay on Andros Island (page 209), Ay. Nikolaos Bay on Kea Island (page 213), and in two small sheltered coves on the opposite shore of Evvia.

(a) Kastri Bay, with good holding on firm sand in 3 fathoms.

(b) A bay unnamed 1¾ miles N.W. of Kastri.

Both bays (with fresh-water springs) afford good shelter from the Meltemi; but after the cessation of a strong Meltemi, the steep short sea in this channel can be very dangerous to small vessels.

Kimi, a small caique port protected by breakwaters; the only useful port en route northwards before reaching the Northern Sporades, it has convenient depths, but has nothing to recommend for yachts. It owes its importance to being the ferry terminal for Skyros with good bus communication via Halkis to Athens.

The Inner Passage via the Gulf of Evvia

This makes a very pleasant cruising ground for a small yacht with the choice of so many attractive anchorages close at hand. During the summer months the Meltemi may cause short choppy seas, but shelter is always near.

Passing by the Petali Gulf to Halkis and thence the Gulf of Evvia, altogether 76 miles, the passage first leads between the uninteresting narrow island of Makronisi (formerly a military area) and the Attic shore. Here are some sheltered bays suitable for temporary anchorage, but of no particular interest to a yacht:

Gaidaromandri is a shallow but well-sheltered cove with a few fishermen's cottages: suitable for a small yacht night anchorage.

Approach. Enter the bay and then steer to the N.W. carefully avoiding the wreck of a Turkish steamer showing one foot above the water. The depths inside the cove are about 2 fathoms, thin weed on sand.

Berth at the head of the cove alongside the T-head of the main jetty, owned by a modern shipyard—Olympic Yachts S.A. (Postal address is Lavrion).

Facilities. Water and fuel can be made available by the yard and certain spare parts can be obtained, but the main interest of Olympic Yachts is the building of fibre-glass craft and winter laying-up. Provisions can be obtained at Lavrion.

5   Skiathos. The boat basin often used by small yachts.
The new quay lies beyond. *See p. 56*

6 Port Skopelos. *See p.* 57

Lavrion, an open roadstead with an ore port and a large village, ore-tips and quays around the bay. A Port of Entry. Of no interest for a yacht.

The mines which were renowned for their silver in the 5th century B.C. were out of production by the time of Pausanias. Re-opened in 1860, the mines now produce zinc and manganese, and from the rubble rejected by the ancients modern methods now enable small quantities of lead and silver to be extracted.

Rafina, which is without interest to a yacht, is the ferry port for Karistos. Many Athenians come here in summer on account of the good bathing beach.

Port Raptis, 15 miles from Sounion, was a charming anchorage beside a summer residential settlement in the green hilly surroundings of the Attic coast, but hotels are springing up along the coast.

> **Approach.** Chart 1630. On the small but steep island, which forms the protection for the bay, stands a marble statue of a headless tailor, from which the place takes its name. This is a splendid seamark and enables one to identify the port.
>
> **The Anchorage,** with convenient depths on a clear sandy bottom, is off the small hamlet of St Spyridon close offshore by some trees. It is open to east and S.E., and though some swell may come in, the wind does not blow home.
>
> **Facilities.** There are hotels and tavernas, fresh provision shops, and general stores. In the summer months, buses run frequently to Athens in about an hour. Fuel and water can be obtained near the landing place.

This little port, which now has a loading quay for caiques in the S.W. corner, appears to be increasing in importance. A large number of villas have been built on the slopes near the hamlet.

> **Early History.** The origin of the headless statue is obscure. It could belong to the sixth century B.C.; but it is also said to be of Roman origin. It is believed that during the period of the Confederacy the annual ceremony of transporting the Theoria to Holy Delos took place here. In later centuries when sailing vessels from the west used these waters, the shelter of Raptis was well known: John Sellers states in *Sailing Directions* of 24 July 1677 'Port Raptis is one of the best and most commodious havens of all that are found in the archipelago to sail into in stress of weather.'

Petali Islands

lie close to the Evvia coast and provide a sheltered anchorage in all conditions. The best is close off a fine villa on S.W. corner of Xero Island where two large yachts are often moored. These all belong to a Greek shipowner whose estate surrounds the anchorage. The retainers who live near the villa are helpful and water can be obtained from a tap near the quay.

The channel running south from this anchorage shown on Chart 1597 as having a depth of 1 fathom has a depth of 2-3 fathoms except for a narrow ledge of rock at the narrowest part of the channel where the depth is 8-9 ft (lead sounding).

On the S. side of Megalo Island is the deserted sandy bay of Vasilico. This is sheltered on all sides except south and is a pleasant place to bring up. Anchor off the beach in 3 fathoms on a sandy bottom.

That man is little to be envied whose patriotism
would not gain force upon the Plain of Marathon.
DR JOHNSON

Marathon is a large bay mainly of interest for its historical associations. There is anchorage in convenient depths off some small houses in the pinewood at the northern corner of the bay, where the peninsula projecting southwards affords some protection except in southerly winds; but it has little attraction. The modern summer village on the N.W. side of the bay usually has a few boats moored off, but this place is too exposed to the afternoon breeze.

Early History. Behind the 'Dog's Tail' (Cynosura) lies the anchorage of the Persian fleet, and where the pinewoods now grow is the site of the evacuation of the Persian army. It was here in 490 B.C. that the Athenians drove them back to their galleys drawn up on this beach. The famous tumulus where 192 Athenians lie buried has been tidied up, and there are now trees and gardens as well as a small pavilion for tourists.

Proceeding northwards is another archipelago of uninhabited islands. On the east side of **Stira** is a rocky islet which provides partial shelter for temporary anchorage on a sandy bottom in depths of 3 fathoms with room to swing; but better places to anchor for the night are on the Evvia coast, only 10 miles from Marathon at

Almiro Potamos, a long attractive fjord.

Anchorage—At the entrance to a cove on the western shore (opp. '15' on chart 1597) in 5 fathom depths, with room to swing, open only to E. Also anchorage with better shelter in a cove in the N.W. corner of the fjord in 4 fathoms.

The village, with a bus service, lies in the bay E.S.E. of the islet.

Opposite Almiro Potamos on the Attic coast is the bay of Ay. Marina. Here the Greek navy has extensive recreational facilities and a pier in the northern part of the bay. Anchorage here is prohibited.

Buphalo (Voufalo Cove). This is a charming sheltered little cove at the head of a small creek with only half a dozen cottages and some small fishing craft. The country around is grazing land and cornfields. A number of beehives painted green can be seen on the hillside.

Approach and Anchorage. Chart 1597. There is deep water everywhere except near the projecting sand spit from the eastern shore. Anchor in the middle of the small basin in 3½ fathoms on firm sand. Here there is nearly all-round shelter and sufficient room for a medium-sized yacht to swing.

Aliverion. A mole provides good shelter off a village, recognized by an Hellenic tower and Venetian castle. A yacht should round the mole-head (Chart 1597) and berth stern to a quay by the village close to a water-tap, and a restaurant nearby. This little place has been dwarfed by the nearby Pyrgos where a huge power plant has been built close by the water-front; it is not worth a special visit.

Eretria is Evvia's busy ferry port terminal; it can also be useful for a yacht wishing to gain shelter for the night and visit the ancient acropolis.

Approach. Chart 1554. A safe course into the middle of the port is about 020°, taking care to avoid the shoals indicated on chart.
Anchorage. On account of the depths and ferry traffic, one is limited to the small area in the S.W. near the root of the sunken mole. Depths here are about 4 fathoms, sand and mud bottom open only to S. The ferries are continually crossing to Oropos on the opposite shore conveying lorries and cars but also a regular bus service which reaches Athens in just over 2 hrs. Land in the dinghy at the quay.

Eretria, now a village of about 2,000 people, was once a city state. Remains of the ancient acropolis can be seen on the hill above the village and also a Greek theatre. In modern times during the Greek War of Liberation refugees from Psara, when sacked by the Turks, fled to the hospitality of Eretria.

Oropos, an open bay on the green and hilly Attic shore, has anchorage off a stone pier near the S.W. corner. Ferries are continually coming and going, conveying lorries with produce from Evvia to Athens.

So they passed by Crouni and Chalkis a land of fair streams
ODYSSEY XV

Halkis (Khalkis or Chalkis) is a pleasant, modernized town with 25,000 inhabitants; a sliding bridge connects the island of Evvia with the mainland. The narrow winding channels through which a vessel approaches from the south are interesting from the pilotage point of view as well as the scenery; the fortress, defended towers, and campanile are all Venetian.

At the narrowest part of the Strait, crossed by a bridge, the tidal streams run swiftly changing direction about every 6 hrs, but considerably influenced by wind and barometer. The stream can occasionally run as fast as 6 knots and it begins almost immediately after the turn of the tide. Yachts are only allowed to pass at slack tide when the bridge is opened for a very short period and signals (see under) are hoisted to indicate which side will be accepted first. Yachts must be ready to seize this opportunity and must recognize the appropriate signal. (*Enquire and pay fee at Port Office west of the Bridge.*)

About 15 min. before opening the bridge the following signals will be hoisted:

(*a*) Cone (point up) above 'hour-glass' shape means that traffic from N. to S. will have priority.

(*b*) Ball–Cone–Ball signifies that the traffic to move first is from S. to N.

Sailing Directions may be consulted for slack water predictions.

Approach. Chart 2802. There is no difficulty in beating up the channels even against a strong Meltemi and then berthing temporarily to await the opening of the bridge.

South of the Bridge. A yacht may either anchor off the railway station, or berth at a quay on the eastern shore. The quays are reserved for small craft unloading into the customs area of the port, but yachts are allowed to secure here behind a small jetty quite out of the current. The jetty itself is normally reserved for harbour ferries. A fuel station here supplies duty free fuel. In an emergency it is possible to embark fuel by arrangement at the fishing boat station at the western side of the narrows.

North of the Bridge. Make fast to the new quay which is out of the tide and sheltered from a northerly blow. There is a restaurant very close but no other facilities nearby.

Facilities. The quays on the eastern side of the channel, south of the bridge, accommodate small steamers, but a yacht is advised to anchor. Fuel and fresh water are available at the yacht station.

There is an excellent market. The modern hotel, some good restaurants and shops have given Halkis a new and thriving look. A train service connects with Athens in 1½ hrs. There is also a half-hourly bus service which is slightly quicker than the train.

After leaving Halkis and entering the northern part of the **Gulf of Evvia** the scenery now becomes more grand and the Evvia mountains reach their greatest height—nearly 6,000 ft of limestone cliff—standing almost sheer above the green coastline. A sailing yacht should keep towards the mainland shore, as the mountain squalls can be hard; moreover the anchorages are all on the Boeotian coast of the mainland.

Larimna (Larymna), the present name of the ancient port of Larmes, lies 16 miles N.W. of Halkis, at the mouth of the River Cephissus. Off the small village are convenient depths for anchoring, but the interesting approach is somewhat marred by the buildings of an ore company, the smoke belching from their furnaces often covers the surroundings with an oily dust. Ferro–nickel is one of Greece's most valuable exports.

An alternative anchorage can be found by a small yacht in an attractive small bay about 2 miles S.W. of Cape Larmes. It is open only to the east and holding is excellent. It could be affected by the smoke from the ore furnaces but only if the wind were S.E.

The ancient river still flows and provides cooling water for a bathe at the anchorage. Formerly running underground, it was used to drive the mills of the early Greeks, and shafts were sunk to enable men to descend and prevent blocking. Some of these shafts may still be seen.

Continuing N.W. one reaches:

Atalandi Island. Off its western shore an islet forms two small coves with a quiet anchorage in each.

Port Armyro although a small mining port, seldom used, is a delightful summer anchorage, but rather near the noisy motor highway.

> **Approach.** The dangerous sunken rock at the entrance is sometimes marked by a buoy, but recently it has been reported as unmarked and the port unused.
>
> **Anchorage.** A yacht should anchor, before reaching a line of stakes, in a depth of about 3 fathoms. Alternatively she can anchor more peacefully in the cove immediately north of the loading jetty. The lines of stakes at the head of the bay should be treated with respect as they are not all visible.

Atalandi Jetty. In settled weather it is pleasant to anchor off a small jetty where a road leads to Atalandi village standing on a hill about 3 miles distant. Unfortunately this anchorage is also near the motor road from Athens to Salonika which follows close along the shore passing two ferry landing points:

Arkitsa. Close under the cape is the car-ferry terminal linking the Athens bus route with Edipsos and the north of Évvia Island. Although this little bight in the coast is of no interest to a yacht the communication route can be useful—see under Orei.

Ayios Constantinos (Vórlovou), a wide bay with modern summer village at the foot of a green crescent-shaped mountain range, is the ferry point linking the Athens bus route with the steamer to Skiathos and Skopelos.

> **Anchorage.** In fine weather only, on the E. side of the bay near an old river mouth; good holding in 3–4 fathoms on mud, but very exposed. Alternatively berth off the steamer quay (which lies N. and S.); anchor in 7 fathoms, stern to the quay.
>
> **Facilities.** As for a summer resort, hotels, restaurants etc. Bus from Athens 2½ hrs, steamer to Skiathos 3–4 hrs, but the service is not daily.

The Evvia Shore. In fine weather when there is not a fresh N. wind it is interesting to cross to the Evvia coast and follow it westwards from the point where the steep-to mountains recede from the shore. Here the green slopes become more gentle with forestry, olive groves, vineyards and cultivation generally. At the foot of each torrent bed is a hamlet with small houses lining the water-front and usually an olive oil factory. Limni, the largest village, has nearly 3,000 people, but most places are only a cluster of houses. Before sighting the large hotels of Edipsos one passes a bay beneath the monastery of the Prophet Elias, standing boldly on a spur close under the 3,000-ft Mt Balanti.

Unfortunately none of the places along this charming Evvia coast have a suitable anchorage, and a yacht should always bring up for the night at one of the anchorages described on the mainland coast.

At the end of the Evvia Gulf and 42 miles above the bridge of Halkis, are the **Islands of Likades** with passages leading into the Oreos Gulf to the N.E., and the Maliakos Gulf to the west. The narrow N.E. Passage (350 yards wide) between Evvia and the small island (see plan, Chart 1196), is quite practical by day. Here the tidal stream can run at 3 knots but its direction cannot be accurately predicted as it is much dependent upon the wind; a yacht can always anchor under the red cliffs to await a favourable tide. In the main channel the tide runs at about half this velocity. (See also sketch plan on p. 52.)

One should not be discouraged from making this inshore passage; it is necessary to pass within 200 yds of the point to avoid underwater rocks on the western side of the fairway and to keep a cable from the Evvia coast until the N. shore of the northern islet bears West. Then keep half a mile offshore.

It is not proposed to describe the western or Maliakos Gulf which leads to the ore and bauxite loading quays at Stilis with the pass of Thermopylae beyond.

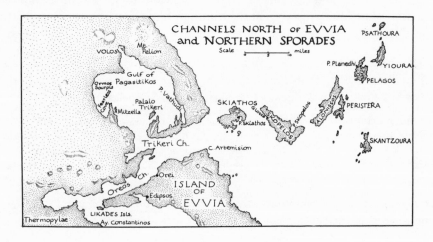

This gulf has no appeal. Turning eastwards, however, is the **Oreos Channel** which separates Evvia from the Thessaly coast and leads past the Gulf of Pagasitikos (or Volos) towards the attractive islands of the Northern Sporades. Every afternoon in summer the N.E. breeze blows freshly down the gulf and whips up a short, steep sea.

There is only one good harbour in the gulf; this is on the northern coast of Evvia:

Orei, a pleasant modernized fishing village with a small harbour protected by a mole against the prevailing winds.

> **Berth.** Chart 1521. Should there be room berth stern to the mole near its extremity in depths of 3 fathoms. Alternatively anchor off the pile pier and haul in the stern. The harbour is clean, the bottom sand, shelving towards the quayside. The little port is apt to be crowded with fishing boats.
> **Facilities.** Water at a tap on the mole (own hose required). Ice and very limited fresh provisions can be bought close at hand. Post office and telephone nearby. Two tavernas with tables under the tamarisks on the water-front. A daily caique ferry runs to Paleo Trikeri Island and Volos. Bus service to Edipsos, thence car ferry and bus to Athens (4 hrs altogether).

By the village square stands a marble bull of early Greek times recently recovered from the sea by fishermen. Beyond it are the ruins of a Venetian fort built on the foundations of an early Greek boundary wall, and S.W. of it is a canning factory. The village was built near the site of ancient Histiaia after which the present village on the hill is now called. The foundations of a marble temple are still to be seen.

On the mainland is the small village of Glifa. A car ferry now operates from here to the opposite coast of Evvia. The two coves in this bay, E. of the ferry point, though appearing suitable anchorages for a small yacht are, in fact, too deep for convenience.

Ormos Vathikelon, lying 1½ miles west of Glifa, is a deep but well-sheltered cove. Anchor in 7 fathoms and run out a warp to a tree. The place is attractive, being well wooded and devoid of habitation.

GULF OF PAGASITIKOS (VOLOS)

On entering this large gulf one sees to the N.E. a substantial village perched on the mountain side. At its foot lies the Skala:

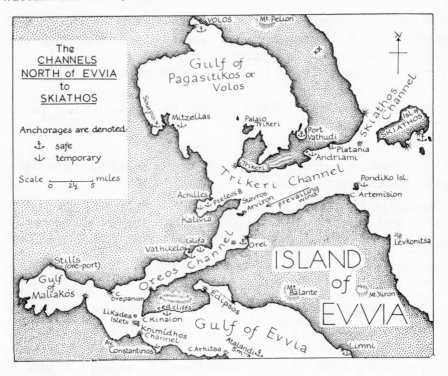

Trikeri, an open bay with a primitive hamlet, Skala Trikeri, guarding the approach to the Gulf of Volos.

Approach and Berth. There is no difficulty by day for the water is very deep and the village is conspicuous on the hill. On account of the sea-bed rising too steeply to permit anchoring off, a vessel must proceed to the N.E. corner of the bay, letting to in 10 fathoms and hauling in the stern to a small pier. (A couple of mooring buoys lie close off, whose ground cables should be avoided.) The mail steamer calls daily.

Historical. A spirited action took place in this little bay during the Greek War of Independence. On 23 April 1827, Captain Abney Hastings, then fighting for Greece, was commanding one of the earliest aux-steam gunboats, named *Karteria*. This 4-masted vessel was built of iron, with a tall thin funnel, fore and aft rig with square topsails, and also driven by paddles. She had already harassed the ships of the Turkish Navy then blockading the Greek coast off Volos, and on this occasion her opponent was a large Turkish brig moored close to the shore and protected by a battery on the hill above.

She was sighted by *Karteria* who, approaching from seaward, immediately prepared for action. Driven by her 40-horse-power engines she rapidly closed the enemy. Meanwhile, in the boilers—each 23 ft long—cannon shot was being heated and when within range Hastings opened fire. The red-hot shot soon had the brig alight and in an hour she was completely burnt out. Hastings has not been forgotten by the Greeks, for his statue stands in a prominent position in the Garden of Heroes at Messalonghi.

Island of Palaio Trikeri is the larger of two wooded islands inside the E. arm at the entrance to the Gulf. Its most prominent feature is a monastery which has recently become an hotel. Although most of the inlets have been examined with a view to finding convenient anchorages, none have been found. The best place to secure temporarily in a small yacht is at the Skala—a charming cove with three or four small houses on the S. coast. Let go the anchor in 7 fathoms and haul in the yacht's stern to a wood pier where the Volos caique-ferry berths.

A small well-sheltered bay will also be found east of the Skala.

In the S.E. corner of the Gulf is

Vathudi. Chart 1556, plan. This is an attractive wooded bay affording shelter and convenient anchorage at the mouth of any of the small coves in depths of about 3 fathoms. During the Meltemi the best shelter is S.E. of the shipyard beyond the caique moorings.

Facilities. Limited provisions, including fish and ice, can be obtained at the café-store belonging to the shipyard. This has been building large caiques for some years and has recently accepted yachts for slipping and laying-up. (Caiques have moorings S.E. of the yard.)

This large enclosed bay is quite unspoilt and inhabited only by a few peasants. It is well worth a visit, being cooled in summer by an unfailing day breeze.

Petraki, lying a mile north of Vathudi, is a charming cove with olives and shrubs.

Approach and Anchorage. North of Alatas Islet can be seen a quarry, and then the cove opens to the N.W. Anchor in 2–3 fathoms, complete shelter. Temporary anchorage can be found in a cove close west of Vathudi entrance, and also under a small headland S.E. of Cape Maratea.

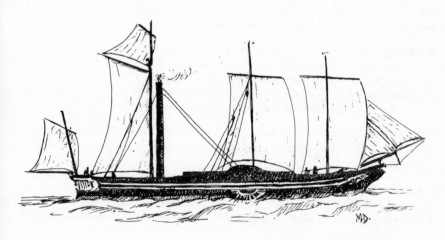

Inside the western arm of the gulf is

Pteleos Bay, a long mountainous inlet with two villages believed to be where Achilles set off for Troy.

> **Approach and Anchorage.** Charts 1521 and 1556. The best place for a yacht to make for is **Pigadia** (or **Paralia Pteleou**) village. Anchor off the ramp in 3 fathoms—sand. Alternatively anchor 200 yds westward in 6 fathoms where shelter from the day breeze is better. The whole gulf is exposed to the prevailing N.E. breeze coming in from the Trikeri Channel and there is always a swell after the wind has fallen off in the evening.
>
> Off the larger village of Achilleion at the head of the Gulf, where the fishermen land their catch for Volos, the anchorage is very exposed; and under the shelter of the Achilles Tower peninsula the depths are too great. Off Pigadia village is the best choice.
>
> **Facilities.** Pigadia is only a poor little hamlet with a road to Volos. The taverna sells basic provisions including fish.

The Achilles Tower is part of an early medieval stronghold with foundations of defending walls and much piled-up rubble. The view from the top of the hill is rewarding, for apart from the magnificent country surrounding the gulf, one can see the Achilleion peninsula with its ancient port, now silted, beside it.

Further N. Westward is

Mitzellas (Chart 1196, plan), or Amalioupolis, a small village with a stone pier off which a yacht can anchor and haul in the stern. A taverna and a water pump are close by. At night with N. winds, one should proceed to an anchorage in the large cove off a sandy beach in the N.W. corner of the bay where there is shelter from the swell caused by the day breeze.

Fearless Cove leading off Ormos Sourpis is a delightful place among pines and olive groves; a perfect anchorage with excellent shelter and almost deserted. Known only as Loutraki Amalioupolis to the Greeks.

> **Anchorage.** Chart 1196. Let go off the beach, about 5 fathoms, sand and mud. A couple of caiques have permanent moorings here and in winter one or two yachts lay-up afloat. Shelter is claimed to be all-round. Land in the dinghy at a stone pier.
>
> **Facilities.** The village of Amalioupolis is 15 mintues' walk over the saddle. Fish and simple supplies can be bought. A bus service on a new road plies to Volos.

Volos, a town of 70,000 inhabitants, lies at the head of this large gulf. Though the port is clean and sheltered, it is seldom that a yacht makes this long detour for a special visit.

The Port

> **Approach and Berth.** Chart 1196. The entrance is straight-forward by day or night. Yachts and coasters usually berth stern to the quay off the yacht station, near the centre of the town;

the bottom here is soft mud. In the summer months the afternoon breeze is usually from the southward.

Port Facilities. Good water is available from a hydrant at the root of the mole, and a hose is provided. Diesel fuel and petrol can be bought and ordinary repairs undertaken. Some yachts lay-up here in winter, the shelter being adequate, and the assistance of mechanic, carpenter and sailmaker being available. (A skid-cradle is used for slipping at Port Vathudi.) At the eastern end of the town is a small but unique collection of painted stellas.

At Volos modern hotels have been built and there are some good restaurants on the water-front. There are frequent buses to Larissa, Athens and Salonika, and sea communication with Skiathos and islands of the Northern Sporades. Air connection with Athens.

Officials as for Port of Entry.

Volos has developed considerably since the Second World War and is now the fourth largest town in Greece. It suffered early in 1955 from a severe earthquake when a number of the older buildings were destroyed, but prompt action by the authorities soon restored the town to working order.

The country round Volos, both on Mt Pelion itself and on the coast beneath it, is attractive. To avoid the heat of Volos in the summer evenings, a drive to Portaria (half way up Pelion) or Macronitsia is recommended; each is picturesque with hotels, good restaurant and a terrace with plane trees. Along the coast are little villages among olive groves where one may also dine simply but well. Returning to the *Trikeri Channel* and then proceeding north-eastwards along the Magnesian promontory one comes to two coves suitable for temporary anchorage:

Andriami, well sheltered in attractive scenery affording anchorage in 3 fathoms in the N.E. corner of the bay. Chart 1556.

Platania, with its small hamlet in wooded surroundings, and an anchorage in 3 fathoms on a sandy bottom. There is a small hotel, provision shops and bus connections to Volos. Of the two coves, Andriami provides the better shelter from the day breeze.

Following the *southern* shore of the Trikeri Channel and heading north-eastwards one reaches Cape Artemision where in 480 B.C. a hundred Athenian warships had their first brush with the invading Persian fleet. There is no anchorage here, but on the south side of the offlying islet of **Pondiko** is a small attractive cove affording convenient anchorage for a small yacht.

Historical. Only a few years ago, with the discovery of a white marble slab at Troezen, details came to light of the naval strategy employed by Themistocles to save Athens from the coming Persian invasion. The writing on the slab explains the employment of delaying tactics to be adopted by the Athenian warships off Cape Artemision: it directs that the trireme's crew should consist of a captain, 20 marines and 4 archers; and it gives the disposition of the other 100 triremes which were to lie off Salamis and the Attic coast to 'keep guard over the land'. Before these details were found, it was never realized how carefully Themistocles had planned the Battle of Salamis. Herodotus adds that a force of Greek galleys had been stationed at Skiathos in order to give warning of the enemy's approach by fire-signal.

NORTHERN SPORADES

Including Skyros there are nine islands, some of which are of great interest and beauty. Chart 2072.

Island of Skiathos

has green and gentle slopes, relatively low-lying and thickly wooded. There is an attractive little village standing on two hills. This was built early in the last century, after the abolition of piracy, and has now eclipsed in importance the early capital Kastro, perched on a rocky spur on the other side of the island. The island's population today is nearly 4,000, but with the growing tourist development and its many large hotels and villas the summer population is greatly inflated. (See photograph, fac. p. 44.)

The Harbour has fair natural protection.
Berth. Chart 1196, plan. The new quay (N. and S.) north of the small wooded islet enables yachts to berth here stern-to; alternatively there is anchorage behind the island in 3 fathoms, where the bottom is thin weed on sand. The depths shoal rapidly close to the quay.

There is also a quiet anchorage at the head of the large bay, half a mile N.E. of the town, 100 yds off a small chapel. (Closer inshore the bottom is fouled by old cables.) A farm nearby, with a jetty, can supply water, eggs and vegetables; they can also ferry one to the town. The shipyard here was still busy repairing caiques in 1973.
Facilities. Off the town quay is a fresh water tap and a fuel pump by the yacht station. Provisions and ice are available by the main pier. Two or three good restaurants. The island is reached by steamer daily from Volos, and from Athens by bus to Ayios Constantinos and thence by steamer in 7 hrs altogether.

Apart from the statue to the local Greek writer Papadiamandis and the shipyard at the head of the bay, there is nothing particular to see near the village. The place has much charm and the gardens of the little houses grow an abundance of flowers.

The Aegean's best bathing beach, **Koukounaries** (meaning stone-pine) lies only a few miles to the westward and affords convenient anchorage in calm weather.

Island of Skopelos

is green and rocky with sharply defined mountain ridges. Some of the wooded valleys lead steeply upwards to attractive monasteries still inhabited mostly by nuns who have recently established a weaving industry, selling blouses and skirts to the tourists. Skopelos, the capital, is unfortunate in having an artificial port so exposed to N.E. gales that sometimes it becomes almost untenable. It lies in a lovely setting, with the houses of the town, rising like the sides of an amphitheatre almost overshadowing the port. Above are olive groves; here and there clusters of cypresses, and vineyards beyond.

Port Skopelos

Approach. Chart 2072. The breakwaters have recently been rebuilt and the harbour dredged. Shelter has been improved by extending the outer mole. A yacht should not attempt to enter the port in a strong Meltemi, but seek shelter instead at an anchorage on the S.W. coast.
Berth. Proceed to W. side of the harbour and secure stern to the quay off the yacht station. Should the Meltemi blow strongly it is best to shift berth to the centre of the harbour and ride to the anchor, or ease off the warps if moored to the quay. Depths at the entrance are 3 fathoms shelving to 2 at the quay; the bottom is mostly firm mud.
Facilities. Water, fuel, fish and ice at the quay; an excellent market garden south end of the quay. Baths at Tourist Pavilion and the new hotel. A mechanic is available at a workshop on the water-front. Restaurant and tavernas nearby. Bus service to Glossa for Skiathos. Steamer services almost daily to the mainland connecting with Athens and Volos.

Two monasteries can be seen in a commanding position on the slopes high above the port; a 4th-century church with frescoes lies north of the town,

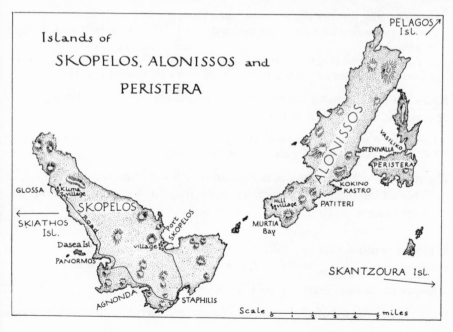

and to the S.E. is a pottery works. Charming scenery forms the object of some delightful mountain walks. (See photograph, fac. p. 45.)

On the S.W. coast of the island are the following anchorages:

Glossa (Klima) is a pleasant small harbour with adjoining hamlet protected by a mole: used by caiques and during strong N. winds, by the mail-boat for landing passengers from the mainland.

> **Approach.** The long breakwater has been further extended, but in 1968 the light was still 50 yds inside the mole's extremity.
> **Berth** inside the breakwater at a quay which until half-way along affords sufficient depths. A new mooring-quay has been built and the mole extended to 220 yds; the harbour dredged to 16 ft.
> **Facilities.** Water is laid on at the quay. Two tavernas are at the port and ice can be ordered (24 hrs). The village, above, can be reached by following a donkey track, or there is an occasional bus, which connects with Port Skopelos.

The walk up the hilly slopes is rewarding, for not only are there fine views from the top, but one passes through luxuriant vegetation with masses of fruit trees including plums, an island speciality.

Panormos Bay, a charming small cove, at the S. end of the island, affording complete shelter for not more than two yachts.

> **Berth.** Entering the cove one sees some ruined cottages at its head. Anchor in 5 fathoms, bows N. and run out a warp to a pine tree on the beach. Winds are only N. or S., no swell, complete shelter.
> **Facilities.** The main road from Glossa to Skopelos passes by. Occasional buses, but no amenities nearby. There are two houses, both occupied during the summer months.

Agnonda is a charming steep-to bay with a pebbly beach at its head and one or two little houses in the N.E. corner.

> **Anchorage** is about 70 yds off the beach in 3 to 5 fathoms on a sandy bottom. Open only to S.W.: a convenient Meltemi anchorage. Land in the dinghy at the quay.

The road to Port Skopelos passes by and there is a café by the water-front. In hard N. winds the ferry-steamer for Port Skopelos sometimes puts in here although space is very restricted.

Staphilis, a more open bay, affords the nearest safe anchorage to Port Skopelos in the event of a strong Meltemi. A few houses and a camping site.

> **Anchor** off the sandy beach in 3 to 5 fathoms, on sandy bottom.

Staphilis was named after the son of Theseus and Ariadne. In recent years his alleged tomb on the rocky peninsula has been excavated and certain gold treasures recovered, which are now in the museum at Volos.

Island of Alonissos has a rocky forbidding N.W. coast without inlets; this contrasts with the S.E. shores which have some attractive anchorages suitable for a small yacht. On the summit of the S.W. peak, nearly 1,000 ft up, is the attractive unspoilt village of Alonissos which is worth a visit. A yacht should anchor in 4 fathoms (mud on sand) 100 yds off the beach in the western-most cove in **Murtia Bay** on the S.W. of the island. A mule track ascends to the village—half an hour's climb.

Patiteri (Patitiri), a small cove partially protected by a short mole with a growing summer hamlet at its head.

> **Approach and Anchorage.** Steer for the centre of the small buildings leaving the mole-head to starboard. A small yacht may anchor off the beach in 3 fathoms on a sandy bottom. Open between E. and S.E. With increasing tourist activity this small port is often crowded with caiques and small ferry craft. The mole was extended in 1972.
> **Facilities.** Some new small hotels and a taverna near the quay. During summer there is a steamer and caique service between here and Skopelos with connection to the mainland.

Stenivalla (Chart 2072) lies midway along the coast almost opposite the most southerly projection of Xero. It is a very small cove with just sufficient room for one yacht to swing when anchored in 4 to 5 fathoms.

> **Anchor** off a small jetty (3- to 4-ft depths at its head) and run out a warp ashore, or anchor off; partly exposed to S.W.
> **Facilities.** A taverna with excellent fish, and a small hotel. Ice may be bought.
> **Note.** Kokino Bay also affords some shelter.

Island of Peristera (Xero), lying close S.W. of Alonissos; barren and uninhabited, with some small inlets at its southern end. The principal bay:

Vasiliko is almost landlocked and except for a couple of cottages there is no sign of life.

> **Approach and Anchorage.** Chart 2072. Passing between Alonissos and Peristera, a yacht should anchor in 3 or 4 fathoms at the head of the bay.

Island of Pelagos is wooded, tall, and almost uninhabited; two delightfully green mountainous anchorages and all-round shelter. The two main anchorages are:

Ayios Petros, a remote cove on the S. side of the island.

> **Approach and Anchorage.** Make for the furthest E. cove and anchor in 3 to 4 fathoms on

sand and stone bottom in very clear water. Almost entirely sheltered. Room for 3 or 4 yachts to swing. No sign of habitation, only large herds of goats.

Port Planedhi

Approach and Anchorage. Chart 2072. There is no difficulty by day, and *Sailing Directions* gives a good description. Though the channel is only 90 yds wide at its narrowest point, there need be no difficulty in beating through. The W. corner of the cove off a beach (where one can run out a warp to a boulder ashore) as well as the S.E. arm, are suitable anchorages; here the bottom is firm mud, and shelter is complete.

Despite the fact that the anchorage is entirely enclosed by high mountains, it is refreshingly cool and there is a potent scent of herbs. The only summer visitors are the fishing boats and caiques that call here for charcoal which is prepared close to the shore and then shipped to Salonika. In 1968 a herd of wild horses belonging to the monastery were roaming over the countryside.

The monastery lies on the E. side of the island towards its southern end and in 1968 was occupied by only one monk. The group of white buildings may be sighted from seaward standing above a small and rather open bay, where a yacht can sometimes anchor and run out a warp to a large rock on the E. side of the shore. Here one can sometimes land; the 11th-century church with some interesting icons makes the expedition worth a visit. The views from here across the sea and islands are beautiful. This area provides good fishing which helps to augment the budget of one or two shepherd families; this is probably one of the more primitive communities in Greece.

The remaining three islands lying to the N.E., **Yioura,** a naval island (controlled landing), **Piperi** and **Psathura** are uninhabited and without suitable landing places.

Island of Skantzoura en route to Skyros can be of use to a yacht wanting a night anchorage. Behind Parausa Islet is a small bay, with partial shelter; but on the west coast in Ormos Skantzoura is good shelter from all but S.W. winds in depths of 3 fathoms on a sandy bottom. At the south end of the island is anchorage in 4 fathoms off a sandy beach.

Anchorages
(a) Parausa; in the bay are 3-fathom depths on a sandy bottom with weed.

(b) a bay on the Ormos Skantzoura end of the island has better shelter with more room to swing, but barely depths of 2 fathoms, weed on sand. Shelter from east winds.

Island of Skyros

is rugged, mountainous and partly wooded, with a village of the same name lying inland on the shoulder of the tall mountain. There are two harbours: Linaria Bay containing the very small main port for Skyros and Linaria Cove (an excellent anchorage) beside it; in the south is Port Trebuki an anchorage more suitable for steamers. (See photograph, fac. p. 62.)

The Port of Linaria

Approach and Berth. Chart 2048. The passage north of Valaxa Island has slightly less depths than charted; one cannot depend upon more than 2½ fathoms and the passage should not be attempted at night. By the small harbour entrance the white house and the green flashing light are easily distinguished; beneath them a 50-yd mole trends northwards and has been recently extended. The short quay, also on the S. side of the port, has depths of only 4 to 6 ft, but this too is being built out to afford depths alongside of 6 to 12 ft. When berthing in a yacht one should lay out the anchor northwards and haul in the stern towards the quay. (Every morning and evening the quay is taken up by the Kimi ferry-steamer.) The bottom is clay or mud and it rises steeply; when letting go care must be taken to avoid heavy mooring cables of the caiques which can usually be seen through the clear water on the sea-bed.

Facilities. A water tap is on the quay by the nearer taverna. Petrol and diesel fuel may be bought. Basic provisions are obtainable. Ice arrives daily by the ferry-steamer and is sent to the Chora (Skyros village). Two tavernas and two modest hotels have recently been built. A bus runs to the Chora twice daily. The Piraeus steamer calls and so does the Kimi ferry.

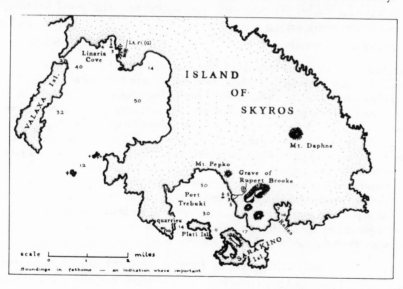

Linaria Cove. In the event of the harbour being too congested, there is good anchorage in 5 fathoms in Linaria Cove—weed on clay and mud. This is the best place for newly arrived vessels and a useful anchorage in unsettled weather.

The Island of Skyros, with a population of about 3,000, has its main village, or Chora, on a rising slope on the east side of the island. It can be reached in

20 minutes by bus and is well worth a visit. There are some interesting houses, the Byzantine church of St George and local crafts, also a well-arranged small museum. A new Xenia Hotel is on the beach at the foot of the village.

In ancient times the acropolis stood just above the present village, and the walls connecting it with its port beneath can still be traced; the mole is shown on Admiralty chart. Until the end of the last century Skyros exported wheat, wine, honey, oranges and lemons; nowadays goats are grazed and sent by caique to Athens.

The original herd of wild ponies sometimes to be seen in the country is now largely diminished, and the remaining ponies are cared for by a British organization.

The statue to Rupert Brooke stands in an imposing position north of Skyros village looking across the brilliantly coloured sand and over water of many shades of blue towards the distant islands beyond. Brooke died on St George's Day 1915 on board the French hospital ship *Duguay Trouin* at Port Trebuki when on the point of sailing for Gallipoli.

Port Trebuki (Tres Boukes), a large enclosed bay surrounded by barren hills, is unsuitable for yachts. There is only one anchorage with good holding, but with northerly winds strong gusts sweep down from the mountains and spoil the tranquillity. The only interest here is the grave of Rupert Brooke.

Directions. Anchor off the river-mouth (see plan), in depths of 3 to 5 fathoms; bottom is weed and sand, good holding. Position: from river-mouth Mt Daphne bears 045°, N.W. point of Sarakino Island 195°. The mouth of the dried-up stream can be identified by a loose stone cairn; on landing here, one can follow its course and presently reach an olive grove. The grave will be found on the west side of the stream, about 20 minutes' walk.

For those visiting the poet's grave, a brief description of the burial written immediately after the ceremony by Edward Marsh may help to recreate the scene on 23 April 1915:

'We buried him the same evening in an olive grove . . . the ground covered with flowering sage, bluish grey, and smelling more delicious than any flower I know. The path up to it from the sea is narrow and difficult, and very stony; it runs by the bed of a dried-up torrent. We had to post men with lamps every 20 yards to guide the bearers. The funeral service was very simply said by the chaplain, and after the Last Post the little lamp-lit procession went once again down the narrow path to the sea.'

Winston Churchill, writing to *The Times* on 26 April said, 'A voice had become audible, a note had been struck, more true, more thrilling, more able to do justice to the nobility of our youth in arms engaged in the present war than another. . . . The voice has been swiftly stilled.'

> *If I should die, think only this of me:*
>   *That there's some corner of a foreign field*
> *That is for ever England.*

7   Skyros. *See p.* 60

8   Prosforion Tower, Chalkidhiki. *See p.* 70

9   Thasos: the harbour from the acropolis. *See p.* 75

10 Athos: Simon Petra monastery

11 Athos: Dionysiou monastery

12 Local craft: Bratsera with Trehandiri hull. *See p.* 237

13 Local craft: Gagava

Akladi Cove is reputed to have prehistoric dwellings, visible on the bottom in clear weather; but an examination of this cove in 1968 failed to locate anything of interest. The holding here, weed and fine sand, is unreliable.

Renes Bay, deserted and rocky, has a small cove in the N.W. corner. Although well-sheltered, one must anchor in not less than 7 fathoms to ensure room to swing. The bottom is weed on fine sand, the holding poor.

The south coast of Skyros is almost forbidding; only a few goats are to be seen, and the rubble mounds of early quarries on the hills. The bays on the west coast are used by small fishing craft, but are not recommended for yachts.

Glifadha Cove, on the south side of Sarakino Island, affords anchorage in 3 fathoms on a sandy bottom, open only to south.

> **Mythological notes on Skyros.** It was here that Thetis decided to protect the young Achilles by disguising him as a maiden among the daughters of Lycomedes. 'What songs the Syrens sang, or what name Achilles assumed when he hid himself among the women' wrote the witty 17th-century writer Sir Thomas Browne 'though puzzling questions, are not beyond all conjecture'.
>
> The bones of Theseus were also found on the island, and according to Thucydides were then conveyed to Athens to be enshrined in the Theseon.

COAST FROM NORTHERN SPORADES TO GULF OF SALONIKA

This coast is straight and without shelter for 100 miles. The predominating feature is Mt Olympus, nearly 10,000 ft, and the high mountains in the vicinity. Chart 1085.

The Thermai Gulf leads into the Gulf of Salonika and, though there are some night anchorages close off the coast, they are completely open and practical only in flat calm weather.

The Meltemi can blow in strength from the Axios River (formerly the Vardar, and renowned for the duck shooting) down the gulf. This happens for periods of only 2 or 3 days, often followed by a S.W. sea breeze blowing up the gulf every afternoon.

SALONIKA (Thessaloniki)

The second city of Greece, with a large commercial port, has been the capital of Macedonia since earliest times. It is a Port of Entry.

The Marina

> **Approach and Berth.** Chart 2070 and plan below. A yacht marina completed in April 1973 lies 12 kilometres on the motor road S.E. of the city in Thermaikos Bay. One hundred and fifty yachts (max. length 100 ft) can be accommodated in depths of 3 to 4 metres.

Officials. Port authorities. A British Consul-General.

Facilities. Water, fuel, telephone, power; shops and restaurant nearby. Hauling out arrangements are planned. Berthing charges slightly less than at Zea.

Salonika is connected to Athens by air (1 hr); train and bus (about 7 hrs). Express to London 2½ days.

Officially known by its ancient name of Thessaloniki, the modern city, with a population of nearly half a million, presents a great contrast to the walled, oriental town captured from the Turks in 1912. The large cemeteries outside the

town are evidence of its occupation by Allied troops during the First World War. Between the two wars some progress was made in rebuilding, but in 1940 with the German invasion the place sank to a low ebb. However, all these misfortunes have now been forgotten and one sees the bold façade of a modern and prosperous-looking city with esplanades, public squares, large hotels and skyscrapers; many of the inhabitants are workers at the new industrial plants growing up inland on the outskirts of the city. Unfortunately the pollution caused by industry has had a contaminating effect on the fish normally caught in the gulf.

In Roman days the port became more important when the Via Egnatia was completed. This great military highway from Dyrrachium (now Durrës, Albania) linked Rome with her eastern empire. It passed through Thessalonica, Amphipolis and Phillipi before reaching Byzantium.

The guide-book describes the town's associations since the days of St Paul, and the historic Byzantine churches; together with the ramparts and the White Tower they should be visited.

Mount Olympus is within close reach.

> *. . . yet here will I*
> *Upon Olympus' lofty ridge remain,*
> *And view, serene, the combat;*
>
> ILIAD XX

Climbing. Information on the ascent of Mount Olympus can be obtained from the office of the Greek Alpine Club either at Salonika, Athens or Litochoron, the village from which the climb begins. There are now three huts, one low down, one three-quarters of the way and one on top. Only the last few hundred feet involve a climb. Mules may be hired for the first two stages of the ascent; the second stage passes through wooded country and is much the more attractive. A guide is compulsory for the last stage. Three days are necessary for the expedition which can be made from late June to the end of August.

This chapter covers the seaboard of Grecian Macedonia* and Thrace.

THE CHALKIDHIKI PENINSULA

Paliourion
    Port Koupho
    Sikias Bay
Port Dhimitri

The Holy Mountain
    Daphni
    Vatopedi Bay
    Plati (Ierissos Bay)

Island of Ammouliani

STAVROS TO THE TURKISH FRONTIER WITH THE ISLANDS

Stavros Anchorage
Elevthero (Deftero) Cove
Kavalla
Keramotis

Island of Thasos
    Port Thasos

Vistonikos Bay (Porto Lago)
Alexandroupolis

Island of Samothraki
    Kamariotissa

Island of Limnos
    Port Mudros
    Kastro Merini

Island of Ayios Evstratios (Strati)

    * Greek Macedonia was acquired in 1913 after the Balkan Wars, and Thrace from Bulgaria after the First World War at the Treaty of Lausanne.

4

The Northern Coast

The western part of this coast, especially the Chalkidhiki (or Chalcydice) Peninsula and the island of Thasos, is of great beauty. Here, the summer winds blow with considerably less strength than in the southern Aegean.

THE CHALKIDHIKI PENINSULA

Looking at the chart, this unusual shape appears like a folded hand with three fingers sticking out into the Aegean. These are the peninsulas of Kassandra (Pallene), Sithonia and Athos or Akti. All are green and wooded, with hilly or mountainous country.

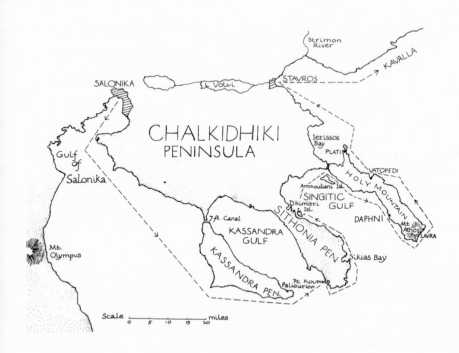

Kassandra, which is mainly pastoral and agricultural country, has a canal across its neck, which has been allowed to silt so much that there is a depth of barely 7 ft. The only suitable anchorage on the Kassandra shores is

Paliourion, near the eastern extremity of the peninsula, a recently advertised port of call, where fuel and water are available and a small hotel.

Across the Kassandra Gulf on the Sithonia peninsula, but 80 miles from Salonika, is the beautiful landlocked harbour of

Port Koupho (or Koufo) lying in an attractive setting amid pinewoods and olive groves with some small houses and farms nearby. There is room for several yachts to anchor here in excellent shelter.

> **Approach and Anchorage.** Chart 1679. Plan. The approach is easy day or night. Proceed to the head of Goras Bay and either anchor in 4 fathoms or haul in the yacht's stern to the Yacht Station pier (9-ft depth at extremity). Bottom is fine weed on sand, shelter is all-round. The port is little used in summer, but in winter is a base for fishing craft.
>
> **Facilities.** Fuel can be obtained at Nea Marmara 7 miles N.W. There is only one café, and provisions are practically unobtainable. There are some interesting caves on the hillside west of the hamlet. A new road is being built round the shoreline of the peninsula and there is reported to be public transport to Thessaloniki.

Sikias Bay. Barely a dozen miles from Port Koupho, it lies close to the mouth of the Singitic Gulf—a pleasant deserted sandy bay, sheltered on three sides, and worth a call.

> **Approach and Anchorage.** Chart 1679—inset. There is no difficulty day or night. The best anchorage is in 3 fathoms where indicated in the southern corner of bay. It is firm sand, and a perfect bathing beach. If it blows from the N.E. this anchorage is no longer comfortable.
>
> An anchorage 3 miles southward (2 miles N. of Cape Pseudhokaves), behind a rocky spur in a sandy bay, is sometimes to be preferred in N.E. winds.
>
> **General.** The hamlet of Sikia is 1½ miles inland, otherwise there is no connection with civilization.

Port Dhimitri. Lying deeper in this gulf is the lovely island of Dhimitri providing landlocked coves between it and the mainland, suitable for small yachts. The country is hilly and green with clusters of poplars and cypresses near the shore merging into olive groves close behind; a background of dark green pinewoods rises to the skyline beyond. There are only one or two small houses belonging to fishermen temporarily on the island; and on the mainland a number of farmhouses by a road connecting with Salonika. See plan.

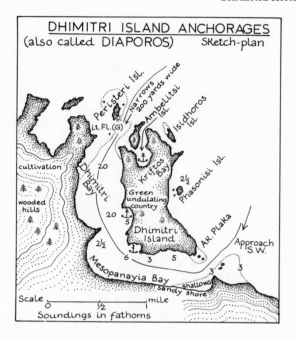

DHIMITRI ISLAND ANCHORAGES
(also called DIAPOROS)   Sketch-plan

Approach—*Sailing Directions* explain it in great detail; the sketch-plan is intended to simplify this.

There are two entrances:

South Entrance—This should be approached in a S.W. direction; the rocks are above water and clearly visible.

North Entrance is between the two wooded islets of Peristeri and Ambelitsi (the outlying rocks are above water and clearly visible). The channel leads through a narrow passage (200 yds wide) which at night is covered by the sectors of a flashing green light.

Anchorages close under Dhimitri Island are shown in the plan. There is also the pleasant sheltered anchorage of Kriftos Bay, entered by passing eastward of Ambelitsi islet.

Forming the eastern side of the Singitic Gulf is the narrow isthmus of the Akti or Athos Peninsula where Xerxes in 481 B.C. dug a canal to enable his galley fleet to pass in safety and avoid the much-feared storms off the headland. Landing at Tripita and walking inland, some of the diggings can be discerned, and though the land here must still be about the same level above the sea as then, the sea-bed close-by has sunk. In 12-fathom depths traces of large stone blocks can be seen and also the outline of early wharves.

Island of Ammouliani. Lying a mile off the isthmus, this island has a small fishing population. Though indented and irregular in shape, it is unattractive and rather barren. Certain coves indicated on the chart afford useful anchorage to small vessels, according to the weather.

In the summer months there is daily communication with Salonika by caique which brings provisions and ice.

On the Peninsula towards the frontier of the Holy Mountain is the prominent seamark of Prosforion, a Byzantine tower.* In contrast, the adjoining village of Pyrgos (which means Tower) is very new, having been built to accommodate the Greek population deported from one of the Princes Islands, in the Sea of Marmara, after the First World War. The construction of a modern hotel for tourists has brought some benefit to the villagers and the place is still growing, but apart from the hotel there are no amenities for a yacht.

Close offshore a long reef on which the seas break heavily during storms extends more than 2 fathoms underwater. The sea-bed on the southern side of the reef falls away quickly and at one place the Cyclopean walls of some early construction, long since submerged, can still be clearly seen.

In fine weather it is convenient to anchor in 2½ fathoms 200 yds N.W. of the Tower. (See photograph between pp. 62–3.)

The Holy Mountain (Mt Athos or Akti Peninsula)

Less than a mile from the Tower is the frontier of the Holy Mountain with its dwindling population of less than 2,000 monks, still leading a monastic life. There are altogether twenty monasteries with their sketes and kellia, undoubtedly seen at their best from seaward and, therefore, a yacht should sometimes stand in close or when desirable go alongside a jetty. Some monasteries were built in the second half of the 10th century; others at later periods. Most of them stand dramatically on various mountain spurs, or are tucked into the mouth of some green valley, or have grown up on fertile land close to the sea. With the exception of one or two relatively modern ones, each monastery is usually a heterogeneous cluster of Byzantine buildings in colourful shades of red or blue and conspicuous for their domes and cupolas. Though varying considerably in size and shape, when seen as one unit they nearly all look attractive in their green mountainous setting. (See photographs between pp. 62–3.)

The peninsula, which is nearly 25 miles long, is rugged and steep on its western side, whereas the eastern slopes are gentle and covered in a great variety of trees. Close to the ridge itself on both sides there is afforestation—beech and chestnuts above, oaks and plane trees below—also a flowering undergrowth. The long ridge forming a backbone reaches a bare peak (Mt Athos) near the extremity of the peninsula where it rises to over 6,000 ft; here it is rather bare and stands abruptly out of the sea.

* See *A Fringe of Blue* by Joice NanKivell Loch (John Murray).

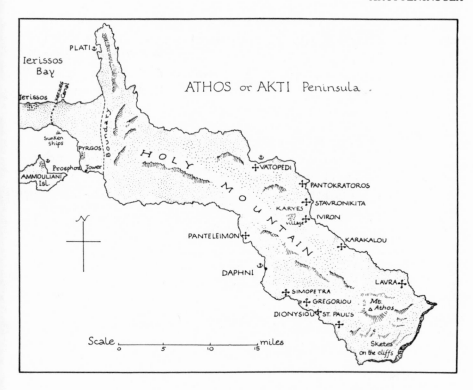

Daphni is the Control Port for the Holy Mountain—a temporary place of call if landing on the Athos Peninsula—and lies about half-way along the shores of the Singitic Gulf.

A Customs Officer and Police are stationed here to examine papers and possessions of visitors to the Holy Mountain. Women may not land, and men intending to do so must have the Greek Foreign Office permit. In 1969, after a thousand years of monastic rule, it was learnt that a civil administrator is to be appointed. Regulations regarding visitors might change.

Approach and Berth. About 100 yds S.E. of a light-tower is a small quay with a stone pier, having a depth of 6 ft at its extremity. The sea-bed rises sharply, and 70 yds off is a heavy mooring-buoy suitable for steamers; but near the pier-head is a patch of sand (which is not good holding) sufficient to hold off a yacht's bows when temporarily hauling her stern up to the end of the pier.

The prevailing wind does not blow home and though entirely open, one may expect sufficient shelter from the curvature of the coast during ordinary summer conditions.

General. There are one or two rather modest little shops, and a fresh water tap close by. The mule track leads to Karyes, the principal village of Athos, where permits to land on the Holy Mountain are again examined.

Continuing along the shore one sees the striking monastery of Simon Peter built solidly into the cliff, reminiscent of those fortress-like structures in Tibet. Further towards the top of the peninsula, and standing on the steep mountain-side, appear small houses. They are in fact the abodes of hermits and occasionally a monk may be seen under the shade of his black umbrella climbing up to one of these solitary habitations; some, even more primitive, appear as mountain caves, and are accessible only by ladder; others seem to have no visible mode of access at all and cling to the steep cliff like swallows' nests.

The sea off the extremity of the Cape can be very disturbed, and under certain conditions violent squalls sweep down from the mountain slopes. Mardonius experienced a phenomenal storm in 491 B.C. when from a clear sky a sudden Levanter blew up and wrecked the invading Persian fleet of 300 vessels.

Rounding the massive headland and approaching the north-eastern shores of the peninsula you come to one of the oldest and most attractive of the monas-teries, Lavra—here, one may land to climb the mountain; the Lilliputian harbour cut into the cliff close under the monastery can accommodate caiques up to 35 ft in length. Other monasteries have short piers where landing can be made in calm weather. There is only one summer anchorage on the N.E. shore of the peninsula and this is beneath the large monastery of

Vatopedi

Approach and Anchorage. Steer for the monastery buildings and let go 100 yds off the small stone pier in 4 fathoms. Holding is good, but the bay is open to the northern quadrant.
General Information. A policeman is on duty at the quay to check the coming and going of visitors and local people who have no direct connection with the monasteries.

During part of the summer a few of the fishing fleet are based here. The monastery still has its ancient aqueduct, and there is plenty of water available in the buildings today.

The only good shelter on the N.E. coast is in the large bight of Ierissos at the deserted cove of

Plati. This is a pleasant anchorage in which to bring up, and convenient for making a day excursion to those monasteries with jetties when the sea is calm.

Approach. Chart 1679. Pass to seaward of the islets off Cape Arapis as the inside passage has shoaled since the last survey.
Anchorage is almost anywhere in Plati Cove in 4 to 5 fathoms, light weed on sand—open only across the bight to S.W.—a fetch of 5 miles, but normally only the night breeze is from here, although wind direction in the cove changes frequently. Room for half a dozen yachts to swing. The surrounding land is relatively low-lying and the anchorage peaceful.

A number of fishing boats make use of another cove and some use Ierissos, the village opposite, where one can get limited supplies.

Continuing northwards, you approach the mountainous wooded slopes at the head of the Gulf of Strimon. On the sandy shores lies the village of Stavros and behind it an extensive cultivated plain reaching to the foothills beyond.

Stavros Anchorage. Plan on Chart 1679.

The setting is appealing, though the anchorage off the pier by the village, being no longer sheltered by the mole shown on the chart, is exposed to the southerly swell. North of the village the waters of the Rendina River, flowing from Lake Volvi (Beşik), enter the sea. The green and wooded gorge is attractive and may be followed along the motor-road for six miles as far as the lake; it is also partly navigable by boat, though the stream can flow swiftly in places.

STAVROS TO THE TURKISH FRONTIER WITH THE ISLANDS

Ten miles N.E. a more important river, the Strimon, empties its muddy waters into the Aegean. This is the first of the Macedonian rivers which flow from the Bulgarian mountains and empty into the North Aegean. There is also the Nestos (east of Thassos), the large lake at Port Lago fed by two rivers, and finally the Evros River forming the boundary between Greece and Turkey. The mouths and estuaries of these rivers are interesting to explore on account of the variety of wild birds; both the indigenous and the temporary visitors.

In Graeco–Roman days the Strimon formed an artery to the port of Eion close to the city of Amphipolis sometimes visited by St Paul. There are still a few Roman remains, and by the bridge across the river stands the large Amphipolis lion. Unfortunately the river no longer supports a fishing industry, for in recent years the rising levels of mercury, copper and lead are reported to have contaminated the fish.

Some 15 miles beyond the east entrance of the Strimon Gulf is

Elevthero Bay (Devtero), a dull but well-sheltered large bay with some loading wharves for steamers in the northern corner. The best anchorages for a yacht are near the medieval fortress (see Chart 1679, plan) or the north corner. A change of wind may quickly alter the sea level.

Kavalla, seven miles E.N.E., is the pleasant modernized commercial port (ancient Neapolos) which during modern times has been Greek only for about fifty years. With a population of nearly 50,000 the modern part of the town was built after the First World War to house refugees from Turkey.

Its earlier associations are shewn by the presence of a Roman aqueduct stretching across the town, and the Byzantine fortifications beyond its eastern suburbs. The modern, well-built port is often busy with medium-sized steamers in the tobacco trade, and during the summer months it is active with ferry-boats plying to Thasos with tourists.

It was recently announced that considerable natural gas deposits had been discovered close outside Kavalla.

The Port

Approach and Berth. Chart 1679, plan. No difficulty when entering day or night, but the yacht station is very exposed and has an inconveniently high wall for landing. Small yachts can usually shelter behind the S. mole.

Officials. A Port of Entry. The Harbour Office has been moved to the centre of the town.

Facilities. Water and fuel are available at the yacht station. A 25-ton crane and a 5-ton crane are available. Most things can be bought in the town; laundry, mechanical repairs etc. available. Some modern hotels, restaurants and tavernas are nearby. Daily air service to Athens. Frequent ferry-service to Thasos.

In the town is the old Turkish university founded by Mahommet Ali, now an old people's home; the house where he was born has become an interesting museum.

St Paul landed here on his way to Phillipi, whither a short excursion to the ruins may now be made by car from Kavalla. It was at Phillipi that St Paul gained his first European convert, Lydia, a purple-seller. Also, in A.D. 42, two years after the murder of Caesar, Antony and the young Octavian won a decisive victory over Brutus and Cassius.

Keramotis is a low-lying ferry port about 16 miles S.E. of Kavalla. This small port is the nearest point to Thasos, but is of no particular interest to a yacht except for the fish hatchery and the local delicacy of dried mullet roe.

Berth. Chart 1679, plan. Stern to the S. side of the quay (lit at night). Anchor in convenient depths—good shelter.

Facilities. Water and fuel are available. Ice at the root of the quay. Some tavernas nearby.

The mouth of the River Nestos lying immediately east of Keramotis is much frequented by wildfowl. Between the channels is a delta where pelican and sheldrake are frequently seen, also egret and heron fly across from Thasos where they breed. Many smaller marsh birds are also to be seen.

Island of Thasos

Tall and wooded, is largely of marble, one of the most beautiful islands in the Aegean. Though the green mountains are visible many miles off, the low walls of the old Greek harbour cannot be seen until close to. See photograph between pp. 62–3.

Port Thasos

Approach and Berth. Chart 1679, plan. When entering the harbour a yacht should keep in the middle where there are depths of 16 ft all the way in as far as the end of a short stone pier extending from the middle of the S. shore. Here, if space permits, a yacht should berth stern-to off its extremity with anchor laid in a N. direction. Depths towards the shore become very shallow. Harbour lights are exhibited and shelter is all-round.

Outside the harbour a few hundred yards westward is the ferry quay, but ferries, being now so numerous, occupy much of the harbour.

Facilities. Water and fuel, but there is also a water tap near the stone pier in the harbour. In summer provision shops are good but since much of the produce comes by ferry-boat from the mainland in the afternoon, it is wise to shop late. This includes ice which must be ordered by telephone from Kavalla. There are some good modern hotels in the new village and beyond, and tavernas by the harbour. Car ferries operate several trips daily both to Kavalla and to Keramotis.

The modern village of Thasos has expanded appreciably in recent years and is now much visited by tourists. The ancient town recently excavated by the French was surrounded by 2½ miles of walls with a dozen towers and gates. It rises to the acropolis standing on the hill among pines and olives behind the port. One may climb leisurely to the sites of temples and a theatre enjoying at the same time splendid views of both the port and the green wooded mountain valleys behind. Some of the finds from the acropolis have been assembled in the small museum by the port.

The countryside, similar to the Tyrolese landscape, should be explored; there is a variety of trees and birds; running streams are everywhere. The bus service is helpful in getting one to mountain villages.

In early Greek days Thasos marble was sent to Samothraki and used in the construction of the temples and for statuary. Among distinguished early visitors were Thucydides, historian and admiral, and Hippocrates, the famous doctor of Kos. Today the island exports no more marble, but mostly olives, honey and timber. One cannot predict its future role, but on 14th February 1974 the Greek Prime Minister announced the discovery of substantial high grade oil deposits only 6 miles south of this lovely island.

From Thasos Strait the low uninteresting coast of Thrace stretches eastwards for 70 miles towards the last Greek port, Alexandroupolis, close to the Turkish frontier. About halfway lies the large land locked lagoon.

Vistonikos Bay (Porto Lago) consists of the small port of Lago lying at the head of a low sandy bay, and a larger lake fed by a number of streams.

> **Approach.** Chart 1679, plan. After passing a light buoy 1 mile N.W. of Akri Fanari the harbour should be approached on a course 023°. The channel is marked by pairs of buoys and light-perches. After entering the lagoon turn to port and keep in the middle where a depth of 2 fathoms is maintained until near the concrete pier.
>
> **Anchorage.** Let go before reaching the pier and haul in the yacht's stern. Anchor should be to S.S.E.; depth about 11 ft, less off the quay.
>
> **Facilities.** Some small shops and tavernas. Ice; water from a tap and fuel. Some good bathing beaches.

Between the lake and the sea a large number of birds can be seen most of the summer months. Many may be seen alighting on the saltpans and lagoons; waders and sandpipers are common, while pelicans, herons and white tailed eagles fly in from Thasos to feed on the lake.

The coast between Lagos and Alexandroupolis is reported to have shoal-water extending further to seaward than charted, especially the shoals near Ak Makri not marked on the chart. Vessels should keep at least one mile off.

Alexandroupolis, formerly the wretched shallow Bulgarian port of Dedeag-atch, has been improved by the Greeks. The small town has become important on account of its communications by air, road and rail with Turkey. It lies near the mouth of the Evros River, marking the Turkish frontier. This is the largest of the rivers on this coast and it helps to augment the outflow from the Dardanelles and cause a south-going stream often apparent in certain channels of the Aegean.

On the river estuary are fisheries and on the banks upstream mulberry groves with a flourishing silk industry. In the delta a variety of birds are often to be seen; ibis and plover breed here; black storks, golden eagle, Egyptian vulture, falcons, woodpeckers, martins, and a number of smaller birds are often sighted. The best approach to the marshes is from the road near Perai.

Approach and Berth. Chart 1679, plan. Proceed to northern basin and berth at cement loading pier. Though rather dirty, the W. end is recommended where the berth is safe.
Facilities. Water and fuel, good provision shops, mechanical repairs. A 5-ton crane is available at the quay, also a 5/7-ton floating crane. Daily air service to Athens. Express to Istanbul in 12 hrs. Harbour authorities undertake to look after a yacht in event of the owner wishing to travel. Daily ferry-service to Samothraki.

The town has been given a new look and the water-front especially has been smartened up. Alexandroupolis is a Port of Entry.

The islands of Samothraki, Limnos, Ayios Evstratios and Imbros (now Turkish and mentioned later) all belong to the North Aegean.

Raised aloft like a woman's breast. STRABO

Island of Samothraki (Samothrace)

is a 'great lump of marble' rising from the sea. Shaped like Fujiyama this 5,000-ft mountain is partially covered in woods and on its western side a low spit of cultivated land helps to form some natural shelter for the small new harbour of

Kamariotissa. This is convenient for visiting the splendid archaeological sites.

Approach. One can enter harbour day or night. The curved breakwater, which has recently been extended by 100 yds, reaches from the western shore and trends in a S. direction. The quay has 2- to 3-fathom depths, and yachts should berth stern-to, anchor E.S.E., soft mud bottom, poor holding. Some yachts prefer to berth alongside if the ferry-steamer's berth (at the extremity of the mole), happens to be free. The Port can be crowded with fishing vessels. Shelter is good; only in S.W. winds can the harbour be uncomfortable. The Meltemi seldom blows here before the autumn months and causes little concern.
Facilities. Excellent water is available at taps on the quay. Basic provisions including fish are available at the hamlet close by. Ice comes daily by the ferry-steamer from Alexandroupolis. Bus and taxi (10 minutes) to archaeological sites at Paleopolis, where there is an hotel.

The Panhellenic Shrine, 'Sanctuary of the Great Gods', now being excavated by the Americans, is well worth a visit. The whole setting in a charming green valley lies beneath the great mountain peak without any modern infringement. It has an air of peace similar to Delphi before the tourist invasion. Near the theatre the famous 'Victory of the Samothrace' was discovered by the French Consul in 1863. In the well-arranged museum are some of the more precious finds.

The island is well worth visiting and in 1968, apart from an occasional call by a cruise ship, relatively few tourists came over by the ferry-steamer from Alexandroupolis, but it was planned to extend other transport services.

Island of Limnos

lying 40 miles to the southward of Thasos, is a dull, sparsely cultivated island, somewhat low-lying with a few hills, and the large harbours of Mudros (Moudrou) and Kondia which were used as fleet bases during the Dardanelles Campaign in the First World War. They are of little interest for a yacht today, and one should put in at Kastro Merini instead.

Port Mudros. Yachts should make their way towards the substantial modern village standing above the shore on the N. side of this large bay.

> **Approach.** Chart 1661. There is no difficulty but by day it is interesting to identify some of the hills. There are
>
> YAM Hill
> YRROC Hill
> EB Hill
> DENMAD Hill.
>
> By reading these names from right to left one learns what the British surveyors thought of their captain, whom they considered had worked them too hard and also had stopped their leave.
>
> **Berth.** Yachts may berth off one of the piers, still sometimes referred to as Australia Pier, Egyptian Pier etc. All were built originally in 1915 for landing troops and vehicles when army hospitals and depots ringed the shores of this great bay.

Kastro Merini (Limin Mirinas) is the only convenient harbour for small vessels and yachts, though this is liable to be crowded with caiques. A Port of Entry, and a convenient place for obtaining clearance if intending to visit the Dardanelles.

> **Approach and Berth.** Chart 1661, plan. Note that the light is positioned inside the Genoese Castle. A yacht should berth at the new pier stern-to in convenient depths. Good shelter.
> **Facilities.** Water and fuel at the yacht station. Good shops for provisions and other stores. Some good tavernas. Mechanical repair facilities.

Limnos, although fertile only on its eastern side, supports a population of about 25,000. It has steamer connection with Piraeus and Salonika, and air communications about four times a week with Athens.

Island of Ayios Evstratios (Strati), about 17 miles southward of the S.W. corner of Limnos, appears from seaward as a barren lump of rock without interest. It does, however, grow some agricultural produce which is exported only with difficulty, for the island is without a harbour or suitable shelter except for the small cove on the west coast, 4½ miles N. of Cape Tripiti. The village is over the hill on the E. side. Until recently political offenders, banished by the Greek Government, were sent to this island.

Introduction to Turkish Waters

Introduction to Turkish Waters

Before reaching Istanbul a visiting yacht sailing up the Dardanelles and Sea of Marmara will get an impression of rural Turkey which is dispelled on reaching the Golden Horn.

Istanbul, described briefly on page 92, is a westernized once-Byzantine city, something quite apart from the country towns and villages where three-quarters of the population live.

On the Anatolian coast the scenery is often very beautiful and there are expeditions to be made to ancient Greek sites,* many of the greatest interest; but the amenities in the small ports are apt to be disappointing. The villages may well be without dependable drinking water, fuel supply or electricity, and lacking a doctor or technician. The Government are making efforts to better social and industrial conditions, and have greatly improved the roads, although local transport is often by donkey or camel, and cars are few. Bus services now link up towns and villages, but unfortunately drivers generally cannot be trained fast enough to keep up with the increased transport, and Turkey is said to have the highest accident rate in the world. Nevertheless fairly reliable taxi-drivers are usually to be found in the small towns for those wishing to make a country expedition.

Turkish officials are almost invariably polite and welcoming, but their bureaucratic ways still make the entry and departure at even the smallest port an endless session of formalities. At one or two ports these have been expedited and it is hoped that as more visiting yachts appear formalities will be simplified.

Food is sometimes difficult to obtain when away from the towns, although with a few words of Turkish one can forage in the village and sometimes find eggs and tomatoes, an assortment of fruit and the local flat brown bread eaten by the peasants. Fish can usually be bought or caught (fishing by net is prohibited) and sometimes a farmer will sell an old fowl 'on the hoof'. In the towns food is

* It is recommended that every yacht should carry on board a copy of those excellent books *Aegean Turkey* and *Turkey—beyond the Meander* by George E. Bean.

14 Lesbos: Port Sigri. *See p.* 109

15 Amphorae from Sifnos being landed at Port Sigri.

16 Izmir, the old port, still suitable for yachts. *See p.* 116

abundant, good and cheap. Market-day is usually Friday, but it varies for different areas.

Some Food Terms:

bread	*ekmek*	fruit	*meyve*
meat	*et*	orange	*portakel*
veal	*dana*	apple	*elma*
vegetables	*sebse*	cherry	*visne*
water	*su*	apricot	*kayisi*
fruit drink	*serbet*	figs	*incir*
milk	*süt*	nuts	*findik*
wine	*sarap*	ice	*buz*

Steaks	cooked medium	*iyi*
	rare	*az*
coffee	with sugar	*sekerli*
	without sugar	*sekersik*

Fish (Balik). On the Turkish seaboard fish is greatly to be preferred to meat. Some of the more popular fish are:

small tunny or bonito	*kiliç*	grouper or rock cod	*orfo*, or *ofoz*
gilthead bream	*isipoura*	whitebait	*gümüs*
red bream	*mercan, fangri*	sardines	*sardelya*
white bream, or dentex	*saryos*	anchovy	*hamsi*
sea bream	*manda göz mercan*		
small species of bream	*sinagrda*	prawns	*karides*
red mullet	*barbunya*		
grey mullet	*kefal*	crawfish	*böcek, istakoz*
mackerel	*uskumru*		

Few people realize the quantity of fish to be found in these waters and in the Marmara. Over eighty varieties are said to exist and yet fishing has been as little exploited here as at other places on the Anatolian coast. The mackerel, according to local opinion, are unsurpassed in quality anywhere, and this is believed to be due largely to an abundance of plankton on which the sardine and anchovy feed; they are eaten by the mackerel which in turn is devoured by the bonito. Tunny frequent these waters and occasionally the blue shark.

The tunny which pass into the Mediterranean early in spring are keenly fished off Sardinia, Sicily and other places before they reach the Aegean and Black Sea to spawn. They enter the Black Sea along the coast of Asia and return along that of Europe, a peculiarity noted by Pliny who, following a theory of Aristotle, supposed that the fish see better through the right eye than the left! Yachts should be cautious about fishing in Turkish waters, and to avoid suspicion by Turkish officials prior permission to fish should be obtained through Tourist authorities. Net fishing, aqualung or lamp fishing by night are prohibited.

Fuel is seldom available at the quay and must be fetched from pumps in the towns.

Fresh water though plentiful is not easily accessible and sometimes of doubtful purity. It has been found to be good at Aivalik, and Fethiye, also at certain village wells. Marmarice has a hydrant on the pier, but it is not always in order.

Ports of Entry are as follows: Çanakkale, Istanbul, Ayvalik, Dikili, Çandarli, Izmir, Çesme, Kusadasi, Güllük, Bodrum, Datcha, Marmarice, Fethiye and Kaş. The authorities whom it is necessary to visit if they do not come aboard are: *Sağlic ve sosyal yardim bakanliği* (Health); *Polis* (Police); *Liman Baglama* (Port Captain); *Gümrük* (Customs). In each case a yellow bill of Health has to be obtained from the Health Officer, a passenger list (two copies) given to the Police, and a paper from the Port Captain (to whom dues are paid) has to be stamped by Customs. On leaving it is necessary to visit these officials in the order stated.

Military Areas are apt to vary from year to year, but for a long period the following were prohibited to yachts:

(a) *The Dardanelles, Sea of Marmara and Bosporus*
    The two islands Imros and Bozcaada (Tenedos).
    The area by Kumkale (south side of Dardanelles entrance), and by Cape Helles opposite.
    The Isthmus of Gallipoli—an area extending about 10 miles E.N.E. and W.S.W. of the old Bulair Lines.
    At Büyük Çekmece which touches the coast at Eregli for only about 2 miles.
    The N. entrance to the Bosporus on both shores of the Black Sea and for 7 miles inside the Bosporus.

(b) *The Aegean coast in the Gulf of Smyrna*—Approaches to Izmir
    A small area extending southward from Eski Foça.
    Uzun and Hekim Islands.
    A small frontage on the S. shore close to Izmir.

Turkish Nautical Terms may be traced back through the centuries and it is interesting to note that so few words stem from the Ottoman tongue, the majority of terms and expressions have come in via the Greek and betray their Venetian origin. This is hardly surprising when one remembers that at about the time of the Norman Conquest of England the Turks only began to occupy Anatolia. Ionian Greeks were then building and manning all the trading craft which they continued to do until 1920, and for at least two centuries during this long period the Venetians controlled the Anatolian ports.

The following glossary of sea terms may be of help on some occasions:

bow	pruva, bas	jib	flokos
stern	kic	mizzen	mezzana
deck	güverte	halyard	mandari
mast	direk	'pay out'	lasca
boom	bumba	'haul in'	vere, çekmek
keel	karina, omurga	port	iskele
mainsail	pani, yelken	starboard	sanjak

Pilotage Notes. In this section certain names are spelt according to the common English practice, e.g., Dardanelles, Gulf of Smyrna, Mytilene, Rhodes, etc.; others are in Greek or Turkish according to the present sovereignty of the places. This diversity of nomenclature sometimes presents a difficulty when wishing to explain to the port authority of one country the yacht's destination which may be a port of the other; Tenedos (near the Dardanelles) known for centuries by this name, is Bozcaada to the Turks, Samos is called Sisam. Fortunately Turkish harbour officials are often supplied with British charts and misunderstandings can be overcome.

In *Sailing Directions* the language difficulty sometimes arises, also, when referring to capes, bays, gulfs, islands, etc. To clarify a few of the more common words on the chart, the following brief glossary may be of help:

ENGLISH	TURKISH	GREEK	ENGLISH	TURKISH	GREEK
castle	hisar	kastro	new	yeni	neos
customs	gümrük	telonion	old	eski	palios
great, large	büyük	megalo	river	nehir, irmak	potamos
gulf, bay	körfez, koy	ormos	sky blue	gök	galaxios
island	ada	nisi	small	kücük	mikro
harbour	liman	limani	strait	bogaz	stenon, dhiavlon
headland, cape	burun, burnu	akri	tower	kale	pyrgos
hill	tepe	vouno	valley, stream	vadi, dere, su	koilada, vrýssis
lighthouse	fener	faros	village (main place)	Kasaba, köy	khora or chóra

GALLIPOLI AND THE DARDANELLES

Cape Helles
Çanakkale—(*Port of Entry*)
Lapseki
Gelibolu (Gallipoli)

SEA OF MARMARA

South Coast
Karabiga
Marmara Island
Pasha Liman Isl.
Erdek Bay
Mudanya
Gemlik
Armutlu
Yalova
Paulo Liman or Paulo Aydinli
Pendik
North Coast
Ereğli or Erekli
Silivri
Büyük Çekmece

PRINCES ISLANDS—'THE ISLANDS'

Büyükada
Heybeli
Burgaz
Kinali
Yassi
Sivri
Sedef
Tavşan

ISTANBUL—(*Port of Entry*)

Moda

THE BOSPORUS

Bebek Bay
Therapia or Tarabya
Büyük Dere

5

The Dardanelles to the Bosporus

GALLIPOLI AND THE DARDANELLES

The Western coast of the Gallipoli Peninsula consists of cliffs and sandy beaches with minor indentations suitable for anchoring only in the summer months. The background rises gently to hills of less than a thousand feet largely covered in scrub. Though Chart 1800 gives plans of both Arapos Bay (Gulf of Saros) and Suvla neither is suitable for yachts, and one should therefore make for the entrance of the Dardanelles.

It is impossible to sail past these shores without being moved by the sight of the Allied War Cemeteries. More than a dozen burial places of varying sizes were laid out, usually near where men fell in battle—a reminder of our heavy casualties in the campaign of the First World War where a million men fought for possession of the peninsula. Unlike the usual war cemetery elsewhere, the graves on Gallipoli are marked by plaques of marble lying horizontally on the ground, which is lavishly planted with cypresses and flowering shrubs. The southern end of the peninsula at Cape Helles is marked, not only by a Turkish lighthouse, but by the 70-ft British War Memorial, an obelisk cut in stone shipped from England. A French memorial can also be seen inside the entrance, and now the Turks have recently set up a large symbolic gateway on the high cape east of Morto Bay near the site of a famous battery called after Baron de Toth, the French engineer who modernized the defences early in the last century.

The Passage to Istanbul. From Cape Helles the distance to this former capital of Byzantium is about 150 miles, and much of the route passes through interesting scenery.

The Dardanelles continues for about 40 miles from the entrance until reaching Gelibolu where it begins to broaden out into the Sea of Marmara. The tall European banks broken by steep ravines are mostly covered in scrub with occasional clusters of trees. The land supports only rough grazing, and apart from the village mentioned, is sparsely populated. A foul current estimated to average at least 1½ knots should be allowed for.

Although the approach may be made at night this is not recommended; for, added to the embarrassment of steamer traffic, is that of the searchlights at Seddulbahr, which sometimes like to focus their beams on each approaching vessel. Also, if compelled to anchor off the Cape (a small bay known by the British in the First War as V-Beach) or in Morto Bay, it is possible that the

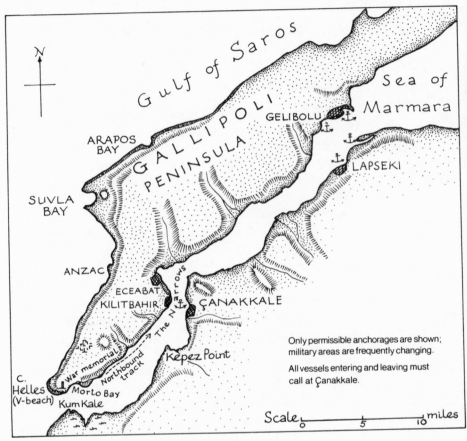

Only permissible anchorages are shown; military areas are frequently changing.

All vessels entering and leaving must call at Çanakkale.

Scale 0 — 5 — 10 miles

military would interfere. A yacht should therefore aim at entering the Dardanelles soon after dawn to be sure of completing Control formalities and reaching a suitable night anchorage later.

Route. Chart 2429 (with plan) shows that it is practical to follow close under the European shore, thus avoiding the full force of the outflowing current. At the entrance the current off the Asiatic shore often flows at 3 knots, but close under Cape Helles it is only half this velocity. Towards the Narrows it seldom exceeds 2 knots, except in strong north winds when a velocity of 5 knots has been known. All vessels, whether north-bound or south-bound, must call at Çanakkale for clearance, even if they come from another Turkish port.

The Current. Sailing vessels seldom used to attempt to sail up the Dardanelles against the current without a fair wind, and often waited outside many days until conditions were favourable. On one occasion in 1807, Duckworth, anxious to press on with his squadron to Constantinople, had to remain at anchor off Tenedos for nine days awaiting a fair wind.

Since the days of Leander many attempts have been made by swimmers to cross from one shore to the other.

On 3 May 1810, Lord Byron in company with a young lieutenant swam from Sestos to the Asiatic shore in 1 hr 10 min. On board the frigate *Salsette*, which was at anchor nearby, it was calculated that the distance from the place where they had entered the water on the European shore to the finish of the swim below the Asiatic fort was upwards of 4 miles although the width across the Strait was only one. In the summer of 1923 some naval officers accomplished the swim without difficulty, but in later years the Turks raised official objections to prevent a repetition of the performance.

The chart of the Dardanelles is now marked with the positions of wrecks, some of them British and French battleships sunk by German mines and Turkish guns on 18 March 1915 when the Allies were attempting to fight their way through this vital passage to gain the greater prize of Constantinople. This date was a decisive one for both the Allies and the Turks; for the Allies because they had to abandon any further attempt to force the Dardanelles by warships alone, and were thus compelled to raise a military expeditionary force, while the Turks, profiting by this delay, gained the necessary respite to enable them to continue the war.

On a hillside by the Narrows, in large characters formed of white stones, may now be seen '18 March 1915'. But all the forts have vanished, and except for an old Genoese castle there are no visible signs of defensive works today.

Çanakkale, lying on the Asiatic shore of the Narrows, is the Turkish Control Port for all vessels entering or leaving the Dardanelles. Sometimes a Customs boat puts off to the newly arrived yacht with other port officials necessary for Clearance. Although Çanakkale can now boast of one or two modest hotels and a museum displaying some Hellenistic and Roman objects from Troy, it is still poor and squalid, its houses and dusty streets presenting a depressing picture from seaward. It is also the residence of the Allied Graves Commissioner for the War Cemeteries on Gallipoli, which commemorate 40,000 British and Commonwealth dead. One can visit Troy from here; a car may be hired, and in about an hour one arrives at the scene of Schliemann's excavations which can be best appreciated by a previous study of Professor Blegen's book *Troy and the Trojans* (Thames and Hudson).

Anchorage. It is difficult to anchor off the port on account of the steep slope of the sea-bed and the changing swirls of the current. See Chart 2429. Anchor N.N.E. of the loading piers in the deeper water, or anchor temporarily at a wooden pier. There is also a small basin where a yacht may berth alongside to obtain clearance. On the opposite shore (Kilid Bahr) is Eceabat, a small port with a breakwater extending in a S.E. direction affording space for two or three yachts. Provisions may be bought. Also a ferry from the Asian shores calls.

Approaching Nagara above the Narrows, where the width is only a mile, the current usually runs at 2 knots, and rather unexpectedly flows faster at the sides than in the middle. It was here that Xerxes built his bridge of boats for the vast invading army he was leading into Europe in 480 B.C. The bridge crossed a little higher up than Abydos and touched the European shore between Sestos and Madytus. Herodotus wrote: 'And now as he looked and saw the whole Hellespont covered with the vessels of his fleet and all the shore and every plain about Abydos as full as possible of men, Xerxes congratulated himself upon his good fortune; but after a little while he wept.'

It was at Abydos that Alexander first set foot in Asia.

Today there is almost nothing to be seen at Sestos and only a few poor dwellings at Abydos, one of which, now a petrol dump, was the house where Byron stayed on his voyage from Smyrna to Constantinople:

> *The winds are high on Helle's wave*
> *As on the night of stormy water*
> *When love, who sent, forgot to save*
> *The young—the beautiful—the brave.*
> *The lonely hope of Sestos' daughter.*

In the Dardanelles twenty foreign steamers may be passed in the day, proceeding to or from Istanbul or the Black Sea ports, of which almost half may be flying the flag of Iron Curtain countries. Local caiques are also to be seen, ferrying either passengers or cattle from one shore to the other; but their graceful form has now changed. No longer do they resemble the Greek caiques with a low waist rising with a gentle sweep to a high pointed bow and stern. The modern design demands a high built-up waist where the weather screens used to be, and a raised poop on which is a wheelhouse. From head on, especially when lightly laden they appear not unlike the original Roman freighter. There are no sails—only a stump mast and derrick.

Further northwards the undulating countryside on the banks becomes more attractive, and in early summer yellow-brown cornfields suggest England at its best.

Continuing up the Dardanelles it will be necessary for a sailing yacht to find an anchorage for the night, as the summer breeze normally drops immediately after sunset.

NIGHT ANCHORAGES IN THE DARDANELLES

Lapseki, on the Asiatic shore, is a country town with a convenient roadstead protected by a stone pier.

> **Anchorage** is off the pier-head in about 3 fathoms; well sheltered except between N.W. and N.E.
>
> **Facilities.** Bread, fish, wine and fruit can be bought.

Lapseki, capital of the province, lies in an attractive position by the water-front amidst vines and olives with a background of wooded hills. Mostly of modern construction, this small town was once the sacred city of the Priapus cult.

Should the wind be unfavourable for anchoring here, a yacht may cross to the European side and anchor at:

Gelibolu (Gallipoli). There are suitable depths in line with the town jetty well-sheltered from the N. wind, alternatively the N.W. corner of the bay near a stone pier by a clump of trees near a hospital with an officers' mess. One can land by dinghy at the jetty where restaurants and shops are close by.

If wanting to press on to Istanbul it is recommended in summer to keep under the northern shore of the Sea of Marmara where the wind, especially at night, is better and there is shelter under the land. The coast however is of no interest, except for a couple of night anchorages which can be used by smaller yachts. The southern shores are interesting to follow:

SEA OF MARMARA

On the South Coast

Karabiga. A delightful anchorage behind the promontory of Kale Burnu, conspicuous for its medieval walls.

> **Anchorage.** Chart 844 plan. Anchor either off the village or N.E. of the above-water rock. Open to E. and S.E.

Marmara Island has the port of Marmara on its S.W. shore. A large breakwater provides excellent shelter and the small town is growing as a tourist resort with many shops.

Pasha Liman Island has an attractive landlocked bay with a primitive village.

> **Approach.** Chart 2242. It is easy to enter by day although the fairway buoy in the West Pass is sometimes missing, also the ruin forming part of the leading marks. There are no lights at night.

The Anchorage is off the village in 2- to 3-fathom depths on a sandy bottom. Perfect shelter. **Facilities** are few, though water and bread can be obtained.

At the eastern end of the Erdek Gulf there is good anchorage in the open bay off a small summer bathing place.

Approach and Anchorage. Chart 2242, plan on Chart 884. The channel between Tavsan Island and mainland has at least 3½-fathom depths. The island off the town has been almost connected by a causeway. The bay so formed is beautifully sheltered from all directions. **Facilities.** Summer hotels. Simple provisions.

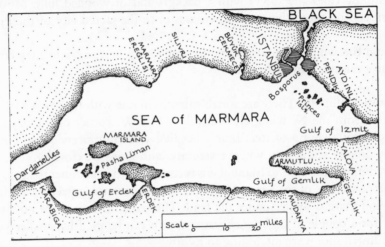

Mudanya is a commercial port with a substantial town, convenient for visiting Bursa (Brusa) and climbing the Uludağ (one of the many mountains called Olympus). See Chart 908, plan on Chart 844.

Anchor behind the breakwater, but clear of the ferries; somewhat exposed to N. winds. **Facilities.** Provisions of all kinds, hotels. Ferry-boats from Istanbul land tourists here who continue to Bursa by road.

The following are unimportant open anchorages:

Gemlik, a small summer bathing place at the head of the gulf.

Armutlu, opposite Mudanya, lies on the promontory—a bay well-sheltered from N.

Yalova has become a popular little ferry-port for tourists from Istanbul when visiting Bursa. Their cars are embarked at Kartal (near Pendik) and landed here at a pier. Both Yalova and nearby Çinarcik are completely open anchorages.

Eastward of Yalova the Izmit Gulf leads towards the naval base, an area prohibited to yachts.

Aydinli has the attractive and secluded Mankafa Bay, well-sheltered except during fresh W. and S.W. winds.

Anchorage. Charts 224, 497. Let go in Mankafa Bay E. of the barren and uninhabited Andreas Island S. of Paulo Burnu. There is a choice of small coves according to the weather.

Pendik affords good anchorage except in strong W. winds when yachts must move close under the lee of Pavli Island. Water, provisions, hotels and fuel available.

On the North Coast

There are some partially sheltered bays, none of which are worth visiting except for temporary anchorage:

Ereğli or Erekli, Chart 2604, plan. A yacht may anchor N.W. of a military jetty, but this is permissible only in event of bad weather, for the place is a military area. During approach the lighthouse must be given a wide berth.

Silivri, sheltered only from N. Nothing here of interest. A small hotel; provisions can be bought.

Büyük Çekmece affords anchorage off the beaches near some hotels, but it is very exposed to S. and S.W.—a bathing resort.

Before reaching the southern entrance of the Bosporus are the six Princes Islands (Adalar), formerly used by the Greek colonists as summer resorts. They are popular with Turkish tourists who pour out of the ferry-steamers from Istanbul to enjoy the fresh air, the flowers and the absence of motor traffic.

Princes Islands ('The Islands')

These islands, reached by a ferry service from Istanbul, are largely green and wooded. Some have become peaceful summer resorts, motor cars being prohibited, and afford anchorage for a yacht.

Büyükada, large and mostly wooded, was known to the Greek colonists as Prinkipo. It is a fashionable summer resort with hotels, villas and cafés by the sea front.

Anchorage off the sea front is too exposed, and the quietest place is in the southern bay of the island; open only to south.

Büyükada has a permanent population with a small village, and provision shops, but it lacks sufficient water.

Heybeli, attractive and wooded, is also inhabited and much frequented by summer tourists.

Anchorage is in the south bay of the island, pleasant scenery and quiet.

The island was inhabited during Byzantine days; from this period some buildings survive and have been embodied into the naval college. The old church of Theotocos is worth a visit. There are pleasant walks in the pinewoods, and if passing by the N.E. corner of the island one can see the grave of Sir Edward Burton, one of Britain's Elizabethan ambassadors.

Burgaz, lying close to Heybeli, has similar terrain and an anchorage behind a sunken mole whose root lies 100 yds south of the ferry pier.

Kinali, also inhabited, is without particular interest.

The four small islands are mostly uninhabited:

Yassi, sometimes used by the Navy, was once owned by Sir Henry Bulwer, who at the beginning of the last century built himself a mansion which has now become a ruin.

Sivri came into the news sixty years ago when the Turks rounded up all the dogs in Istanbul and put them on this island for extermination. **Sedef** and the small island of **Tavşan** (close S.E. of Büyükada) are without interest.

ISTANBUL

Chart 2286. Yachts on arrival should anchor off Dolma Bahçe out of the tideway and haul their sterns into the quay. Here there are depths of 6 ft, but west of the palace by the mosque there are 2 fathoms 10 ft from the quay. The Turkish authorities do not board newly arrived yachts, but expect the owner to come to the office with Ship's Papers. While port formalities are being completed, one may watch the never-ending flow of traffic; large steamers, local craft and fast motor-boats all straining to enter the Bosporus and Golden Horn. (Chart 1198.) At the same time one should not miss the opportunity of seeing the naval museum inside Dolma Bahçe.

Clearance may be obtained by visiting Yokµlu Salonu on the 'old city' end of Galata Bridge. At the Police Office is an information centre with an interpreter who is there to lead one to all the officials concerned.

After obtaining clearance, one alternative for a yacht is to anchor in comparative peace in the open bay of Moda near the Yacht Club Deniz. This has the disadvantage of a longer journey to reach Istanbul than if one went to the Bosporus Anchorages—see page 94, but on the other hand it is pleasantly cool and sheltered from the prevailing N. wind.

Facilities. Club Deniz can be most helpful to a foreign yacht. All provisions, ice etc. can be obtained with its help.

Water is available from a tap in the boat harbour and it is possible for a yacht to berth near the head of a small pier and take in water by hose with the assistance of the Club boatman.

A small repair shop is available at the Club, both for limited shipwright work and sail-making.

Petrol and diesel fuel (*motorine*) can be obtained in drums or one's own cans at one of the filling stations in Kadikoy.

To reach Istanbul a taxi is necessary.

> *Tall minarets, shining mosques, barbaric towers*
> *Fountains and palaces, and cypress bowers.*
>
> HEMANS

THE CITY. Guide-books describe the many interesting places to be seen in Istanbul, yet one is apt to forget that this city with its 3 million population has only recently acquired a western look. As late as the twenties the alleys and bazaars were crowded with men nearly all wearing the red fez and clad in Asian costume. There were Arabs, Persians, Kurds, Armenians, Circassians and Greeks, all to be distinguished by their dress. The few women to be seen were veiled. In the narrow streets were Dervishes, lemonade-sellers with their huge brass apparatus, story-tellers, letter-writers and barrel-organ players. Threading their way through this gossiping crowd, laden donkeys would pass with their drivers, and porters bearing heavy loads.

On 1 November 1922, these outward signs of an eastern world began to change, for Kemal Ataturk had come to power. By deposing the Sultan many centuries of ancient Turkish tradition and customs were discarded. A new democratic state arose with the Gregorian calendar, the metric system, hand-writing in Latin characters and western clothes. Almost over-night the fez and the veil were swept away and the secular powers of holy men and priests abolished. More than half a century has now elapsed, yet apart from some of its architecture this ancient Byzantine city has shed all outward signs of its oriental past.

THE BOSPORUS

The Bosporus, 16 miles in length and in places only 1,700 yds wide, is remarkable not only for its beauty but for its many types of ships and local craft. On account of the 3-knot current and unpredictable whirlpools it is advisable to proceed under power. Though permission to enter the Bosporus is not required, no vessels may proceed into the Black Sea without notifying the Turkish authorities, and at the same time a study should be made of the prohibited areas.

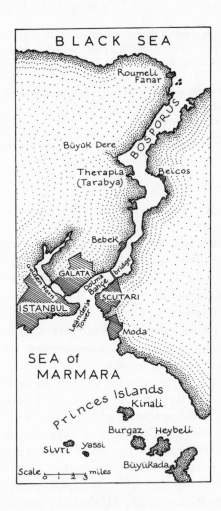

When proceeding to one of the Bosporus anchorages it will be noticed that the Asiatic shore is more peaceful, the traffic being mainly off the European coast. The new bridge joining Europe to Asia crosses the Bosporus between Ortaköy and Beylerbeyi, passing 64 metres above the high water level.

ANCHORAGES IN THE BOSPORUS (*Chart 2401*):

Bebek Bay is probably the most convenient anchorage for getting into the city by road.

Anchorage can be found out of the tideway in 2 or 3 fathoms where a number of local yachts have moorings, making the place very crowded. Holding is poor, and space being limited one cannot veer sufficient cable. No suitable place to leave a dinghy. Harbour official prefers use of buoy if available.
Note. When approaching this place from the south the violent current off Arnavut Kioi should be avoided by keeping in mid-stream or even nearer the Asiatic shore.
Facilities. Fuel and ice may be bought. There are provision shops and good restaurants; laundry and dry cleaning. One can land in the dinghy close to a bus stop for the city—nearly an hour's journey following the sea.

Therapia (Tarabya) is also convenient for a yacht to berth when visiting Istanbul

Berth stern to a quay on the S. side of the creek with anchor laid out to N.N.E. in somewhat deep water (about 8 fathoms). Dinghy can be hauled-out on N. shore where provision is made.
Facilities. A few local shops, and occasionally ice is available. An excellent restaurant, modern hotel on the point (baths and showers). Bus service to the city, also minibuses or shared taxis—a 20-min. journey.

Although there is little disturbance from passing steamers, the road traffic at night can be noisy.

Büyük Dere, used by many local craft also provides good anchorage out of the current. This is the official port for entering and leaving the Black Sea.

Berth alongside the T of the jetty by the boat-steps.
Facilities. Provision shops, fuel and ice are available. Drinking water by fire-engine. A good shipyard willing to undertake yacht work. Bus service to the city.

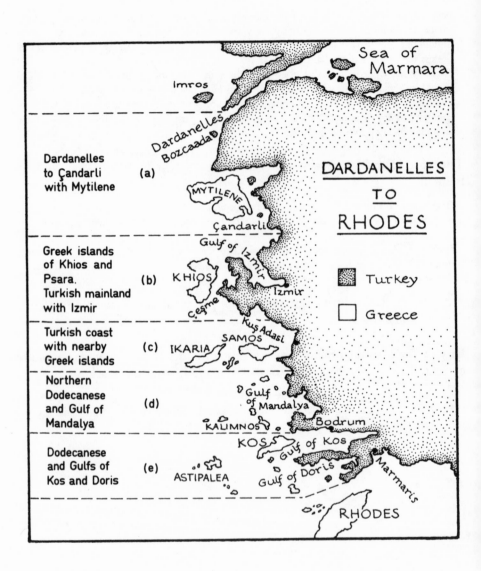

Sea of Marmara

Imros

Dardanelles
Bozcaada

Dardanelles
to Çandarli   (a)
with Mytilene

MYTILENE

Çandarli

DARDANELLES

TO

RHODES

Gulf of Izmir

Greek islands
of Khios and
Psara.   (b)
Turkish mainland
with Izmir

KHIOS

Izmir

Çeşme

Kuş Adasi

Turkish coast
with nearby   (c)
Greek islands

IKARIA

SAMOS

Turkey

Greece

Northern
Dodecanese
and Gulf of   (d)
Mandalya

Gulf
of Mandalya

Bodrum

KALIMNOS

KOS

Gulf of Kos

Dodecanese
and Gulfs of   (e)
Kos and Doris

ASTIPALEA

Gulf of Doris

Marmaris

RHODES

6a–e

Eastern Shores

THE DARDANELLES TO RHODES

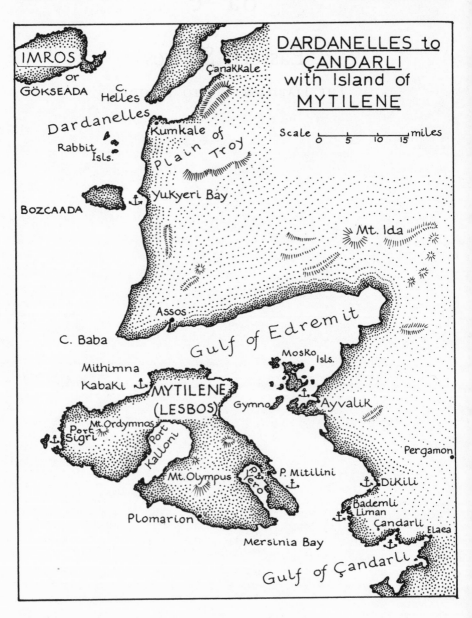

IMROS
or
GÖKSEADA

Çanakkale

C. Helles

Dardanelles

Kumkale

Rabbit
Isls.

Plain of Troy

BOZCAADA

Yukyeri Bay

DARDANELLES to
ÇANDARLI
with Island of
MYTILENE

Scale   0   5   10   15   miles

Mt. Ida

Assos

C. Baba

Gulf of Edremit

Mithimna

Kabaki

MYTILENE
(LESBOS)

Mosko Isls.

Ayvalik

Gymno

Pergamon

Port Sigri

Mt.Ordymnos

Port Kalloni

Mt.Olympus

P. Iero

P. Mitilini

Dikili

Bademli
Liman

Çandarli

Elaea

Plomarion

Mersinia Bay

Gulf of Çandarli

to Çandarli

TURKISH COAST	GREEK ISLAND
Island of Tenedos (Bozcaada)	Island of Mytilene (Lesbos)
The Port	Port Mitilini (*Port of Entry*)
	Port Kalloni
Beşika Bay	Plomarion
Yukyeri Bay	Mersinia Bay
Assos	Port Yero
Ayvalik (*Port of Entry*) for Pergamon	Scala Loutra
Dikili	Mithimna (Molivos)
Bademli Liman	Kabaki (Petra)
Çandarli	Port Sigri
Aliaga	
Yeni Foça	
Çanakia Limani	

6a

The Dardanelles to Çandarli

FROM THE DARDANELLES SOUTHWARD

Emerging from the entrance of the Dardanelles and turning to the southward a vessel passes the green valley of Troy and Beşika Bay, the anchorage where sailing vessels bound for Constantinople sometimes had to await a fair wind.

The small, flat and uninteresting island of Tenedos lies close off the Anatolian coast and, together with Imros in the north, form the sentinels guarding the Hellespont approach. Both were advance bases of the Allies in the First World War and are now the only Aegean islands held by the Turks. Whereas Imros* (now Gökseada) is partly wooded and hilly, with two alternative partially sheltered anchorages, Tenedos is flat and rather bare with a small 2-fathom port, formerly defended by a well-preserved Genoese castle.

Island of Tenedos (Bozcaada in Turkish)

In Byzantine days when Constantinople was dependent upon its corn supplies from Egypt, ships frequently had long delays off Tenedos awaiting a favourable wind to blow them up the Dardanelles. To avoid this idleness of valuable shipping Justinian had a huge granary built to enable vessels to unload there and then return to Egypt for another cargo. Small freighters then ferried the grain up to Constantinople as .opportunity offered. Nothing is left of the granary today; and the vineyards, which 200 years ago were so famous, have now dwindled, and though the quality of the grapes is good only a small amount of wine is produced for the home market. The island, now poor, still has its derelict little harbour to provide shelter for trading caiques, and a ferry-service to Odum Iskelesi, a small village on the mainland a few miles south of Troy.

In 1968 Tenedos had been declared a Military Area, and a yacht should not enter the port without first obtaining permission at Istanbul or Çanakkale.

---

* In 1973 anchoring and landing prohibited.

The Port

Approach and Berth. Chart 1608 and plan 1880. The two breakwaters have been largely destroyed by gales, but their extremities are clearly to be discerned a mile off. The red oil-lamp at the head of the southern mole shows barely half a mile. It is advisable to anchor in the centre of the harbour in 2½ fathoms and then take a long warp ashore. Though open to east, the harbour is quite comfortable in normal weather.

Officials. The island has a Governor, Customs and Police, who do not always appreciate a visit by a foreign yacht.

Facilities. Spring water suitable for drinking is available but must be carried some distance. There are a few provision shops where food is sometimes rationed and an excellent white wine can often be bought.

One or two small deserted coves on the S. shore of the island also afford anchorage and shelter from the north, but they are not recommended.

On the mainland shore is **Beşika Bay** a favourite anchorage for the old sailing ships as well as modern men-of-war. It was here that Admiral Duckworth had anchored his squadron in February 1807 when H.M.S. *Ajax* of 74 guns caught fire and burnt out with the loss of 250 men. Nearly two years later Sir Francis Darwin on a visit to Tenedos described the melancholy sight of the wreck which had drifted ashore on this island.

For a yacht, however, there is a more suitable night anchorage also on the mainland shore, which is a better alternative than the congested little port of Tenedos. This is at

Yukyeri Bay. Close under Kum Burnu where the spit extends much further than shown on the chart, one can normally find a good lee from the north wind in 3 fathoms on a sandy bottom.

Leaving this anchorage and pointing southwards down the straight Anatolian coast a sailing yacht, helped by the south-going current and a fresh north wind in the summer months, is quickly blown towards the impressive steep-to Cape Baba. Some 7 miles before reaching the Cape one must be careful to stand well away from the coast. The shoal water at the mouth of the Tuzla River extends much further westward than charted. A decision must now be made whether to follow the Turkish coast towards the Edremiti Gulf (with Ayvalik and the Mosko Islands) or turn towards the island of Mytilene (Lesbos).

During the Meltemi season the wind off this headland now becomes westerly and again follows the Turkish coast into the gulf usually maintaining its strength until sunset.

About 5 miles past the Cape is the ancient port of **Assos** (now called Behram by the Turks) with its two moles still showing above water. There is nothing much to be seen here now—only the foundations of early walled defences. It is too shallow for a yacht of medium draft but a few local boats use it. St Paul embarked here after visiting Troy and was rowed southwards on his third missionary journey in A.D. 71—described in the twenty-first chapter of the Acts of the Apostles.

He had been in Macedonia and had crossed by sea to Troy, where after walking to Assos he re-embarked for the voyage to the Levant. This was at the period of the Spring equinox; and as St Paul had left barely enough time to reach Jerusalem for the celebration of Pentecost, he had to hurry. He put in at Port Mitilini, Çeşme ('the point opposite Khios'), Samos, Miletus (now some miles from the sea), Kos, Rhodes, Patara and thence to Tyre. Mostly rowing by day—the Meltemi would not have started so early in the season—and resting the oarsmen at night, speeds of at least 4 knots appear to have been maintained during the longer hops when sometimes 50 to 60 miles were made good in the day. (*See map below.*)

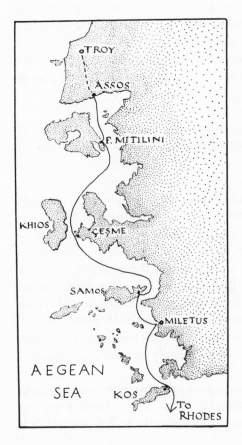

The coast now continues eastward, broken by the Edremiti gulf and the arid Mosko Islands. Here in Roman days (when they were known as Poroselene) Pausanias was an eyewitness of the spectacle of a tame dolphin that came at a boy's call and allowed him to ride on its back. Though confirmed by another witness this story still raises doubt as to its credibility, even though the dolphin was always regarded by the early Greeks as a friend and was not hunted. An 11-ft channel leads to the port of

Ayvalik (Aivali). This little town of 3,000 people thrives on the export of its high-grade olive oil and soap, and more recently on tourism.

Approach. Chart 1672. The interesting narrow Taliani Channel is easy to approach; new beacons are prominent.

Anchorage. A newly-arrived yacht must anchor off the Customs House (just north of the protruding land with a club and cinema) in a depth of about 5 fathoms or anchor south of the pier. The bottom is mud and is good holding. The resulting sea from the day breeze, which during summer blows force 5 from the west from noon until two hours after sunset, makes boat-work almost impossible; only in the forenoon is it calm during Meltemi conditions. A yacht may also anchor off Alibey or in Kumru Koya in the S.W. corner of the harbour. This miniature archipelago is worth exploring by dinghy.

Officials. A Port of Entry: there are Health, Police, İmmigration and Customs.

Port Facilities. There is no convenient place to land in a dinghy. Fresh fruit, bread and meat may be bought in the market and shops. There is a bank, an hotel, a cinema and a club. Ice and petrol can be bought.

A steamer from Izmir calls weekly and buses to Izmir run three times a day (3½ hrs). A caique ferry runs to Port Mitilini weekly. There is a fine bathing beach on the S.W. side of the bay. On the surrounding hills and islands can be seen the ruins of some old monasteries.

On the south side of Ayvalik promontory is a summer anchorage off the open shore at Tatli sa Körfezi. Here are a few tavernas and some houses which are signs of a growing small summer resort.

A car may be hired to drive to the ancient city of Pergamon—an hour's drive and well worth a visit.

PERGAMON is splendidly situated standing upon a hill, and as the ruins gradually appear one is impressed by the vastness of this 'Athens of Asia'. Her port at this time—second century B.C.—was at Elaea, at the head of the Gulf of Çandarli, where the river Caicus formed an artery of transport to the city.

The modern Bergama, a substantial town, is built on the site of the former residential part of the great Greek and Roman cities. It lies at the foot of the Acropolis, on whose steep slopes stand the crumbling tiers of seats of the Greek theatre and the foundations of Greek, Roman and Byzantine walls. Seen from the top, in the light of the setting sun, the view across the ruins towards the green fertile plain beyond is magnificent. Not far down the hill are the ruins of the famous library. Its only rival was that at Alexandria, whither its whole contents were eventually despatched by Anthony. Here it survived until the 7th century when the Caliph Omar gave orders for its destruction.

Our word 'parchment' is derived from the name Pergamon. According to Pliny, the Ptolemies of Egypt, becoming jealous of the growing importance of the Pergamon library, prohibited the export of papyrus from Egypt. This compelled the king of Pergamon to revert to the former use of animal skins for writing upon; but he demanded improvements in the technique, as a result the more delicate skins of calf and kid came to be used and adapted for writing on both sides. This eventually became known as vellum.

The famous Great Altar of Zeus, discovered in the seventies of the last century south of the Acropolis, was excavated by Humann and removed to the Kaiser Frederick Museum, Berlin. Carried off by the Russians after the Second World

War this massive altar with its fine friezes was returned in 1958 and has been re-erected in the Pergamon Museum in East Berlin.

As well as the massive basilica of Hadrian's time there are, across the river-bed, remains of a Roman Theatre and the more remarkable Aesculapium of the fourth century B.C.

Sailing southward one comes to the dull little commercial port of **Dikili.** Lying at the head of a wide open gulf with a village close by, the port of Dikili is partially protected by a breakwater, but it is used only by a few freighters which call to collect produce from the hinterland and also by cruise liners which come to land or embark tourists for Pergamon. There are Health and Immigration officials.

Berth. The breakwater having recently been extended, there is sufficient shelter for a yacht to berth stern-to inside the port; but as harbour dues are demanded some yachts prefer to anchor outside. Good water, available at the dockside, was reported in 1969. The place is of no interest and yachts very seldom call here.

Bademli Liman, a deeply indented inlet with well-sheltered anchorages, lies 6 miles S.W. of Dikili.

Approach. Chart 1617, plan. Keep in the middle of the channel—about 30 yds broad—bordered by steep-to mudbanks.
Anchorage. Let go close S. of 'Factory Ruins' (marked on chart) in 4–5 fathoms. Excellent holding on mud and sand, all round protection; the seas never get inside.
  The inner basin where the chart shows 1½ fathoms has actually silted to 1, and the bottom has thick weed.

One can land for a pleasant walk on the S.E. shores where the fields are well cultivated. To the N. are olive groves, and at the head of the inlet, frequented by seabirds, one may land near a primitive taverna with a minor road leading to Dikili.

The Gulf of Çandarli has some interesting inlets and sometimes the diminishing ruins of Greek Ionian cities. The villages are mostly poor and one cannot expect adequate supplies until reaching Çeşme. The winds in summer are nearly always westerly; an occasional N.E. wind may blow without warning.

Çandarli. Chart 1617. A peninsula of historic interest with suitable anchorage off a poor little village dominated by a fine Venetian castle.

Approach and Anchorage. The castle can be seen 10 miles away and a yacht should anchor about 80 yds offshore on the E. side of it. Depth 4 fathoms, mud bottom, open only S.E. A large yacht must anchor further off in about 8 fathoms. One can land in the dinghy at a low quay which borders the water-front.

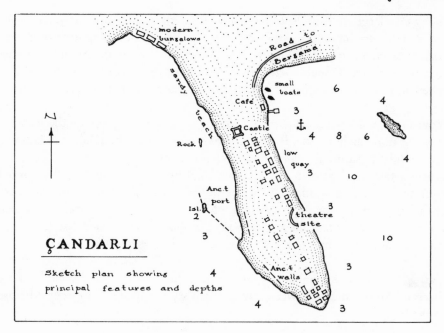

ÇANDARLI

Sketch plan showing
principal features and depths

Facilities. Very poor shops; bread and some fruit can be bought. Bus to Bergama; a taxi is sometimes available.

The present village, built largely of the plundered materials from ancient Pitani, is very poor and of no interest. Almost nothing remains of the ancient city; but, of the two harbours referred to by Strabo the blocks forming the western mole have recently been built up, but the little harbour is still very small. They run from the walled town in a N.W. direction to the islet; and a short distance beyond. They are now submerged in depths of 1 to 1½ fathoms.

The place continued to be of importance up to medieval times when the Venetians built the fine castle which is still in excellent preservation. At some later period the Turks modernized its defences, this being indicated by the presence of guns bearing the arms of George III.

About 5 miles east of Çandarli is the site of Pergamon's seaport Elaea. Only a few mounds remain to show where city walls and the acropolis once stood: but the harbour mole consisting of large horizontal blocks running N. and S. can be seen, and show how well the port was protected.

On the southern shores of the gulf are some ruins of the ancient cities of Gryneum, Myrina, Aliaga and Vyme; but during recent centuries they have been greatly plundered to build new villages, and the original harbours have silted.

Aliaga is a large, well-enclosed bay with a modern country town reaching from the S. shore up the hillside—the centre of a prosperous farming district. A few small local craft moor in shallow water close offshore where the afternoon breeze makes boatwork difficult. Better shelter is under the lee of the western shore, where in 1968 industrial works were in progress and a short mole had been built.

Yeni Foça, a sheltered bay with a dilapidated village lining the southern shore. A yacht may anchor 100 yds off the white building of the Club in 3 fathoms on a sandy bottom. A 50-yd mole extends from the E. shore and provides nearly 2-fathom depths to moor a few small boats. The bay is well-sheltered from the prevailing wind. This former walled village was built by the Genoese in the 17th century for shipping alum which they mined in the vicinity. When Captain Copeland made his survey in 1834 he shows on the chart that the village was then unaltered, but no trace of the walls can be seen today.

Çanakia Limani has anchorage at the head of the small inlet which is now deserted. Some ruined 'tower-houses' (Mani style) still stand unoccupied close to the shore.

'This noble and pleasant Island' STRABO

Island of Mytilene or Lesbos—see plan, page 98

is large and mountainous; now officially known as Lesbos. The eastern part of the island is green and wooded, but on the western side the land around the coast is poor and partially arid. With a population of 100,000 the island attracts many Greeks in the summer months, and it is pleasant to visit in a yacht.

In antiquity the island was made famous by Aesop who wrote many of his fables here, and by Sappho, who is believed to have been born at Eresos, a village on the S.W. coast; it was here she wrote her poems. In more modern times Mytilene was under the rule of Turkey for centuries, and reverted to Greece after the Balkan Wars in 1913.

Port Mitilini, the capital, is a pleasant little town in a delightful setting of partially green mountains, with a port for caiques, fishing craft and local steamers from Piraeus.

> **Approach and Berth.** Chart 1664. Enter the southern harbour and berth in the basin, stern to the broad quay at the yacht station. Yachts sometimes berth outside the port near the root of the mole, where in summer it is cooler. The mole was extended to 300 yds (1971).
>
> **Facilities.** There is a fresh-water hydrant and fuel at the yacht station; plenty of good shops for fresh provisions, and a palatable dry wine may be bought locally. There are some restaur-

ants on the water-front and two modest hotels. Clean hot baths and showers are to be had in a street leading off the Park. There are plenty of taxis. Mechanical repairs can be undertaken by Firestone. There is also an Esso station in the corner of the harbour.

A Port of Entry. There are Health, Immigration, Customs and Harbour Officials. A daily steamer runs from Piraeus, and then sails for Chios; there is also a daily air service to Athens. A caique runs to the Turkish port of Ayvalik.

In the town, apart from the Genoese castle and museum there is not much to see; but to offset this, a number of delightful drives may be taken into the country, passing through mountain forests and many olive groves from which the island derives much of its limited prosperity.

Port Kalloni on the south coast has an interesting mountainous entrance leading into a dull expanse of sheltered water.

Approach. Chart 1668. This is narrow, yet easy by day, for both good leading marks and buoys are now established. Certain lights are exhibited at night, but they should not be relied upon.

Anchorage. Apothiki Bay is well-sheltered from the Meltemi. The holding is good (mud) and the sea is cooled by fresh water from the river.

Facilities are non-existent. The few small cottages near the cove are partly deserted. Some fishermen are based here in summer.

Plomarion, lying between the two large gulfs is a small port protected by two breakwaters.

Approach. Chart 1664. The entrance faces S.E. and the two moleheads are lit at night. The channel, with 2 to 3 fathom depths, leads to the town-quay by the village square. There is room for a medium-sized yacht to swing to her anchor.

Mersinia Bay is an almost uninhabited cove; it lies 3 miles S.W. of the entrance to Port Yero.

Approach and Berth. Chart 1665. Proceed in direction of chapel, marked on chart, and anchor in 5 fathoms at the head of the bay. In the N.E. corner are the remains of an old pier of which the outer extremity (an 8-ft square standing in 9 ft of water) has ring bolts to which warp can be secured. The bottom is thin weed on sand. There is nothing here except a farmhouse with goats and a well of excellent drinking water.

Port Yero is more suitable for a fleet than for yachts. The approach and narrow entrance are attractive, and there are one or two coves here which afford convenient anchorage. The best one is

Scala Loutra, well sheltered, not attractive.

Anchorage is on the E. side off a taverna and shipyard in depths of 3 to 5 fathoms. Mud bottom.

Facilities. Water, ice and basic provisions are obtainable. Bus service to Port Mitilini.

The adjoining cove to the S.W., quite deserted among olive groves and with fresh-water springs, is a very pleasant anchorage.

The harbour authority here is at Perama, a factory village on the W. side of the strait, with a ferry-service across.

The Northern coast of Mytilene facing the Turkish hills 5 miles across the Muselim Strait is the most beautiful. Before reaching Cape Molivos a fine view of its castle suddenly appears through a gap, but on rounding the cape it will be found that the anchorage of

Mithimna (Molivos) is not a comfortable place to bring up for the night. The very small harbour has only 9-ft depths and is usually crowded with caiques. The anchorage, situated dramatically off the village beneath the Genoese castle,

is not suitable, the sea-bed being very uneven with rock; moreover the swell after the day breeze makes the place uncomfortable. A good bathing beach, with modern hotel, extends round the bay, but rocks protrude in places.

A better alternative is to proceed 1½ miles southward to the bay of

Kabaki (Petra). Here is a short mole extending in a southerly direction from the N. shore of the bay. In summer there is excellent shelter during normal conditions.

> **Berth,** stern to the quay near its extremity, anchor laid to the eastward in 2½ fathoms. Sand. (Ballasting at the quayside extends rather far underwater.) Clean for bathing, One or two pleasure boats are kept here.
>
> **Facilities.** The village, where basic provisions are obtainable, is 15 minutes' walk. Octopus and ouzo are specialities. Methimna's beach is 7 minutes by taxi.

The village of Petra is charming and quite unspoilt. One should see the Byzantine church with early frescoes and the old Turkish house. The place is very green with trees, flowers and running water.

Port Sigri on the west coast is a convenient place to shelter from the Meltemi, but not worth a special visit. (See photographs, fac. p. 80.)

> **Approach and Berth.** Chart 1668 should be studied together with *Sailing Directions* giving a view of the approach which is sometimes difficult to find.
>
> There is good protection from the N.E. wind and sea in the bay southward of Sigri village, when the old castle bears N.W. and the depth is 3 to 4 fathoms. The caiques also berth here, and in the event of northerly winds run a warp ahead to the rocks on shore, for the holding (thin weed on very hard sand) is poor. It appears that there is a hard layer of rock immediately under the sand, into which an anchor will not bite. There is better holding in the more remote N.E. corner of the bay, where the caiques often shelter in N.E. gales.
>
> **Facilities.** There is bus communication with Mitilini town every other day—3 hrs.
>
> Bread, eggs and vegetables are obtainable, otherwise supplies must be ordered from Port Mitilini—a 2-day delay.
>
> Water is piped to the village from a spring, and is good, but the few taps are rather far from the landing place.

The village of 600 people is very poor. They were originally brought over from the Asian coast in exchange for the former Turkish inhabitants after the First World War. A rough track ascends to Mount Ordymnos which can be reached in 3 hrs. From the monastery on the summit (1780 ft) there is a grand view of the distant islands.

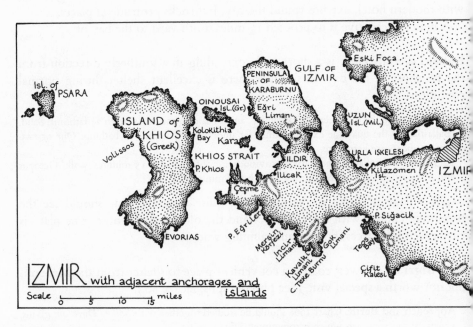

IZMIR with adjacent anchorages and islands

Scale 0 5 10 15 miles

6b

Gulf of Izmir to Körmen Adasi

GREEK ISLANDS

Leave battles to the Turkish hordes and shed the blood of Scio's* Vine.

BYRON

Island of Khios (Chios)

is relatively large and hilly with a bare mountain chain running along its spine. Formerly renowned for its shipping and exports of mastic, herbs and oranges, Khios has been slowly declining and today its population of 25,000 is barely self-supporting. Early in the last century guidebooks described it as 'the most beautiful, most fertile, richest and most severely afflicted of the Aegean islands'. This has greatly changed and nowadays as one approaches along the east coast the island appears mountainous and barren; on landing it does not impress one either with its beauty or fertility, although inland there are some rich plains where agriculture still thrives. On the west and N.W. coast the mountain slopes are still largely green with abandoned terraces where the vines were grown.

From the town one or two excursions are within easy reach by taxi; the most interesting is the drive over the hills to the Byzantine monastery of Nea Moni with its remarkable 12th-century mosaics. The 'School of Homer' with its rotund topped rock, and the poet's alleged birthplace 3 miles north of the town are of moderate interest; there is also the drive to Pyrghi with its medieval walls and some mastic groves nearby.

Port Khios. A spacious sheltered port, with broad quays, and a busy town beside it. A Port of Entry.

Approach and Berth. Chart 1568. The entrance is easy day or night. The yacht station is at the southern quay; a yacht should lay out anchor to N. and haul in the stern—14 ft at the quay. Holding good, but slightly exposed to N. winds. Both quays have recently been extended.

Officials. Harbour authority, Customs, Police (Immigration), all by the quay.

* The Venetian name of Khios in Byron's day.

Facilities. Water from a hydrant at the yacht station is hard, but good; fuel by hose. Ice at a store behind the police building. Provision shops in the street behind the water-front. Many inferior restaurants and tavernas, but one good one at S. end of the quay. The modern residential part of the town, called Bona Vista, has grown up to the southward and is joined by a promenade; here are a modern hotel, dining place, cabaret and tourist attractions. A shipyard on the N. side of the port is sometimes busy slipping and refitting local caiques.

The Piraeus steamer calls daily on its circuit to Mytilene and Kavalla and a car-ferry runs three times a week to Çeşme on the Turkish coast.

Historical. During the past centuries the people of Khios aroused the admiration of a number of travellers largely on account of their marked ascendency over the inhabitants of other Aegean islands. In the 17th century it was recorded that after Constantinople and Smyrna, Khios was the most wealthy and civilized place in the Turkish Empire. Their women had the reputation of being exceptionally good-looking, and Lithgo, a Scot, writing at this period, records:

'The women of the Citty of Sio (its former spelling) are the most beautiful Dames or rather Angelicall creatures of all Greeks, upon the face of the earth, and greatly given to Venery. Their Husbands are their Pandors, and when they see any stranger arrive, they will presently demand of him if he would have a Mistresse: and so they make Whoores of their own wives. . . . If a stranger be desirous to stay all night with any of them, their price is a chicken of Gold, nine shillings English, out of which their companion receiveth his supper, and for his pains a belly full of sinful content.'

At the beginning of the 19th century when the island was thriving on its valuable exports, many wealthy Greek families enjoyed the general high standard then prevailing. In the ill-fated year of 1822 the inhabitants were encouraged to revolt against their Turkish masters who, retaliating quickly, ruthlessly killed 25,000 people and carried off 45,000 inhabitants. The French artist Delacroix painted an imaginative picture of this gruesome event, which is now in the Louvre. Though this calamity wrecked the social structure of the island, vengeance soon came and the spirit of revolt revived when the Greek Admiral Canaris led a small naval squadron with two fireships into the harbour by night and destroyed two large Turkish war-ships, one with 2,000 men on board. General Gordon describes this feat as 'one of the most extraordinary military exploits in history'. The statue to Constantine Canaris is in the park, and there are ships named after this modern Greek hero today. The most recent 'affliction' was a terrible earthquake in the '80s of the last century when 5,000 inhabitants were killed.

Kolokithia Bay is also a sheltered anchorage, used by caiques, but has nothing much to commend it for a yacht.

Evorias, on the south side of the island, is a charming small cove lying between two hills and sheltered on three sides. A few cottages and a taverna have recently sprung up by the shore; ice comes every third day. Some vineyards and groves of mastic shrubs add to the attraction of this peaceful scene.

Approach and Anchorage. This small cove—400 yds in depth—is unmarked on the chart, but it is easy to find. It lies close westward of Cape Kamari, which may be recognized, not by a 'monastery ruin' (shown on chart) but by a couple of modern stone huts. There are no lights. The bottom is of clear sand and runs out 300 yds to depths of 3 or 4 fathoms. There is a 2-fathoms depth about 100 yds off a small stone pier in the centre of the bay with barely room to swing—a warp ashore is recommended. The day breeze blows off the land. The cove is sheltered on the three sides and open only to S.E.

General. A British archaeological expedition dug some trenches here in 1955 and recovered certain Hellenic pottery now to be seen in the Khios museum. Skin-divers also made an exploration of the sea-bed.

Fishermen use the cove as a base during the summer months.

Volissos, a small cove, provides the only anchorage on the west coast of the island. The castle on the hill makes a clear distinguishing mark and *Sailing Directions* describe the approach. The very small boat harbour accommodates fishing craft and the ferry caique for Psara; the village stands on the slope above.

The Growing of Mastic. For more than two thousand years there was great trade with the East in mastic. This is obtained by making incisions in the branches of these six-foot shrubs and draining the sticky fluid into little cups—according to Pliny it is like 'Frankinscense adulterated with resin'. That most highly praised was the white mastic of Khios which in later years had the entire monopoly for supplying the Turkish Empire and consequently brought much wealth to the Khians. The death-knell came when Turkish ladies ceased to chew mastic and other substances took its place in the paint market. Now the culture of these shrubs has declined and although it is still exported this, together with the recession in other industries, has brought some poverty to the island and induced considerable emigration to countries in the west.

A heterogeneous trio slipped for repairs—Port Khios

The adjacent **Oinousai Islands** (Spalmatori) are barren and hilly. They project from the east coast of Khios and have some small bays on the southern shores where a yacht may lie for the night or ride in comfort during Meltemi:

Pasha Bay. Chart 1568. Here is a sandy bottom with good holding in 6 fathoms, and the adjacent coves are also claimed to be good for anchorage.

The only sign of habitation is a farmhouse, and some cultivation in the valleys where vines and figs are grown. The hilly slopes become dried up in summer but in the spring there is sufficient grass for grazing goats.

Mandraki. This is the only village in the group and has a thousand inhabitants, many of whom live here only part of the year. Two modern buildings, a naval school and a technical school, may be seen close to the shore.

Anchorage. One the northern side of the cove is a landing pier with provision shops nearby. The anchorage off the pier is sheltered from prevailing winds, but the holding being soft sand with boulders, is rather uncertain.

The only officials here are Police.

Note. A Radio station has been set up upon the summit of a hill in position 38° 30 N., 26° 17.6 E. A white chapel already exists on a hilltop in position 38° 30.4 N. 26° 17.2 E. The cove S.S.W. of the chapel was a forbidden anchorage in 1967, but a yacht could anchor in the cove W.N.W. of it.

These islands form a splendid barrier and protect the Khios Strait from the lumpy sea caused by strong N.W. winds. As one runs southward the wind becomes more northerly.

Island of Psara, lying 10 miles west of Khios, is small and barren. There is good shelter on the south side off the principal village, either at the anchorage or in 2-fathom depths in the very small harbour; both the approach and break-waters are clearly described in *Sailing Directions* which should be studied. See Chart 1568, plan. (The mole has since been extended by 30 yds.)

Facilities. Barely basic provisions can be obtained, water is scarce. Communication with Khios is maintained by caique which plies to Volissos three times weekly bringing passengers and ice.

The small village, built during the last century, houses most of the 600 inhabitants of the island whose young men nearly all go to sea in merchant ships. The villagers grow only enough produce for local needs and a few fishermen catch sufficient fish. Conspicuous among the small houses are the surviving walls of the fine 18th-century mansions of the great shipowners. These mark the prosperous period when twenty thousand people lived here with an extensive maritime trade in the Mediterranean. The stump towers of several windmills standing on the high ground are also of this period when Russian corn was brought from the Black Sea and resold by Psariot merchants. When Sir Francis Darwin visited the island in 1810 he was impressed by the beauty of 25 ship models then hanging in St Antonia Church. This state of prosperity, however, came to an end early in the last century when Greek patriots rose in revolt against the Turks, and Psariot ships took a prominent part. Vengeance came swiftly when in 1824 a large Turkish expedition landed and completely destroyed the whole village and most of the people. It has never recovered; but Psara has not forgotten her great hero Admiral Canaris, the site of whose house is marked by an inscribed marble plinth.

TURKISH COAST SOUTHWARD

With the exception of Izmir and Çeşme all villages and hamlets mentioned in this chapter are primitive, and fresh supplies are unlikely to be obtained.

Approaching the Gulf of Smyrna (Izmir Körfezi) is

Eski Foça, a village with two harbours, neither of which are suitable for a yacht.

The *South Harbour* with its village lining the water-front, is actually a military area, but there are no objections to a visiting yacht.

> **Anchorage.** Chart 1617. The best shelter from the swell (after the day breeze) is S. of the isthmus protecting the N. side of the bay; but the bottom is uneven, mostly heavy weed with occasional patches of sand. There are also other anchorages, but none convenient.
> **Facilities** are limited, the village having some provision shops.

The *North Harbour* affords excellent shelter behind the low-lying spit described in *Sailing Directions*. Unfortunately the holding in 3- to 5-fathom depths is everywhere bad—thick weed on powdery sand. The best anchorage is to be found on the E. side of the 2-fathom channel. This passage is used by many local boats proceeding from the village to a Club Mediterranée large holiday camp in the next bay. The harbour is very remote and should only be used if seeking shelter.

> Eski Foça was the ancient Greek colony of Phocaea, and lay on the seaward flank of the Ionian–Aeolis frontier. The Phocaeans, like the Phoenicians, had a reputation as early navigators, but with the Persian invasion they were driven from their country, some to become colonists in Italy, others fleeing to Corsica where they took to piracy. Eventually returning to Phocaea, they became busy traders and continued until modern times. Many were massacred at the end of the Balkan War and the colony destroyed 9 years later when the inhabitants were driven out.

Uzun Island is a military area and yachts should keep well away from its shores.

IZMIR (Smyrna)

Turkey's largest Aegean port, a city of 300,000 inhabitants, lies at the head of a large gulf. The objection to a visit by a sailing yacht is that the return voyage beating against the daily Imbat or N.W. wind (similar to the Meltemi) can be tedious.

Many writers have described Smyrna as being among 'the more pleasant places on earth', and though one must concede certain advantages in its natural situation and climate—it was a city throughout historical times—few people today find the present town attractive. It has, however, many antiquities of interest, especially in the country around and for these a guide-book is essential.

During the last century the approach to the port was almost blocked by the alluvial deposit brought down by the Gediz Çay (Ancient Hermus) but in 1886 the river-bed was diverted to its present channel south of Eski Foça and thenceforth the navigable approach, though narrow, has been maintained. A new port on the north of the town, under construction for many years, has recently been opened and has relieved the hopeless congestion of the small port on the western side. (See photograph, fac. p. 81.)

Approach and Berth. Chart 1552. Yachts should make for the old port which the steamers no longer use. Berth stern to the quay, anchor laid out to the W. It is understood that berthing facilities for yachts are likely to improve, although in 1974 the place was still filthy.

Officials as for a Port of Entry. A British Consul-General is established here; N.A.T.O. has a H.Q. in the city.

Facilities. Although away from the town centre, adequate supplies can be got quite near, and a pleasant small hotel with restaurant is nearby. Before taking in water one should make careful enquiries about its purity.

From the time of Queen Elizabeth I until Queen Victoria came to the throne, Smyrna was of considerable commercial interest to Britain. The British Levant company maintained a high prestige in Turkey, and in London their position was so predominant that they used to nominate their own ambassador, consuls and the factors.

For many years a naval guardship was stationed here, and a shore hospital maintained; the large Greek colony was a flourishing community and handled much of the Turkish commerce. After the defeat of Turkey in the First World War Smyrna suddenly became a focal point of world interest when the Greeks, encouraged by certain European statesmen, seized the opportunity to land a military force to invade Turkey. The Turkish army however, unexpectedly rallied by Mustafa Kemal, soon routed the Greeks who, in September 1922, retreated in disorder and fell back on Smyrna. Here were scenes of terrible carnage when most of the Greek and American colonists had to abandon their homes and flee for their lives towards the harbour where already a number of allied

17   The walled village of Siğaçik. To the left a rich farming valley extends across the isthmus to Teos Bay. *See p.* 122

18 Island of Samos, Tsamadou beach. *See p.* 127

warships and transports had been assembled. Meanwhile, to add to the confusion, the whole of the civilized quarters of the town, European, Greek and Armenian, had been set on fire and throngs of destitute men, women and children swarmed down to the quays hoping to board the waiting ships. H.M.S. *Iron Duke* alone embarked 2,000 and during these few weeks an estimated quarter of a million refugees were rescued; among them was Aristotle Onassis and Sir Alexander Issigonis, Britain's outstanding automobile engineer. But there is little doubt that at least 100,000 perished.

The comparatively settled conditions today support a belief that the rich hinterland with an increasing agricultural produce and improved technique in mining valuable ores will ensure the port's prosperity. The modern centre of the town has been building up since the Great Fire of 1922, and in the last decade large buildings have been springing up everywhere.

IZMIR TO ÇEŞME

Urla Iskelesi. A small fishing harbour on the corner of the Gulf used by a few Izmir yachtsmen, but of no interest to a visiting yacht.

Approach and Berth. Chart 1617. The harbour, which is very small, is easy to find by day, for there is a large stumpy white tower on its extremity. (No harbour lights.) With nearly 3 fathoms in the entrance there is sufficient depth to berth stern to the outer extremity of the mole where shelter is all-round.

Facilities. The village seems a poor little place and supports only a few fishermen. A bus runs to Izmir and ferry-steamers sometimes call.

When attempting to sail out of the Gulf northwards one may sometimes be confronted with a freshening N.W. day breeze which soon whips up a short steep sea. If wishing to find temporary shelter there are certain alternative choices:

(a) In **Urla Road**—depths of 3 to 4 fathoms.

(b) **Island of Kilazomen** (connected to the mainland by a causeway) was until recent years the quarantine station of Smyrna. In a wide bay on the east side of the island is good shelter and holding. By the shore are the extensive wings of a hospital; one need not be alarmed at the sight of the inmates for they are no longer detainees for quarantine, but patients with diseases of the bone.

In ancient times, when still an island, it was known as Clazomenae; but after the Persian invasion the causeway was built. Attributed to Alexander, it was referred to both by Pliny and Pausanius. Of the original port on the west side, only a few blocks of masonry are now to be seen on the N.W. corner—possibly the remains of a quay; there is also a short stretch of the ancient city wall. The shallow landing on the western shore now used by hospital boats is of modern construction. The island is sometimes referred to by the Turks as Klazumen.

On the N.W. corner of the gulf is the anchorage of

Port Saip formed under the shelter of the tall islands off the N.E. corner of the massive Kara Burnu peninsula. The village of Saip can be seen above on the hillside. Though sheltered the anchorage suffers from strong gusts of wind off the mountainous surroundings.

The Peninsula of **Karaburnu** is tall and steep-to, but its northern slopes as far as the lighthouse are interesting to look at, being extensively farmed and growing vines on the terraced hillsides. About 6 miles southward of the lighthouse is

Deniz Giren, a cove mentioned in *Sailing Directions*, with a few small houses and fishing boats. This place has silted up and one can see the reeds growing where the anchorage used to be. The rocks extending underwater westward and S.W. from the promontory should be given a wide berth (half a mile off the headland), for in fresh westerly winds the seas break over them.

Eğri Liman. Plan on Chart 1617. This is a deserted inlet with excellent shelter and a good place to bring up for the night.

> **Approach and Anchorage.** A white cairn stands on the tip of the tall headland and helps one to avoid the 2½-fathom patch about 250 yds to N.N.W. One can enter even in strong N.W. winds, and no swell penetrates inside. Anchor off a ruined house in 6 fathoms; plenty of room to swing for one medium size yacht. A white cairn also marks this low sandy point. Bottom is mud. With W. to N.W. winds, the breeze is N. The sides of this islet are very steep-to.

There is nothing here except a little cultivation on the E. bank; an occasional sponge-boat may put in.

After entering the Gulf of Ildir a yacht should make for the anchorage off

Ildir, a deserted village lying inside an archipelago of 5 small islands.

> **Anchorage** (Chart 1645) is at the S. end of a rocky islet midway to the E. shore of Karabag. 4 fathoms, sand with light layer of weed. Excellent shelter among deserted surroundings.

Close southward of the anchorage one can see the village from which the Greeks were thrown out after the First World War. Also to be seen from seaward, but with some difficulty, are the ruins of ancient Erythrae—the city walls, theatre (recently excavated) and the acropolis—but all have been plundered during the last century.

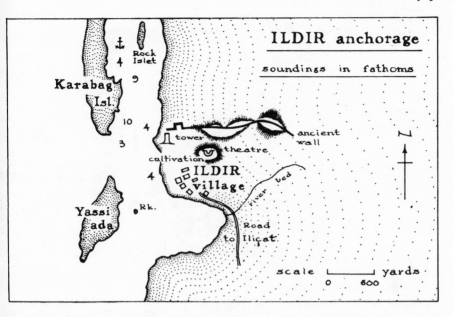

Erythrac, one of twelve Ionian cities, was surrounded by three miles of walled defences, much of which can still be followed. In the 5th century B.C. it was a wealthy commercial city, and as a member of the Delian League preferred to contribute ships rather than money. She had her prophetic Sibyl, but a less famous one than her rival at Cumae in Italy.

Continuing to the S.W. a yacht will come to the bay of Ilicak. On the S. shore of this wide bay is a long sandy beach with numerous blocks of houses and hotels forming a growing resort for the people of Izmir, who now reach it by a fast road in about an hour.

Off **Ilicak** there is no anchorage for a yacht because the north wind blows straight into the bay and in the S.E. corner where a few fishing boats have moorings there is a dangerous submerged mole. The only shelter is at the mouth of Corsair Cove which has now silted to less than 2 fathoms.

When making for Çeşme, it is necessary to round Cape Üç Burunlar; on a clear day a yacht can pass safely inside the off-lying shoals. The islet of Topak is most conspicuous.

Çeşme is a bay, open to the west, with a large village overlooked by a Genoese castle. Apart from Izmir this is the best place on this stretch of coast for taking in supplies.

Approach. Chart 1617, plan. The Kaloyer reef, though no longer marked on its S.E. corner by a post, is easily avoided. It has recently been marked by a large buoy.

Turkish Sponge-boat

A *Trehandiri*, with rubber suit and ladder being prepared for a diver's descent. They are almost the only survivors of traditional local craft now to be seen on the Anatolian coast.

Anchorage. Let go about 1 cable west of the castle and north of the pier in 2 or 3 fathoms on a bottom of fine mud. Shelter under normal conditions is good, for the projecting point to the northward deflects the sea caused by the local N.W. sea breeze, and the wind does not blow home. A pile pier, recently built, now extends from the castle for about 80 yds in a westerly direction. There are generous depths at its extremity for steamers to berth, but yachts ride better to their anchors.

Officials. A Port of Entry: Health, Customs, Immigration, Police.

Facilities. It is normally possible to land at the water-front by the square, and when calm to leave the dinghy here. The shops sell a wide range of fresh provisions, including fish; the fruit and vegetables are remarkably good. Ice at the factory on the water-front near the Customs. Fuel and water can be obtained at the pier subject to some delay. A good restaurant by the square. A fast road leads to Izmir—bus and minibus service 1¼ hrs. Passenger caique to Port Khios 3 times weekly during the tourist season.

The fine castle with two rings of walls and gun towers was originally built by the Genoese in the 15th century, and subsequently seized by the Turks. It protected the Roads where in the summer of 1770 the Turkish fleet had come to anchor. On 5 July they were attacked by three Russian squadrons and almost entirely annihilated. The Russians after refitting in England had sailed out from the Baltic to operate independently in the Mediterranean, and after seeking the Turks elsewhere in Aegean waters eventually found them here. The Russian victory was complete, and not without interest to the British, for on board the Russian ships were Admirals Elphinstone and Greig, while of the three fire-ships which caused such havoc, two of them had British captains. This was the period of Russian naval expansion when Catherine the Great had obtained British support to train and equip her navy with a view to its crushing Turkish sea power and thus enabling the Russian Black Sea fleet to break through the stranglehold of the Dardanelles and operate in the Mediterranean. At the time of writing, some two hundred years later, the Russian Navy has recently started to operate Russian warships in the Eastern Mediterranean, but this time without the assistance of a foreign power.

FROM ÇEŞME TO KÖRMEN ADASI

On leaving Çeşme a yacht proceeding southwards will round Ak Burun, and before reaching Teke Burnu (20 miles S.E.) must pass half a dozen inlets under the hills of the deserted Anatolian coast. Chart 1645 shows the choice of anchorages, but it may be noted that only two places have all-round protection, of which Incir Limani is the best. For the first three ports plans are published on Chart 1568.

Except for Eğriler (Alaçati Limani) all are uninhabited and without cultivation; the hilly slopes are mostly covered with scrub.

Eğriler Limani with a hamlet (often called Ağriler) at its head is too large and uninteresting to attract a yacht. A plan is shown on Chart 1617.

Mersin Körfezi—a completely deserted bay with shelter from S. formed by the island at the entrance. Here the above-water rocks are conspicuous and a yacht can pass on either side.

> **Anchorage.** Best shelter is in N.E. cove; anchor in depths of 3 to 4 fathoms on a sandy bottom with plenty of room to swing.
> **Facilities.** See *Sailing Directions*. There are no fresh provisions; nothing to be had.

An unnamed cove midway between Mersin and Incir has a conspicuous beach at its head with summer camp equipment set up.

Incir Limani provides excellent all-round shelter in South Cove for any size of yacht. Anchor in 4 or 5 fathoms on firm sand. Completely deserted.

Kavalki Limani, a long steep-to fjord without habitation, provides good anchorage at its head in 4-fathom depths, bottom of sand. Partial shelter from southward is provided by a small projecting point on the west side of the fjord. After rounding **Cape Teke Burnu** you enter the Gulf of Siğacik with the sheltered anchorage and village of Siğacik in the N.E. corner. One should put in en route at

Gök Liman, a charming well-sheltered inlet with anchorage in N. cove with room for a small or medium yacht to swing; and towards the head of the cove, with warps ashore, there is room for a large yacht.

Sığacik has a sheltered anchorage with a village built inside a ruined fortress. The place is of interest for the ruins of the early Ionian city. (See photograph, fac. p. 116.)

> **Anchorage.** Plan on Chart 1606. Head for conspicuous minaret and let go in 4 fathoms about a cable N.W. of the ruined castle. Good holding on firm mud, excellent shelter; but during strong N. winds boatwork is difficult.
> **Facilities.** Basic provisions.

One must land to see the ruins of ancient Teos; they lie in the middle of the isthmus, a mile from the landing place by the castle. This town of about the 3rd century B.C. originally extended from there to Teos Bay where the harbour quay can still be seen. Of the town itself the theatre, temple of Dionysos, the odeon and some paved streets are worth visiting. At Sığacik, the ancient mole can be followed underwater from the corner of the castle in a N.W. direction; near it is a curiously-shaped block of stone of the same period, evidently lost during shipment; there are several others within this area, but the reason for cutting large blocks in a sort of cubist style is mystifying.

Teos Bay, lying on the S. side of the isthmus, is a better place to lie than Sığacik during strong N. winds.

> **Anchorage.** Let go in 2½ fathoms about 150 yds east of the ancient mole. Bottom is sand and holding good. (S.W. of mole the holding is poor.) Land in the dinghy close to the wall of the ancient quay.

To visit the ruins it is best to make across the fields to the theatre, for from the top you get a fine view round the whole of the green isthmus with its many cultivated fields and a great variety of trees. The theatre itself is somewhat disappointing, for although the stage has been excavated and restored, the stonework from the cavea has completely vanished.

Running down the coast for eight miles one reaches a tall steep-to rocky islet joined to the coast by a partly submerged causeway. This is

Çifit Kalesi, 'Mouse Island', or ancient Myonnesus. In calm weather one can anchor off the causeway, but with fresh N. winds alarming gusts shoot down from this perpendicular wall of rock. On its northern face can be seen a number

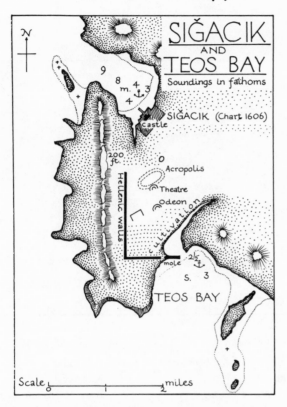

of ruins one of which is a remarkable section of Cyclopean wall. Passing on the west side is a great cleft which almost splits the rock in two. It seems extraordinary that such a small islet could have attracted the attention of ancient writers; but Livy records an incident when a Roman galley fleet was chasing some pirates who had escaped and were defending themselves on the islet. The Roman galleys, while sheltering under the perpendicular cliffs, were so afraid of the prospect of lumps of rock being dropped on them from above that they abandoned their quest and set off for Teos instead.

Another mile southward is the islet **Körmen Adasi** which helps to form a small sheltered inlet; but here again a yacht might need shelter from the N. wind, violent gusts make the anchorage untenable.

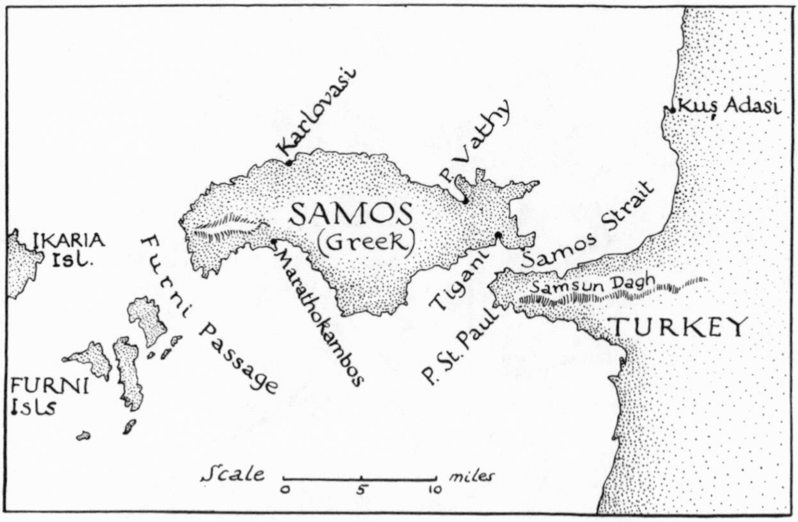
Karlovasi
P. Vathy
Kuş Adasi
SAMOS
(Greek)
IKARIA
Isl.
Furni Passage
Marathokambos
Tigani
Samos Strait
Samsun Dagh
P. St. Paul
TURKEY
FURNI
Isls
Scale
0
5
10
miles

THE TURKISH COAST

Kuş Adasi (*Port of Entry*) for Ephesus
- The Marina

Port St Paul

THE GREEK ISLANDS

Island of Samos
- Karlovasi
- Port Vathy or Port Samos (*Port of Entry*)
- Tigani or Pithagorion (*Port of Entry*)
- Marathokambos

Island of Ikaria
- Ayios Kirykos

Furni Islands

6c

Kuş Adasi to Port St Paul

TURKISH COAST SOUTHWARD

Following the Turkish coast southward the first important place is

Kuş Adasi. It is the most convenient port from which to visit Ephesus.

Approach. Chart 1546. If coming from the direction of Samos both Petroma Reef and Karakaci Bank should be carefully avoided.

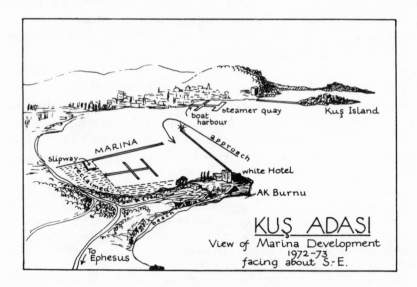

KUŞ ADASI
View of Marina Development
1972-73
facing about S.-E.

The former island of Kuş has now been joined to the mainland by a causeway which, in addition to providing shelter, makes a pleasant walk for those visiting the old fort, now a night club.

Berth.

(a) The old harbour, on the S.E. side of the bay, provides berthing for tourist steamers and local craft. A yacht of modest draft can still berth stern to the stone pier inside the steamer quay.

(b) The new marina, and the N.W. side of the bay, will not be completed before 1975, but already the pontoons with mooring rings are in position. The holding mostly on weed is reported to be extremely poor.

Officials. Customs, Harbour Master and Immigration. Pilotage fees if over 50 tons. Berthing fees are charged.

Facilities. The place having become a summer resort, there are hotels, restaurants and cafés close by and along the beach. Fuel may be obtained from a Shell depot nearby and water from the end of the main quay, but its purity is questionable and some yachts prefer not to fill their tanks here. Water is also available by lorry, but this too cannot be depended upon. Bread, meat, excellent fruit and vegetables may be bought at the shops. Ice is obtainable. Excursions can be made by car to Ephesus, Priene, Miletus and Didyma; minibuses and taxis are available in the square by the old harbour.

Kuş Adasi has a population of about 6,000 and is expanding. Many are employed in the olive oil industry and in agriculture, and an increasing number in the tourist trade. Much has been spent on modernizing the town which now has an occidental Riviera look. Even the old fortress has been restored and converted into a Club Méditerranée Hotel.

Ephesus can be reached in 30 min. The ruins are interesting and extensive; at least half a day should be allowed to see what is left of this once greatest city in Asia whose temple was a former Wonder of the World. The museum in the village at Selçuk should also be visited.

The road follows the old course of the Cayster River, along which St Paul was rowed when visiting Ephesus nineteen centuries ago. Now completely silted, part of it has become meadows where the camels graze; but outside Ephesus where the old harbour has become a marsh the quays can still be traced. From here a broad street, perfectly preserved and paved with marble, leads up to the city and the large theatre, estimated to hold an audience of 25,000.

Historical. It is easy to re-create here the historic occasion of the demonstration by the silver-smiths after St Paul had been preaching here for some months. Summoned by their leader, Demetrius, they met together to protest against the ruin of their souvenir trade in selling small silver goddesses to the Roman tourists. They became infuriated against St Paul and a riot ensured. Rushing into the amphitheatre they shouted 'Great is Diana of the Ephesians'. (*Acts of the Apostles* 19.)

Even in Greek and Roman days this 'largest emporium of Asia Minor' had its difficulties in keeping the river navigable for sea-borne trade. Strabo writes:

'The mouth of the harbour was made narrow by the engineers, but they, along with the king who ordered it, were deceived as to the result—for he thought the entrance would be deep enough for large vessels . . . if a mole were thrown up at the mouth which was very wide. But the result was the opposite, for the silt thus hemmed in made the whole harbour as far as the mouth more shallow. Before this time the ebb and flow of the tide would carry away the silt and draw it to the sea outside.'

But whatever steps were taken by man to keep open the ancient Greek ports on the west

Anatolian coast, subsequent silting throughout the centuries has proved that the forces of nature predominate. Other examples of these city ports may be seen at Priene and Miletus, both of which are well worth visiting from Kuş Adasi. (See p. 144.)

Lying on the Turkish shore close across the S. entrance of Samos Strait is

Port St Paul, an almost deserted sandy cove. It is the usual anchorage for a Turkish Customs patrol boat, and is well-sheltered from the strong winds in the Strait.

After the battle of Salamis, some of Xerxes' galley crews which had escaped from the action were resting ashore in this cove and at an adjacent inlet when they were attacked and mostly destroyed by some of the Spartan ships.

The origin of the name—no longer printed on British charts—is obscure, but by tradition St Paul on one of his voyages down the Anatolian coast put in here for a night's shelter to rest the oarsmen.

THE GREEK ISLANDS

Thus all their forces being joined together, they hoisted sail towards the Isle of Samos and there gave themselves to feasts and solace.

PLUTARCH, writing of Antony and Cleopatra.

Island of Samos (Sisam)

This large, wooded and mountainous island, separated by barely a mile from the Turkish mainland, is one of the most attractive in the Aegean. Since the days of Polycrates it has been famous for its forests and vineyards. Today there are 60,000 inhabitants in Samos distributed among a number of hill villages as well as at the three major ports. (See photograph fac. p. 117.)

Samos produces a dry white wine most of which is now exported to Germany, France, Holland and other European countries; it can however still be bought locally, but is more difficult to obtain than the less palatable sweet wine. The best pinewood for caique construction is grown here and there are still three or four small building yards but their activities are declining. Tobacco is grown and processed for export, and an unusual species of sweet olive is also shipped to America. Notwithstanding these assets the trade of the island is barely holding its own. The pottery for which Samos was famous in Hellenic days is no longer produced. It should not be confused with the dull-red 'Samian Ware' sometimes dug up by archaeologists on Roman sites in England. This pottery, though it took the name from Samos, was imported into England by Roman merchants in the 1st century A.D. and was actually made in France. Samos was fortunate in avoiding the destruction suffered by Khios and other islands early in the last century. Although under the suzerainty of Turkey for nearly a century she prospered as an independent principality with a flourishing commerce in the Eastern Mediterranean and at the same time cultivation was efficiently maintained. After the Second Balkan War in 1913 Samos became part of Greece.

On the north coast of the island is the rather dull port of

Karlovasi which has been repaired and dredged.

> **Approach and Berth.** Chart 1568, plan. There is no difficulty day or night. Berth near the Customs House but clear of the steamer quay which is in daily use. Holding is poor, but the port is well protected by its long breakwater against the prevailing N. winds.
> **Facilities.** Water by tap close to Harbour Office. Restaurant on the waterfront. A few shops for basic provisions. Bus service to Vathy. Piraeus steamer daily in summer.

The small village with a church on a pinnacle rock makes a pleasant walk from the port, and the mountainous country behind is impressive; the oldest church on the island lies in the next bay to the westward. Otherwise there seems little inducement for a yacht to call here.

The mountainous coast from Karlovasi eastwards towards Port Vathy is one of the most beautiful in the Aegean. Terraced slopes with carefully tended vineyards alternate with pine forests on the mountain sides, while here and there are villages of red-roofed houses tucked into the green valleys above.

Port Vathy (Port Samos), the capital of the island, lies at the head of a wide inlet bordered by wooded hills. Protected by a short mole where the steamers berth the port is subject to a disturbing swell in Meltemi conditions. This is a Port of Entry.

> **Approach and Anchorage.** Chart 1530. An above-water rock not shown on the chart extends for about 100 yds N.N.W. of Cape Kotsikas whose light structure cannot easily be discerned. The mole light is Lt. Fl. (R). A yacht can anchor about 100 yds E. of the mole and run out a mooring ring on the water-front (5-ft depths). Alternatively berth stern to the steamer quay close to the root of the mole (10 ft); but in this berth a yacht can be endangered by the screw wash when the Piraeus steamers are berthing, and it is recommended to leave before their arrival. The holding is good.
> **Officials.** As for Port of Entry. Offices are near the mole. A British Vice-Consul has his residence on the water-front near the yacht berths.
> **Facilities.** Water has always been in short supply, but it is hoped that by now the shortage will have been overcome. Harbour authority can usually arrange for small quantities. Ice can be delivered daily. Provision shops at the town centre; dry Samos wine can be bought close to the mole. A few tavernas, and a Xenia hotel. The archaeological museum in the town is worth visiting, also the Byzantine museum in the Mitropolitis and the portrait gallery above the Post Office. Daily air service (weather permitting) to Athens, and in summer also a daily steamer (16 hrs.).

The town is attractive and the views across the mountains are beautiful. The disadvantage of Port Vathy is that there is no satisfactory place to berth a yacht especially during the Meltemi. Mountain excursions can be made by car and bus; a pleasant half-hour's drive is to the monastery of Zoodochos Pigi, or further afield to the more interesting Brontiani above the village of Vourliotes.

Tigani (Pithagorion), a well-sheltered little port of great antiquity beside a pleasant small village lining the water-front.

Approach and Berth. Chart 1568, plan. When passing through the Samos Strait during Meltemi conditions very strong gusts will be experienced from the high land of Samos. It is sometimes wise to lower the mainsail. The outer harbour is easy to approach day or night, the breakwater extremity being marked by a Lt. Fl. (R). The inner harbour which is frequently dredged has an average depth of about 14 ft—off the quays about 10 ft. Care must be taken to keep in the centre of the entrance channel, i.e., pass midway between a white port-hand beacon and the extremity of the mole. A yacht may berth comfortably off the Customs House where there are several mooring rings, and a water hydrant is within reach. Although a few gusts of wind may be experienced in the port, they are relatively mild compared with those outside. The fuelling berth is much exposed to the easterly winds from the Samos Strait, and in winter the southerly gales occasionally surmount the breakwater making the harbour untenable.

Officials. As necessary for a Port of Entry.

Facilities. Fresh-water taps and two hydrants on the quay but water often uncertain. Fuel and water at the yacht station (10-ft depth alongside). Ice at corner of quay by main street. Provisions by the quay. Small hotel, excellent restaurant (1968), and three tavernas on the

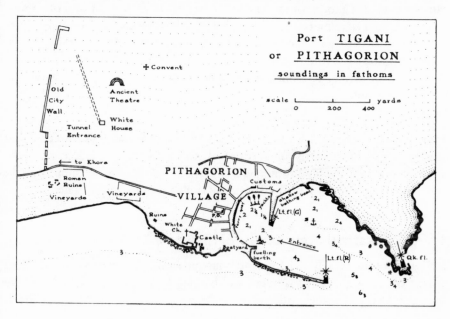

quay side, which is well shaded by eucalyptus and mulberries. Air service to Athens daily (weather permitting). Car-ferry to Kuş Adasi, three times weekly. Bus service to Port Vathy, four times daily.

In 1945 the Greek Government decided to rename Tigani (which it had been called for some decades) Pythagorion (spelt Pithagorion on the chart) in honour of the great mathematician's birthplace; but it is even more famous for the 'great works' of Polycrates, still to be seen today. At the time of Herodotus it was considered to be one of the most important cities in the world. In the port itself, the inner harbour is much as Polycrates built it, and on the hill above can be seen his walls, fourteen feet thick, which encompassed the old capital. A number of drums of columns and some capitals from the buildings of the old city have been plundered from the ruins and brought to the port for use as bollards, stands for water-taps and sometimes flower-pot stands outside the houses. The famous water-tunnel, now 2,500 years old, is interesting though difficult to explore and one cannot emerge at the other end, as it is blocked; the uneven and slippery nature of the limestone ledge on which you walk and the fact that the water conduit is unfenced have sometimes brought the most intrepid visitors to disaster. Temporary electric lighting was installed in 1973.

The village has been tidied up in recent years. It has much charm, and in the coolness of a summer evening it is pleasant to be on the water-front enjoying an evening meal under the mulberry trees.

New roads in the island have recently been under construction and not only can one reach the mouth of the tunnel by car, but cover a great deal of Samos.

There is rich farming country in the broad valleys on either side of Pithagorion, vines, tobacco and corn being grown extensively. An interesting drive leads along the coast to the temple of Hera, and another excursion takes one to the mountain hamlet of Koutsi where a small hotel has been built beside the mountain stream.

Marathokambos is yet a fourth harbour lying on the south-west coast, but it is very little used partly on account of storm damage, and because of the violent squalls off the high mountains which during the summer months strike across Marathokambos Bay. The principal shipyard of the island is here.

Island of Ikaria (Nicaria on the older charts)

is a long, tall and largely barren island lying only 5 miles west of Samos. Its main village of Ayios Kirykos has hotels and bathing beaches, and also radio-active springs which in summer entice many sufferers of rheumatism from the Greek mainland. It has hardly ever been visited by yachts partly because it has little attraction and also because it had, until now, no harbour.

In Meltemi weather yachts should keep well clear of the south coast which is notorious for the violent squalls off the mountains.

Ayios Kirykos on the S.E. side of the island is the new port with a 200-yd mole and quay extending eastwards; completed in 1969 it affords only limited protection. Here in summer many tourists arrive daily in the Piraeus steamer. The anchorage is exposed to easterly winds and swell; also with fresh N. winds, strong gusts sweep down from the mountains.

In settled calm weather the steamers also call at Evdilos and Armenistis, two bays with hamlets on the N. side of the island.

The island derived its name from the legend of Icarus, son of Daedalus, who having incurred the displeasure of Minos made wings of feathers and wax for himself and his son so as to escape from Crete. But, rising too high, the sun melted the wax of Icarus's wings and he fell into the sea near this island.

Furni Islands

lying between Samos and Patmos are barren, rocky and indented with several coves. Together with Ikaria these islands are administered by the *Nomark* of Samos. Their few inhabitants live on the main island close to the narrow strait, which is shown on Chart 1568 (plan) together with details of some deserted sandy bays—ideal places for anyone wanting complete isolation.

The Furni Islands were formerly a lair for pirates, one of whose captives, an Englishman named Roberts, writing after his escape in 1692 states: 'They go to Furnes and lie there under the high land hid, having a watch on the hill with a little flag, whereby they make a signal if they see any sail; they slip out and lie athwart the Boak of Samos, and take their prize.'

Today one may walk up this hill and enjoy the same view across the strait towards Samos.

Northern Dodecanese

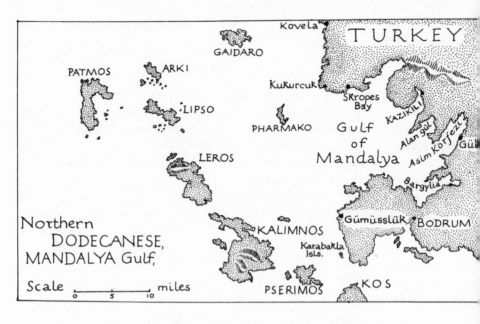

NORTHERN DODECANESE (GREEK)

Island of Patmos
  The Harbour
  Anchorages outside the Port:
    Meloyi Bay
    Livadhi Bay
    Kambos Bay

Island of Arki
  Glypapa Cove
  Avgous
  Campo
  Marati Islet

Island of Lipso

Island of Gaidaro (Agathonisi)

Island of Pharmako

Island of Leros
  Alinda Bay
  Pandeli (Panali Bay)
  Xerokambo
  Port Laki
  Partheni Bay

Island of Kalimnos
  Port Kalimnos
  Vathy
  Borio Bay
  Telendos Island
  Linaria Bay
  Cape Kephalo anchorage

Island of Pserimos

and Gulf of Mandalya

TURKISH COAST

Kovela (Ancient Gulf of Latmos)

GULF OF MANDALYA (Güllük)
Kukurcuk
Skropes Bay (Altinkum) for Didyma
Kuru Erik Limani
Akbük Limani
Kazikili Limani
Saltaluthea
Asim Körfezi
Asim Liman, Port Isene (Anct. Iassus)
Güllük (*Port of Entry*)

Sheiro Bay
Varvil Koyu (Anct. Bargylia)
Salih Adasi
Kuyucak Harbour
Güvercinlik
Ilica Bükü
Türk Bükü
Büyük Farilya Bükü
Gümüsslük (Myndus)
Karabakla Islands with Yassi Islet

(*For Bodrum see* 6(*e*))

6d

Northern Dodecanese and Gulf of Mandalya

THE DODECANESE

THE DODECANESE, which lie so near to the Turkish gulfs, are described simultaneously with the Turkish coast of similar latitude in Chapters 6d and 6e.

The 'Twelve Islands' with their mountainous formation, rugged grandeur and indented coastline, make an attractive sailing area for a yacht. Also called the Southern Sporades, these islands appeared to the early Greeks as 'lean wolves'. So close are they to Anatolia that their extremities sometimes jut into the Turkish gulfs.

After being under Turkish rule for many centuries, these islands were ceded to Italy after the First World War and handed back to Greece after the Second. Kos and Rhodes still reflect the recent influence of Italian occupation, the other islands are sparsely populated but offer some delightful, solitary anchorages, each different from the other in size, shape and character.

The Dodecanese are under the central administration of Rhodes (described in Chapter 7) and have separate Customs regulations from the rest of Greece, whereby many foreign imports are allowed to enter either free or with very little tax.

The Turkish coast opposite these Greek islands has some attractive deserted inlets. The summer winds being suitable, it is recommended to cross over between respective Ports of Entry and then return to Greek waters to top up with water, fuel and provisions. One must bear in mind, however, that although they are more cordial towards a visiting yacht, Turkish officials are usually very bureaucratic and exacting with their lengthy procedure which may mean wasting the best part of a day before obtaining Clearance. Some yachts prefer to pay the local agent to overcome the difficulties and thus save much time and irritation.

NORTHERN DODECANESE

Close southward of the Furni Islands lies

Island of Patmos

Nearing this island from the eastward a vessel passes some rather forbidding rocky spurs, and enters the large sheltered bay; thence a long inlet leads to the Scala, the little port buildings, in modern Italian style, to be seen in the distance.

On the hill behind lies the principal village, Chora, dominated by what appears to be a medieval stronghold. It is, in fact, the Monastery of St John the Divine.

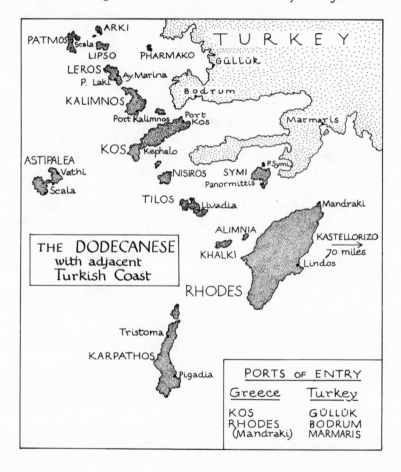

The Harbour

Approach. Charts 3927 and 1669, plan. Sailing into the inlet one should make for the modern ex-Italian buildings on the water-front.

Berth. Extensive harbour works were recently completed to give 750 ft of deep water quay for Cruise ships. Yachts have been provided with a quay close southward. See sketch plan.

Good anchorage can be found at the head of the bay among other craft in 3½ fathoms. This is nearly a mile from the village by land; there is dinghy landing at a decrepit wooden jetty close by, whence a road runs to the village; alternatively use the dinghy to reach the Scala.

General. The island is so far unspoilt by tourists who go only to the monastery; the islanders remain most friendly.

Facilities. Water (sometimes ferried in drums) and fuel are available at the quay where it is also convenient for shopping. Ice can no longer be obtained. A good hotel with baths is near and some modern restaurants, also a Post Office.

On account of the monastery and the island's biblical associations, many tourist ships enter the anchorage, berthing at the quay for a few hours' stay.

Close to the Customs House, a bus or taxi is available to climb the new, well-graded road that spirals up the hill. Half-way is a small shrine built around a grotto, where St John is said to have written the Revelations after having been condemned by the Emperor Domitian in A.D. 96 for preaching the Gospel.

Crowning the hill immediately above the small village is the fortress-like monastery built in the 11th century—a complicated structure with chapels, treasure room, museum and library beneath unsymmetrical roofs and 'bell-cotes' at different levels. At one time it was full of treasure, some of which, during the last century, found its way to London, Leningrad and Vienna; the most valued asset remaining today is the thirty-three leaves of St Mark's Gospel, written in the 5th century on purple vellum, called the Codex Porphyrius, but there are many other treasures.

The superb view from the roof of the monastery must not be missed. Looking towards the Anatolian coast the massive mountains of Asia can be seen in the far distance behind the outlying islands of the Dodecanese. An easy walk through the village and then downhill soon brings one back to the harbour. There is nothing remarkable about the village, but when the French traveller Tournefort came here two hundred years ago he expressed surprise at finding twenty women to every man. (See photograph, fac. p. 188.)

Anchorages outside the port. Chart 1669. Unless one wants to stay in port close to the shore amenities it is more pleasant for a yacht to come outside the harbour and anchor at one of the following coves on the N.W. shore of the large Patmos Bay:

Meloyi Bay, the nearest to the harbour has room for two or three yachts.
Anchorage is off the sandy beach in 5-fathom depths, weed on sand. Two small houses, and tamarisk trees line the shore.

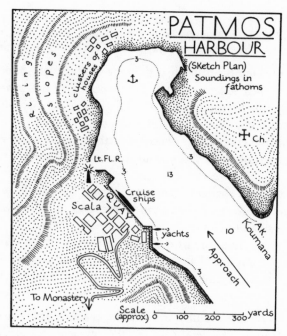

PATMOS
HARBOUR
(Sketch Plan)
Soundings in fathoms

Rising slopes
Clusters of houses of

Scala
QUAY
Cruise ships
yachts
Lt. Fl. R.
Ak Koumana
Approach
To Monastery
Scale (approx) 0 100 200 300 yards

Livadhi Bay, slightly more attractive, is better sheltered and attracts a few bathers who come from the port by small ferry-boats. Anchor as convenient off the beach.

Kambos Bay is more populated with one or two summer villas, a jetty, taverna, shop for basic provisions. An hourly ferry-service with the port. Anchorage as convenient off the sandy beach.

All the above coves are connected by road to the village. There are also other small coves on the eastern side of Patmos not described, but easy to discern on the chart.

Island of Arki

lies among a small group of barren islands east of Patmos. It is long and narrow with some attractive sheltered coves suitable for small yachts. Normally only a few local fishermen make use of them. The three main coves are on the S.W. side of Arki:

With Chart 3927 this is easy by day, but quite impossible by night. The principal cove **Glypapa** or Augusta is that recommended by *Sailing Directions*; the second cove southwards, **Avgous** or Stretto, has uncertain holding but is better for swinging room. **Campo** also affords anchorage.

Glypapa Cove affords 2-fathom depths well beyond the elbow where the inlet turns northwards.

Anchorage. On anchoring it is well to run a warp ashore to steady the bow of a yacht during Meltemi when, except for the gusts, shelter is excellent. In mid-channel the bottom is sand and the water clear. The depths are actually greater than shown on the chart.

Half-a-dozen fishing boats berth at the head of the inlet, some of them being crawfish boats which sell their catch at Patmos. The headman of the island lives in a house on the shoulder of the hill separating Glypapa and Avgous inlets. In summer a small tourist steamer calls twice a week.

For a large yacht there is good anchorage with plenty of room in less attractive surroundings on the opposite shore from Arki at the adjacent

Marati Islet, where a sheltered sandy bay opens only to E. with convenient depths on a sandy bottom. The bay can be recognized by the white church on the hill and two small houses.

About 150 people live on these islands in two or three scattered hamlets. Though nothing is produced for export, the inhabitants grow enough to live on; an occasional caique runs to Patmos with fish and returns with stores.

Island of Lipso lying to southward of Arki, is a dull little place with its small port on the S.W. side. The depths behind the new and insignificant breakwater are not enough for a yacht of medium draft to anchor, and outside the holding is bad. Fortunately, farther out and close under the land to the westward, holding is better, though strong gusts from the Meltemi sweeping down the hills, spoil the tranquillity of the anchorage.

The small village adjoining the port is uninteresting and rather poor, though very recently it has been improved with a new quay and concrete roads.

There are two unimportant islands off the Turkish coast:

Island of Gaidaro (Agathonisi) is small and barren. Barely 200 people live here, mostly at the head of the large cove on the south coast where comfortable summer anchorage may be found for a medium-sized yacht.

Anchorage can best be found about 150 yds from the head of the cove in 5 to 6 fathoms on a bottom of sand and mud with a thin layer of weed. Good holding and room to swing. Meltemi gusts from the hillside. Open only to south.

Most of the inhabitants live at the top of the valley above the head of the cove where there is some sparse cultivation. Cattle, including goats, sheep and cows, are bred for export and the inhabitants grow sufficient to live on. Water is collected by some catchments visible on the hillsides. On the water-front are only a couple of fishermen's houses whose inhabitants invariably welcome a visiting yacht. The local people, who have known no other but this simple way of life, appear to be a happy community. Some have never been away from the island, and their only link with the outside world is the weekly caique, a small steamer and Radio Athens.

Island of Pharmako lying to the southward, has gentle slopes and is partially covered with green scrub. It is not worth a special visit. There are four small coves on the eastern coast, sheltered from the prevailing northerly wind; the north-westerly cove is the most convenient.

> **Anchorage and Approach.** This cove can be recognized by a small white church on the hill above and by four arches of a Roman villa close by the water's edge. The sea-bed shelves to form a sandy anchorage close offshore in 3 fathoms. Though satisfactory in summer, this temporary anchorage is completely exposed to the eastern quadrant.

The island is largely barren with only one small inhabited cottage. Among some Roman remains may be seen the foundations of two or three villas, and underwater there is the rubble of a former jetty; at the southern part of the island there are further remains. Today the only visitors are Greek fishermen who spend the summer months here. They keep their boats under the shelter of the loggia of a Roman house, and at night poach the fish from the nearby Turkish coast.

> **Historical.** It was here that Julius Caesar spent many weeks in captivity. In the year 77 B.C. at the age of 22, he was on the way to Rhodes to finish his education when pirates captured him at sea off Miletus and brought him to Pharmako. Here he was kept a prisoner, and a ransom of 22 talents was demanded by the pirates. Meanwhile, Caesar, apparently maintaining an ascendancy over his captors, expressed disgust that his life should be assessed at such a low value, whereupon the pirates raised their price to 50 talents (about £60,000). His many weeks of captivity were well occupied and we are told he wrote poems and speeches, took exercise, and jested with the pirates, assuring them they would eventually be hanged. The ransom from Rome was sent to Miletus and thence to the pirate camp at Pharmako. Caesar, on being released, soon raised a punitive expedition, captured the pirates and had them sent as prisoners to Pergamon, where they were condemned to death by crucifixion.
>
> It is said that, bearing in mind their humane treatment of him during captivity, Caesar had their throats cut before they were nailed to the cross!

Island of Leros

lying south of Lipso is 8 miles long; its many inlets and promontories afford pleasant summer anchorages. To the north-west of this rugged coast the long island of Arkhangelos forms a shield against the prevailing winds and provides shelter in the remote bays of the Pharios Channel. There are two main ports and some sheltered anchorages:

Alinda Bay on the eastern coast is easily distinguished from seaward by the imposing Venetian Castle on the high Cape Castello. Off the attractive village of **Ayia Marina,** on the southern side near the head of the bay is a short mole where one or two caiques berth, but it is very exposed and the north wind makes it uncomfortable. Pandeli Bay on the south side of the isthmus is a better alternative.

> **Anchorage.** Chart 1669, plan. The anchorage is easy to find by day or night. In settled weather a yacht should anchor on a sandy bottom off the town of Ayia Marina. If several craft are here it is more convenient to run a warp to the shore close S.W. of the pier with the red light.
>
> **Port Facilities.** At the shops in the port there is a limited choice of fresh provisions, but at Leros village on the saddle of the hill there are better supplies. There are some fresh-water taps near the quay and one or two modest tavernas. Taxis are available.

An interesting half-an-hour's drive by taxi from Ayia Marina leads up the hill through Leros village and then down to Port Laki. There are fine views across the hilly unproductive country of the island.

The British cemetery at the head of the bay recalls the determined, though unsuccessful, attempt to wrest this island from the Germans in 1943. Nearly three thousand men were landed at Alinda Bay and the adjoining coves; despite subsequent reinforcing with troops then in Samos, the Germans in the Aegean proved to be too strong. The British had to withdraw, losing many men; six destroyers were sunk and several ships damaged.

Over the saddle S.E. from Ayia Marina is

Pandeli (Panali Bay), a small fishing village with convenient anchorage sheltered from the prevailing wind.

> **Anchorage.** Off the centre of the sandy beach in 3- to 5-fathom depths, on a bottom of light weed and sand. Open only to south.
>
> **Facilities.** Plentiful provisions can be bought at Leros village, 15 minutes walk up the hill. A modest taverna by the shore sometimes provides fish and ice.

Local fishing boats land their catch on the beach and it is carried by lorry to Leros village on the saddle above the hamlet. In late afternoon the setting sun provides an impressive sight when it shines on the Venetian castle towering on the tall promontory above the colourful fishing boats and the small houses of the hamlet.

On the south coast is the inlet of

Xerokambo with a small fishing hamlet, without particular interest; a convenient anchorage for any sized yacht—light weed on sand. Open only to the south.

Port Laki is the former Italian naval base. Since its destruction in 1944 the buildings of the village have been repaired and an attempt has been made to turn the place into a Greek summer resort.

Berth. Plan on Chart 1669. The yacht station is in an exposed position at the N.E. corner of the harbour (mole extended 1972). A better berth is on the W. side, away from the promenade.
Facilities. Fuel at the yacht station. Water tap at the root of the mole. Ice factory E. of the village. Provisions, including plenty of fish, usually available.

The planting of shady trees on the promenade and redecoration of the houses has given the place a 'new look'. The bathing beach attracts many tourists. A technical school has been set up and also a school for wooden-ship construction.

Partheni Bay on the north of the island is completely landlocked, affording perfect shelter in suitable depths; but the Greek Navy has taken it over, and at the moment of writing, although a prohibited area, there was no objection to a yacht anchoring here.

Approach and Berth. Chart 3926, and plan on Chart 1669. There is anchorage with convenient depths of 4 fathoms in the middle, shelving gradually. Some large mooring buoys have been laid out between the entrance to the bay and Porto di Rina, making an approach by night most hazardous.

Island of Kalimnos

A narrow, well-marked strait separates Leros from Kalimnos immediately southward. The beautiful scenery along the west coast of this mountainous and largely barren island should not be missed, and there are some delightful anchorages here sufficiently sheltered against the prevailing winds.

Port Kalimnos, the home of the famous sponge-divers, has an interesting small town with a large and recently improved harbour. Many of the small houses are still colour-washed in blue, said to have been a ruse of the islanders for irritating their former Italian masters by flaunting the Greek colours.

Approach and Anchorage. Chart 1669, plan. Considerable improvements have been undertaken in the port. Land has been reclaimed at the root of the mole, and the mole itself has been widened with broad quays, affording deep water alongside. Yachts are expected to berth stern to the southern mole near its landward end. In strong northerlies this is uncomfortable and the holding is poor. In such conditions it is preferable to anchor near the northern shore between the two short moles.
Facilities. There has recently been marked progress in raising the standard of the local amenities. No longer is the port the squalid place it was; a broad road with flowering shrubs now leads from the new quay towards the village where there are some modest hotels, tavernas,

cafés and provision shops. Steamer communication with Piraeus and Rhodes daily. A large shipyard which can haul up a dozen caiques, it builds most of the local sponge-boats.

The great occupation of the inhabitants for many decades has been sponge-fishing. Several hundred men have usually sailed after the Greek Easter in perhaps eighty boats for the African coast, and based themselves on Tobruk, Benghazi and even Tunis. These small vessels are mostly the local *trehandiri*, about 35 ft in length built of Samian pine. This fleet has its own divers with both rubber suits and aqualungs, also sponge-fishers with masks for the shallower waters. The sponge-boats are usually to be expected back during October when their return is the occasion for noisy celebrations. Many of their sponges, after local processing, find their way to the American market. During the Second World War when sponge-fishing was denied them, many men from this island, fearing starvation, escaped in their boats, together with their families, to Turkey.

At the beginning of the last century Kalimnian divers were taken to Kithera where in 1802 they retrieved the Elgin marbles, then lying in a wreck in 60 ft of water. (See page 14.)

The island can barely sustain its population of nearly 14,000. It was denuded of trees during the long Turkish occupation, and now only the valleys and a few inland plains are cultivated; this however is sufficient. The island also attracts a few tourists mainly for the radio-active springs. The port, relatively large, is sometimes a busy place accommodating one or two modern freighters and perhaps fifty caiques.

Other Anchorages on the east coast:

Vathy a deep fjord with a hamlet at its head is suitable for small yachts. Although well-sheltered, during the Meltemi strong gusts come down the valley. Basic provisions are available.

On the west coast—Chart 3925—is temporary anchorage at

Borio Bay. It has a small hamlet and offers the choice of two coves for anchoring. Off the hamlet is a stone pier to which a yacht can run out a stern warp. There is a simple taverna and basic provisions.

Telendos Island. There is anchorage off the village, in convenient depths, at the foot of the tall mountain, with impressive views along the rugged barren coast. The island appears to have been inhabited since earliest times, for there are some massive stone blocks of a Cyclopean wall, as well as some Greek and Roman ruins, and the remains of an abandoned monastery.

Linaria Bay has a few summer villas and a partly sheltered anchorage; a road leads to Port Kalimnos.

On the south coast is

Cape Kephalo anchorage. One mile east of the cape is an unnamed cove with a few summer villas at its head. This sheltered anchorage (open only to S.) on a sandy bottom is a pleasant place to bring up for the night.

Island of Pserimos is of no particular interest, and its only sheltered cove is on the S.W. coast; this is used by the Greeks from Kos as a summer resort.

Approach and Anchorage. There is no difficulty by day, but a yacht should beware of a rock awash to the southward of this cove. The sandy bottom in the cove rises conveniently to 3 fathoms, but there is a rocky ledge running across which protrudes about 2 ft above the sand. The Meltemi brings in a lively swell. There are some landing steps on the north side of the cove where tourists from neighbouring islands are landed from caiques.

General. There is a good bathing beach; but apart from a few summer bungalows built close to the shore, no other dwellings can be seen.

THE TURKISH COAST

Kovela lies close southward of the present mouth of the Menderes River.

The Ancient Gulf of Latmos together with the Menderes River have undergone many changes throughout the centuries; this has accounted for the abandonment of important Ionian, Greek and Roman cities whose ruins may now be seen many miles inland.

> *The face of places, and their forms, decay;*
> *And that is solid earth that once was sea;*
> *Seas in their turn retreating from the shore,*
> *Make solid land where ocean was before.*
>
> Ovid's *Metamorphosis XV*, DRYDEN, trans.

The present mouths of the Meander or Menderes River can be seen on Chart 1546, but in early Greek times the waters of this river emptied into the spacious Gulf of Latmos, some 20 miles further eastward. On its shores were the cities of the Ionian Greeks, inherited later by the Romans. Miletus, a prosperous

commercial city with its four harbours—'one large enough to accommodate a fleet', wrote Strabo—was famous for 'its men of destiny, talents and sublime genius'; the best known today is probably Thales, the philosopher and astronomer. Although largely destroyed by the Persians and later conquered by Alexander, Miletus did not actually begin to decline until the silting of the port in the early centuries of our millennium, and during Byzantine days its importance was waning rapidly. In A.D. 52 St Paul came here by sea. Today the extensive ruins of the city are well worth seeing; among them is the theatre, the largest in Asia Minor.

Opposite Miletus on the north side of this former spacious gulf was Priene, a carefully planned city by Alexander's architects—now called Gülbahçe. Its port, as Strabo records, had already silted in his day, and in the 1st century A.D. a channel had to be dredged through the mud to enable shipping to operate. German archaeologists have excavated much of the old city including a theatre, council chamber, and nearly 400 houses. Myus is another of the twelve Ionian cities; there is also Heraclaea, and Magnesia, lying on a tributary of the Meander —most of these places are easily accessible by motor-car from the more sophisticated anchorages mentioned in this chaper. But the waters of the gulf have vanished: 'Furrows take the place of waves, and goats leap where once the dolphins played.' The river-bed has continued to silt and the only part of the original gulf still to survive is the inland lake of Bafa; being connected to the sea, a profitable fishing industry has developed, the majority of the fish being cured locally and exported abroad.

Kovela. The present village of Kovela on the eastern shore is poor and squalid, and the shores having silted, there is no longer shelter at the anchorage: it may be used only in settled weather and not in the Meltemi season. If wanting to see the ruins of Didyma, a yacht should make for Skropes, lying inside the Gulf of Mandalya. This is a better alternative, although the guard-post there may have to call by telephone Police and Customs from Kovela before permitting foreigners to land.

Formerly the ancient port of Panormos, Kovela handled the commerce of Didyma with which it was linked by a road bordered by sphinxes. Today there are practically no remains, but it has port officials and is the headquarters of a coastguard detachment: here one may land in fine weather to visit the ruins, not only of Didyma, but also Miletus (8 miles) and Priene (17 miles). Take a taxi from Yeronda.

THE GULF OF MANDALYA (GÜLLÜK)

This large gulf has an exceptional number of inlets worth visiting in a yacht. Some of them are remarkable for their attractive mountainous surroundings, others for their ancient ruins, and some for both. They mostly afford good sheltered anchorage for medium-sized yachts. During the summer months the Meltemi blows into the gulf from a direction W. to W.N.W. starting in the forenoon, freshening after 1100 and easing off before sunset. Occasionally the hot Poyras (N.E. wind) sets in for a couple of days. Inside the inlets the wind sometimes follows round the contours of the coast and also blows off the nearer mountains in hard squalls. At night there is a light land breeze, each inlet creating its own quite independently. The hamlets are very poor—at some places half-a-dozen little houses. The derelict houses to be seen lining the shore at many inlets are those of former Greek settlements abandoned since the First World War. Although often repairable none of these dwellings have been occupied by the Turks whose village is usually a mile or two from the sea. There is some-times nothing to be bought. Customs guards frequently come off and demand Ship's Papers; it is therefore essential to have made an official entry in order to satisfy these officials with the necessary papers.

In contrast to Greece where every sheltered anchorage has a few small houses, one or two caiques and some small fishing boats, in Turkey this maritime atmosphere is entirely lacking. Only at a commercial port one may find a caique loading timber or charcoal, but apart from the sponge-boats hardly any local craft are to be seen.

Kukurcuk, close east of the Cape Tekağaç are two sandy bays sometimes used by sponge fishermen in the summer months. They have good holding on a sandy bottom and occasionally afford a useful night anchorage when sheltering from the Meltemi.

Since the survey was made for Chart 1546, sand bars have appeared across the mouths of both these bays and the depths are barely two fathoms where the chart shows 3½. The water is unusually clear.

Skropes Bay (Altinkum), a comfortable sandy anchorage and useful for a yacht when visiting Didyma. Recently a large modern hotel and restaurant have been built, and the place is becoming a summer resort.

> **Approach and Anchorage.** Chart 1546. One should give Skropes shoal a wide berth and approach the anchorage from the E.S.E. This shoal is now barely under the surface, sometimes showing above, and may be seen by the discoloured water. Let go 300 yds to the eastward of the small Customs shack in 2½ fathoms, on a sandy bottom. Both holding and shelter are good, the bay being open only to the southward.
>
> **Officials.** A Customs post examines passports and in 1968 omitted the usual formalities, but they may refer them to the authorities in Kovela which can mean some delay.

The village of Yeronda is 3 miles distant by a new road; taxis are available but bargaining is necessary. Beside this village are the extensive remains of the Ionian temple of Didyma.

> **Historical.** Towering above the village the surviving columns of the temple stand 100 ft above the ground and all around lie the drums of many more where they were felled by the earthquake at the end of the 15th century. Though nothing remains of the earlier temple destroyed by Xerxes after Salamis, these are the ruins of its successor, the vast temple put up

by the Milesians. The scale was so great that even after 150 years' work and despite the subsequent efforts of the Romans, it was still unfinished. Had it been completed it would probably have ranked as one of the Wonders of the World. It was approached by a sacred way from Panormos from which Newton, the archaeologist, recovered some seated figures and sphinxes of the 6th century B.C., now to be seen in the British Museum. (See also map on p. 148.)

The following inlets on the northern shore are worth a visit:

Kuru Erik Limani, a pleasant anchorage off Talianaki.

Anchor in 4 fathoms in N.W. corner, or alternatively enter Talianaki Cove where there are 2-fathom depths in the western arm and also 2 fathoms on the east side of the entrance.

Akbük Limani, a somewhat open bay with a hamlet which provides basic supplies.

Anchor in 3 fathoms W.S.W. from the hamlet. Good holding on a mud bottom.

Kazikili Limani, an attractive cove at the head of a bay with nearly all-round shelter.

Anchor in 3 fathoms off a conspicuous ruined house; bottom is mud, excellent holding.

The village which is quite large lies a couple of miles inland and can barely be seen from the anchorage. On the eastern shore are some ruined houses, but the western side is wooded and green, the large pine trees coming down to the water's edge. Inside the woods are some scattered Roman ruins.

Saltaluthea in the open cove at the northern corner of the gulf of Alan Gül Körfezi is an attractive anchorage. The shore is wooded down to the water's edge.

Asim Körfezi (gulf) is the most important of these inlets on account of the Iassus ruins and the Port of Entry at Güllük.

At the head of this inlet is the Iassus Promontory with the crumbling Venetian fortress easily distinguishable at a distance. On its western side is the landlocked bay of Asim Liman (**Port Isene**) suitable for medium-sized yachts, and on the east is Asim Bükü (Isene Bay) suitable for large yachts.

Asim Liman, Chart 1606, plan, which also shows the archaeological sites.

Approach. Keep close to the small ruined tower as a sunken mole projects from the western shore opposite, reaching more than half way across the entrance. This obstruction does not show at all on a dull day with a breeze, although it is only 3 ft underwater.

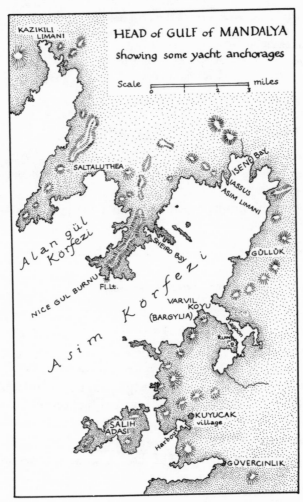

HEAD of GULF of MANDALYA

showing some yacht anchorages

Anchorage. Let go as convenient towards the head of the bay which shelves gradually from 5-fathom depths at the entrance. Bottom is mud.

Officials. They may appear from the ore-port of Güllük, but usually there are none.

Facilities. The hamlet of Kuren at the head of the bay has supplies of fresh fruit, bread etc. and a bar.

The Venetian castle is prominent and among the ancient ruins can be seen the Greek theatre with its Roman additions, including the proscenium. There are remains of the classical walls with subsequent Byzantine restoration. Recent excavations by the Italian Professor Levi have proved that the early Carians lived here for a while before passing on to the Aegean Islands where they set up the earliest civilization in the Cyclades.

Strabo attaches one of the dolphin stories to this place—that of the boy who called it by playing the harp.

Güllük, the only Port of Entry in the Gulf of Mandalya, consists of a hamlet at the head of a bay with a substantial stone pier for berthing freighters.

> **Approach and Berth.** The houses of the hamlet can be seen from Cape Nice Gul, and at night a red light is exhibited on the extremity of the new loading pier. This extends in a N.W. direction from the centre of the bay for about 100 yds and has 25-ft depths at the steamer quay. A yacht requiring practique should anchor in about 3 fathoms on the N.E. side of the pier, good holding on sand, but after the prevailing day breeze this anchorage continues to be uncomfortable. Only when calm can a yacht haul in her stern to the pier.
>
> **Officials.** Health, Customs, Immigration and Harbour Master who board the visiting yacht soon after arrival.
>
> **Facilities** are somewhat primitive, but fruit, bread and fish can usually be bought. Ice is sometimes available. A motel-restaurant is on the coast just outside the hamlet.

Güllük sends away shipments of emery only when sufficient ore has accrued at the dump in the hamlet; it is brought in from the mines, some distance away, in small quantities. Timber and logs are shipped by caique to Istanbul. The village is a poor little place and without interest, although a small modern hotel has been set up to attract local tourists.

Sheiro Bay on the N.E. side of the gulf opposite Güllük is the place to make for if the port should be found untenable.

Varvil Koyu (Anct. Bargylia) is worth a visit for the scenery and the Hellenic ruins, but it is not as sheltered as one could wish. Half-a-mile inside the entrance the bottom comes up very quickly.

> **Anchorage.** About 200 yds off a square, ruined house on the S.W. shore (where the Chart shows 3 fathoms there is in fact 2). Bottom is mud. A swell comes into the cove during the summer day breeze. Land in the dinghy at a wooden jetty, half-an-hour's row across the lagoon.

On the top of the hill are extensive Hellenic and later ruins, very over-grown and difficult to discern. Although unexcavated, the agora, temples and theatre can be found. The view over the marsh is very fine.

Salih Adasi is an island with two pleasant anchorages for small yachts on its eastern coast. At the northern end of the channel is a small cove with a hamlet and jetty at its head and a very restricted anchorage is close off. At the S. end of the channel is a better anchorage, also a small cove with wooded shore where one can anchor in 2–3 fathoms on a sandy bottom.

Kuyucak Harbour (opposite Salih Adasi). A very small, yet completely landlocked harbour with the ruins of a monastery on the isthmus and a Greek village where the river enters.

Anchor in the centre off the western arm halfway between the white ruined church and the shelving N.W. beach in 3 fathom depths on mud and sand. The other arm, towards the village, is shallow and foul, and is reported to be plagued with mosquitoes.

Güvercinlik lying at the head of the gulf is an uninteresting place. The modern Turkish hamlet stands back from the coast; of the former Greek settlement by the water-front only a few houses remain.

The Anchorage is in convenient depths of about 3 fathoms off the port. Land in the dinghy at the ancient mole.

Much forestry work has recently been put in hand on the nearby mountain slopes.

Ilica Bükü is an almost deserted little cove surrounded by pine forests with a very deep anchorage on sand and weed. The head of the bay is attractive and quiet, and you can walk over a good path to the marsh.

Türk Bükü. A yacht may anchor in the western cove as shown on Admiralty Chart. Open to East.

Anchorage is off the village in 5 fathoms, bottom is mud.

There is nothing much to see here, but at the small village one may buy some basic provisions.

Büyük Farilya Bükü has nothing to recommend it other than the shelter in the S.W. corner; but considerable depths force one to anchor inconveniently close to the shore.

Leaving the Mandalya Gulf off the Sandama Peninsula, one follows this rocky coast southward:

Gümüssslük, as the Turks now call Myndus, has little to show of the ancient city beyond some foundations of the old walls: but it provides a pleasant land-locked harbour suitable for a medium-sized yacht.

The harbour entrance is tricky and narrow—during the Meltemi it is almost impossible to enter under sail though the bay is entirely sheltered inside.

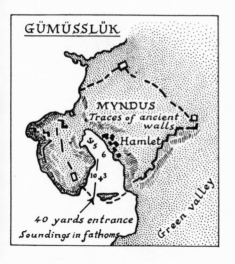

GÜMÜSSLÜK

MYNDUS
Traces of ancient walls
Hamlet

40 yards entrance
Soundings in fathoms

Green valley

Approach and Anchorage. Though Chart 1604 is not clear, the *Sailing Directions* give a good description. As the 40-yds wide channel of entry reaches its narrowest point, an underwater ledge (part of the ancient wall) extends from the W. entrance point. About 150 yds N. of the E. entrance point is the submerged rock referred to in *Sailing Directions*. An examination of the sea-bed in 1968 fixed its position: E. entrance point bore 190°, W. entrance point bore 235°(true); there was about 3 fathoms depth above the rock. By keeping about 30 yds off the western shore it was found that the depths of the channel exceeded 50 ft. A yacht having passed through the narrow entrance should steer a northerly course in the direction of a large ruined house until reaching the anchorage. The only difficulty for a sailing yacht arises when entering in a Meltemi; strong gusts sweep down from the high land, but once inside the wind is fairly steady and cooling, coming in from N.

Anchor in the N. corner of the harbour in about 5 fathoms on a sandy bottom, or nearer the hamlet in 6 fathoms and take a warp to the stone pier (5 ft at its extremity).

Facilities. A simple restaurant, a café, and daily bus service to Bodrum, partly operated by jeep.

The harbour is occasionally used by caiques seeking shelter from the Meltemi when working up the Turkish coast. Although the former Greek houses on the water-front are partly derelict, the valley behind, extending towards Bodrum, is well populated and very green with orange groves and market garden produce. The cattle are well fed and cared for: many cows, donkeys, horses, oriental fat-tailed sheep and camels. The latter may be seen on the sandy shore close to the anchorage being given seabaths and a scrub every morning.

Close southward of Gümüsslük is a group of small rocky islands of which **Karabakla** is the largest. On its eastern side is a bight close to a low-lying isthmus. This provides convenient anchorage in 4 fathoms on a sandy bottom with patches of rock. Shelter here is claimed to be good, even in southerly winds. The island is uninhabited. Close S.W. of Karabakla is the islet of **Yassi** where the hull of a Byzantine ship was recently excavated—see p. 162.

The coast continues southward towards Hussein Burnu where it then turns to E.S.E. forming the northern shore of the Gulf of Kos (Kerme Körfezi). See Chapter 6(e).

Greek Islands: Southern Dodecanese

Island of Kos
  The Port
  Kamares Bay (Kephalos)

Island of Nisiros
  Mandrake

Island of Yali

Island of Tilos
  Livadhi Bay

Island of Astipalea
  Scala
  Maltezana
  Port Agrilithi
  Vathy

Island of Symi (Simi)
  Port Symi
  Pethi Harbour
  Panormittis
  Small yacht anchorages

Turkish Coast

Gulf of Kos (Kerme Körfezi)
  Aspat Bay
  Gumbet Bay
  Bodrum (*Port of Entry*)
  Keramos Bay
  Akbük
  Gökova (Port Giova)
  Gelibolu Limani
  Sehir Adalari
  Sögüt Limani
  Kesr Cove
  Deremen (Değirmen Bükü)
  Guzlemek
  Balisu Bay (Gerenlikli Limani)

Yedi Adalari
  Cape Krio with Büyük Limani
Gulf of Doris (Hisarönü Körfezi)
  Datcha
  Miliontes Bay
  Kuruca Bükü or Kocini Bay
  Göktas Bay
  Bençik or Penzik
  Thiaspori Cove
  Keyif Cove
  Port Kiervasili (Keçi Bükü)
  Port Dirsek
Gulf of Symi (Simi)
  Bozburnu Limani

6e

The Southern Dodecanese and Gulfs of Kos and Doris

SOUTHERN DODECANESE

Island of Kos

A long and partly mountainous island with a well-sheltered small port adjoining a modern resort.

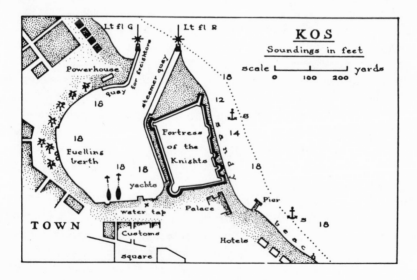

The Port

Approach and Berth. Chart 1616. The harbour entrance, which has recently been considerably widened, is easy to approach day and night. The fortress can be clearly distinguished and one passes between the mole-heads with the new steamer quay to port and the freighter quay to starboard. The wider entrance permits a limited swell to enter the port during strong N. winds and in winter the harbour has recently proved to be unsafe.

The entrance is also apt to silt and must be continually dredged to maintain the uniform depths of 18 ft found elsewhere. Yachts proceed to the south quay and berth stern-to with anchors to northward.

Occasionally larger yachts anchor outside where shown on the chart, but they should keep clear of the steamers which also sometimes anchor off.

Officials. As for a Port of Entry. Offices are close to the quay.

Facilities. Water may be obtained from a tap on the quay by the steps. Fuel available at Fuelling Berth which is shallow, but deepens to 12 ft about 3 yds off. There is an excellent market and many modern shops, a number of hotels (including a Xenia) and restaurants. Early closing Thursdays. Ice can be ordered at a shop next to the Post Office (in street at right angles to the quay); the factory is one mile outside the town. Taxis are available. Piraeus steamers call twice daily in summer, and there is daily air communication with Athens.

Both town and harbour were reconstructed by the Italians after the 1933 earthquake—with the exception of the 15th-century castle built by the Knights of Rhodes. Most places of interest adjoin the port. Yachts berth off the quay at the head of the harbour and caiques off the tamarisk-shaded quays on the west side. The flowering hibiscus and oleanders which border the streets do much towards enhancing the look of the town.

One must see the 18th-century mosque incorporating Hellenic and Byzantine columns, the old plane tree which, according to Hacke writing in 1699, was then 'so vaste that its branches would shade a thousand men'; the local guide explains that Hippocrates used to teach under this tree in the 5th century B.C. but foresters maintain that no plane tree can live for more than 500 years. The castle and the interesting museum should be visited; also some of the more recent Greek excavations on the fringe of the town.

About three miles outside the town is the Asclepeion, the medical school and hospital of Hippocrates, which has been rather over-restored by the Italians; from here the view across the Strait towards the Anatolian mountains is magnificent. One may hire bicycles for this expedition and for exploring some of the villages, one with a small colony of Turks.

Today Kos is a gay little port with plenty of activity; the quays constantly busy with the arrival and departure of small freighters and caiques, and the daily crowd of jostling passengers being embarked and disembarked from the mail steamer. As far as tourists are concerned Kos might be styled a younger sister of Rhodes; but its economy also rests on agricultural produce and honey, fish being sent to Athens and certain canned goods to America.

Historical. When St Paul put in for a night's rest on his third missionary journey from Macedonia to Jerusalem, he probably came to the same harbour as exists today. It silted up in medieval times, but this did not prevent it from being used by pirates. A picture of the place at the end of the 17th century when under Turkish rule is given by Hacke:

'Here being seven half galleys each carrying three hundred men, forty-eight oars, four guns and everyman's small arms. They also have brigantines each carrying seventy men, twenty-eight oars, six patereroes, and small arms each man. These are governed, owned and commanded chiefly by one man who has his commission from the Grand Seigneur; and for retaliation he gathers tribute of the Isles yearly, and by which he is no loser, imposing on rich and poor what he pleases and forces them to pay. And in his progress he takes many Christian slaves.'

The Turks held Kos for almost four centuries until 1912, after which the Italians occupied it until 1948 when it was restored to Greece.

Towards the western extremity of the island's barren south coast is a tall promontory forming the western arm of the open

Kamares Bay where there is excellent shelter in strong northerly winds.

Approach. Chart 3925. Kephalos village stands conspicuously on the hill, and as one nears the head of the bay both Paleo Kastro and the mole of the small port can be seen.

Anchorage. In strong N. winds it is recommended that a yacht should anchor close west of Paleo Kastro in depths of 3 to 5 fathoms on a sandy bottom; good holding and a steady wind.

With fair weather the small port is suitable. Lay out an anchor to the northward and haul in the stern to the extremity of the mole by the light tower. (Lt. Fl. R.) Holding is sand, but the depths decrease rapidly towards the shore. At the mole-head there is nearly 3 fathoms.

Facilities. None at Paleo Kastro. At the port is a small taverna and a water tap. Fruit and bread can be bought at a store near by. A new hotel has grown up.

Small freighters often call to collect the ore (pyrites) which is quarried on the hillside above the port. A Customs Officer is stationed at the port. A few fishing craft are based here to supply the village of Kephalos (2,000 inhabitants). Bus communication.

Opposite Paleo Kastro is a ruined basilica of the 6th century which has been recently excavated.

Island of Nisiros. Chart 3923. Nisiros is square-shaped and largely green with two shallow harbours. The land rises in terraces towards a ring of hills in the centre, surrounding a depression with volcanic craters last active in 1422 and hot sulphur springs. Unlike Milos, the volcanic soil is fertile, the island is wooded, and there are almond trees and olive groves on the hillsides. The three small villages are very primitive.

Of the two small harbours, Mandraki is the more important, but shallow and in the prevailing Meltemi its short breakwater is insufficient to provide adequate shelter; the bottom is of poor holding and most irregular. In the event of a northerly blow, a vessel should make up for the centre of the small and almost uninhabited

Island of Yali, lying 3 miles to the north-westward, is distinguished by its extensive quarries on the hillside; here under Meltemi conditions both shelter and holding are good, but a swell rolls into the anchorage. It is not an agreeable place.

Island of Tilos (Piscopi, formerly Episcopi) is a dull little island with an anchorage in **Livadhi Bay** close to the main village.

> **Anchorage.** Chart 1898. Let go in about 7 fathoms off the entrance to the small boat harbour. Here the bottom is sand; open to north-east, a swell often comes into the bay.
> **Facilities.** The village, 20 minutes' walk along the shore of the bay, is uninteresting but can provide basic fresh supplies. A steamer from Piraeus calls once a week.

There are three villages on the island, whose agriculture has deteriorated; now the only export is goats. The island has never been of historical importance, but during the period of the Knights its security depended upon signalling warnings of enemy approach to Rhodes from a number of watch-towers— hence the name Episcopi, which is also said to have been derived from once having had a bishop.

Island of Astipalea (Stampalia)

is the most westerly of the Dodecanese; its twin mountain peaks make it appear in the distance as separate islands.

From seaward this sparsely populated island appears barren and forbidding, but it affords a choice of good anchorages for even large yachts. Its pleasant little port of Scala offers certain amenities.

Scala lies at the head of a cove with its white houses lining the water-front and ascending the ridge to a ruined Venetian castle on top. There is anchorage for half-a-dozen medium-sized yachts or caiques to swing.

> **Approach and Anchorage.** Chart 1666. Both the ruined castle and the light structure (Lt. Qk. Fl.) are conspicuous. Anchor in 3 to 5 fathoms near the landing pier. With normal summer weather shelter is good and the gusts referred to in *Sailing Directions* are no more alarming than elsewhere. In event of southerly weather shelter should be sought in Maltezana.
> **Facilities.** A limited supply of bread and fresh provisions; water at jetty (caution when berthing), ice at the electricity works. Two tourist hotels with restaurants have been built on the water-front. The Piraeus steamer calls three times a week.
> **Officials.** The Harbour Office is on the terrace close by.

Only a few hundred people live at the Scala which has great charm. The castle was built by the Quirini family who governed the island for 200 years before it was taken by the Turks; the family coat of arms still survives on a plaque by the castle gateway.

Maltezana (Analipsi). Chart 1666, plan, provides nearly all-round shelter.

Anchorage. A patch of sand in 3 fathoms close westward of the white obelisk has good holding, but elsewhere it is undependable and poor.

There are no habitations by the shore, but a road passes leading to Scala.

Port Agrilithi, 2½ miles west of Cape Poulari, affords excellent shelter, in a deserted creek.

Anchorage is in a small cove on the east side of the creek in 5 fathoms on a bottom of sand.

There are no facilities here. The only sign of life is when a caique arrives with workers for a small quarry on the west side of the creek. The land to windward is relatively low-lying and in strong north winds the gusts are mild.

Vathy. Chart 1666, plan, although Chart 3922 gives sufficient detail. This landlocked basin with its barren and uninviting shores appears to be a secure anchorage, but the holding has been reported as being uncertain and the place subject to strong gusts.

Anchorage. After passing the 2-fathom bar turn to port and anchor off some small houses in 2 to 3 fathoms. Bottom is weed on mud, but the water is cloudy. A quarry with power plant has recently been set up close above the shore and two or three cottages were being built in 1969 for the workers.

In Roman days, after the suppression of piracy, warships were sometimes stationed at Astipalea to maintain the safety of shipping. Pirates also used these natural shelters in the later centuries, and in 1812 one of H.M. ships having captured a pirate galley reported:

Yet she rowed fast, possessed a swivel and twenty muskets, and with forty ferocious-looking villains who manned her might have carried the largest merchant ship in the Mediterranean. The pirates had just captured a Turkish boat with five men, four of whom were massacred and the fifth, a Jew, had merely been deprived of an ear!

Apart from the interesting approaches to these natural harbours, this island hardly merits a special visit. Even the mussels, whose quality was praised by Pliny, are no longer cultivated.

Island of Symi (Simi)

Rugged, mountainous and largely barren lies on the eastern extremity of the Aegean within the mouth of the Turkish Gulf of Doris.

It has two main harbours: one, Panormittis, on the western side of the island, affording good shelter in depths of 3 fathoms; and the other on the east side,

Port Symi, lying in a deep inlet surrounded by colourful little houses. Close beside it is the well-sheltered bay of Pethi.

Port Symi lies at the head of a bay with its colourful houses rising up the hillside towards a line of windmills—now dismantled—standing on the ridge above. Approaching the port one can see that although a few houses have been abandoned some of the more substantial ones have been restored and painted in various delicate shades giving one the impression of a small Italian rather than a Greek port.

> **Approach.** Chart 1669. A wooden quay has been built south of the light tower to enable the Rhodes steamer to berth and land her passengers.
>
> **Berth.** The depths are considerable until reaching the head of the bay which becomes shallow and is cluttered with small craft; but there is room to berth in 2½ fathom depths in front of Glitanos Stationianto store. A suitable berth can be found on the south side towards the head of the bay with anchor laid to the northward and stern hauled in to a short projecting quay.
>
> **Facilities.** A small modern hotel stands near the light tower. Nearby is the modest local yacht club with a quay which is too exposed for a visiting yacht to berth there. Provisions and ice are obtainable, also water produced at a solarium recently constructed by a Symiot-American. Restaurants in the N.E. corner of the port.
>
> A small shipyard still builds the trehandiri sponge-boats and could probably help with repairs.

Some thirty years ago Port Symi had a population of 7,000 people, many of whom were employed in the sponge fleet. Today there are only 2,500 of whom only about fifty men go away sponge-fishing in the summer months.

On the front wall of one of the houses is a plaque recording in the English and Greek languages the surrender of the Germans in the Dodecanese in 1944.

A mule-track leads over the mountains from Port Symi to Panormittis: this passes through a wood of pines and cypresses, but it is rough going and takes at least four hours. Also, a walk of one hour takes one to Raukounio monastery with a 5th-century church under the Byzantine one.

Pethi Harbour is a well-sheltered inlet, but rather deep for a yacht wishing to swing to her anchor.

> **Anchorage.** Let go in 8 fathoms in S.W. corner of the inlet; weed on mud. Alternatively a yacht can anchor to seaward off a stone pier (6-ft depth at extremity) and haul in the stern. Gusts are apt to sweep down the hillsides even with light winds.
>
> **Facilities.** Although nothing much can be bought locally it is only 20 minutes' walk over the hill to Port Symi.

Panormittis. A delightful, enclosed, natural harbour in mountainous surroundings with a monastery by the quay.

Approach and Anchorage. Chart 1604. On the N.E. side of the entrance is a ruined wind-mill painted white, which stands out conspicuously to the westward visible at least 5 miles, and by night a light (Fl. R.) is now exhibited. The shore generally is steep-to.

It is convenient to anchor half way between the S.W. headland of the entrance and the southern extremity of the monastery, in 3 fathoms on a sandy bottom. About 30 yds south of the monastery tower is a short stone pier which also has a quay; at the head of the pier are depths of 8 to 9 ft diminishing towards the shoreward end. Though a yacht could berth with her stern to the pierhead for a short while, it is well to know that caiques frequently call here, as well as the Rhodes steamer. In Meltemi weather the best shelter is in the N.E. corner of the harbour about 25 yds from the shore in depths of 12 ft. A warp can be run ashore. There is a slight swell caused by the day breeze.

General. Fresh water is limited, being collected in winter and stored in the monastery cistern; a small general store is in the monastery where tinned provisions and vegetables may be bought; there is also a taverna. Bread can be bought and ice can be ordered by caique from Symi. On the southern shore of the anchorage is a small restaurant. The modern monastery has a charming bell-tower and in its courtyard a 12th-century church, with some interesting carving and icons.

Only a few monks live here, but many Greek visitors stay a few days and eat at the café; there are a few private rooms with showers. In front of the monastery is a memorial to the late abbot who was shot by the Germans in the last war. The custom of ringing the monastery bell as a sign of welcome to a strange vessel (including yachts) is still continued.

Other anchorages for small yachts off Symi

On the East Coast:

An unnamed little sandy cove lies close northward of the entrance to Pethi Bay. An islet off the N. shore of the cove provides adequate shelter for a small yacht; the anchorage being open only through a narrow sector to the east.

Marathouda Bay, lying about 3 miles S. of the southern side of Pethi Bay, has a small sandy cove at its head.

Anchorage is off a quay in 3 fathoms on a sandy bottom; it is sometimes necessary to run out a warp when mountain gusts sweep down. Partly open to east.
Facilities. Only a few vegetables to be bought locally, but a 20-min. walk brings one to Panormittis where there is a wider choice of fresh provisions.

On the West Coast:

Cape Kephalo. East of this peninsula is a very small peninsula (almost an islet). Here is the monastery of Ayios Emiliano, and beneath it a small sandy cove with 2-fathom depths, open only towards the Symi coast.

Turkish Coast Southward

Gulf of Kos (Kerme Körfezi)

This deep inlet extends eastward for 50 miles, reaching Giova, a small trading port lying at the mouth of a mountain stream, at its head. Apart from a small freighter making for Giova not a ship or boat will be seen. The day breeze blows into the gulf from west reaching a strength of 4 or 5 on an average summer's day. The steep, barren, northern shores gradually become more precipitous towards the head of the gulf with mountains rising from the cliffs to heights of 3,000 ft. The last fifteen miles is green and wooded on both shores. On the southern side are some attractive anchorages shown on plans of Chart 1533. These places are completely deserted and well worth visiting in a yacht.

On entering the gulf from the northward a yacht should be careful to avoid the rocky shoals lying half a mile off Hussein Point and beyond. Although Bodrum is the one major port close at hand there are some pleasant coves where according to the wind one can conveniently bring up for the night:

Aspat Bay. Here a yacht can anchor in 5 fathoms on a sandy bottom near some cottages. The peasants take their produce by boat to Bodrum daily.

Gumbet Bay is within close walking distance of Bodrum and is sometimes preferred by a yacht, when that port is too crowded.

Bodrum is the ancient Halicarnassus, former capital of Caria. Its sheltered port is still protected by the original Greek breakwaters.

The site of one of the famous Wonders of the World—the Tomb of Mausolus—is close beside the harbour on the bare rising ground, but today apart from the recent excavation of the foundations, not a stone remains. The only objects of interest here are the Castle of the Knights with its museum, and the market on Fridays.

Approach and Berth. Chart 1606 shows the dangerous rocks off Khator Point which are unmarked but just awash. Otherwise the entrance is well marked. There is now an excellent marina on the southwest side of the harbour, but yachts may find it easier to make first for the town quay below the castle in order to shorten the wearisome Turkish officialdom as the police, customs etc. are close at hand. (The sunken quays to the north of the town quay are marked by a red buoy.) Bodrum has perfect shelter and is an excellent port in which to winter.

Officials. Some efforts are being made to ease the lot of yachtsmen entering Turkey at Bodrum especially if one goes first to the town quay.

Facilities. The water at the marina seems to be drinkable. Ice and fuel are available. Excellent shops—especially vegetables—in the town. There are several small hotels and one or two excellent restaurants. There are two fairly primitive boatyards and a good marine engineer in the town. (Perkins agent.)

The modern Turkish town, mostly built by the former Greek colony, is only of particular interest on market day (Friday), when peasants from outlying villages wearing colourful national costume come in with their wives by camel bringing with them country produce.

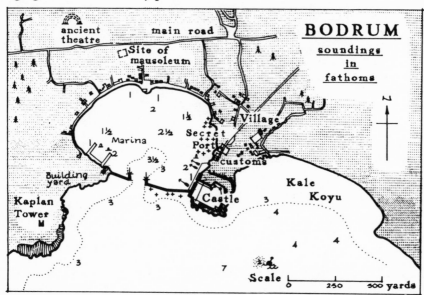

The Castle. On the east side of the harbour standing on a rocky eminence are the well-preserved walls of a large medieval castle built by the Knights of St John. During its construction fragments of the Mausoleum were torn down to embellish the castle and some of them remain embedded in the walls today. The English tower with the coats of arms of Plantagenet Knights still stands, despite a hard knock from a British cruiser's bombardment in the First World War. Among the scattered pieces of masonry one notices a plinth, a jamb or an architrave to a doorway, a marble capital lying on its side, carved with an heraldic device.

The famous Amazon frieze which, in 1856 Newton* with the British Navy's help, removed from the walls of the castle (where the Knights had placed it as decoration) was carried away by H.M.S. *Siren* together with the 9½-ft statue of Mausolus—'the tall handsome man . . . formidable in War!' Both statue and frieze are well displayed in the British Museum.

The castle was used by the Knights for many years, as a base for making sorties against the Turks, and as a sanctuary for escaping Christian slaves. Today much of the stonework has been repaired by the Turkish government and the castle restored to become a great

---

* C. T. Newton, British archaeologist and at that time appointed British Consul in Smyrna. Some captured Turkish reports described him as the 'mad English Consul digging holes in the ground at Cape Krio'.

attraction for tourists. Within the walls are exhibited many of the more interesting early Greek finds—sculpture, pottery, etc. Also very well displayed are the underwater exhibits of the joint Turkish–Pennsylvania Museum archaeological expeditions, led by George Bass and Peter Throckmorton. There are pieces of the hull and parts of the cargoes of a Byzantine period ship which sank about A.D. 620 off Yassi Ada, in the Karabakla Group north of Bodrum, and of the wreck of a Bronze Age ship which went down about 1200 to 1300 B.C. off Cape Gelidonya.

Continuing along the northern coast one comes to some deep and somewhat open bays, where the steep-to mountains cause strong gusts of wind at the anchorages beneath them.

Keramos Bay is rather too deep for a small yacht; the hamlet is close to the shore with a taverna. The ruined Dorian city of Keramos which lies above the plain, formerly gave its name to this gulf.

Akbük affords a pleasant anchorage in wooded surroundings.

Anchorage is in the western corner of the bay, 120 yds off the beach in 7 fathoms on a bottom of thin weed on mud.

There are several peasant houses and a good deal of agricultural activity. At the head of the gulf is

Gökova (Port Giova) where there are two loading jetties (depth alongside 12 ft) where small freighters load chrome ore. Here are port officials and a small hamlet where a bus or taxi is available to go to Marmaris.

On the S.E. shores the coast is well indented, hilly and wooded. See Admiralty Chart 1533 for plans of anchorages which are all quite close together. The first from eastward is

Gelibolu Limani the most open, and least attractive inlet of the four.

Sehir Adalari. Plan on Chart 1533. It provides a delightful anchorage between two small low-lying wooded islands with interesting Greek archaeological remains.

Anchor as convenient in 3 fathoms in the S.W. corner of Castle Island Bay: sand on rock. Perfect fine weather shelter. A sand bar stretches some 50 yds from the mouth of the stream.

The Hellenic ruins on Castle Island are well worth visiting. Best of all is the charming Greek theatre looking across the close-lying islets towards the tall mountains on the opposite shore. Although unexcavated the theatre is nearly

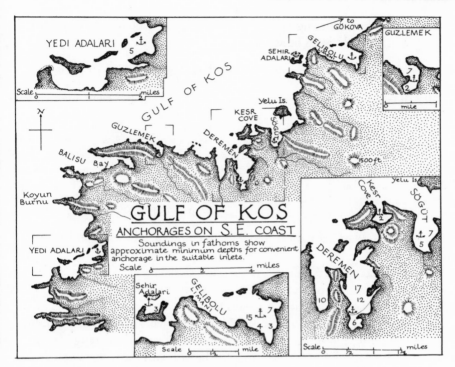

intact, and probably seated about two thousand people. Nearby are fluted drums of temple columns, many well-preserved sections of the citadel walls and some underground passages. It seems amazing to think of this small island as a fortified stronghold enclosing buildings worthy of a large city; one must assume that the adjacent country was then highly populated. Now, only a few peasants graze their goats and look after the olive trees.

Söğüt Limani is a pleasant bay with a good anchorage towards the mouth of a stream at its head.

Kesr Cove (Çanak Limani) is a deserted wooded inlet with all-round shelter at the head, but suitable only for a small yacht.

Deremen (Değirmen Bükü). Chart 1533 (plan). A large deserted fjord with densely wooded banks and attractive anchorages in superb surroundings.

> **Anchorages.** The creeks to N.E. and N.W. are preferable to the 'admiralty anchor' though it may be necessary in the former to put a warp ashore. Perfect shelter.
> **Facilities.** In 1974 there was a small restaurant on the eastern shore—where simple food can be obtained and water is available (hose to the boat).

Guzlemek, a deep winding fjord, the sides densely wooded, with anchorage for only a small yacht at its head.

Balisu Bay (Gerenlikli Limani), a pleasant bay, but shallow at its head.

Yedi Adalari is an interesting long lagoon formed off the coast by a row of small islands.

> **Anchorage.** There is a choice of two places. The safest alternative is S.W. of 7-fathom mark in Götağac Bay. Here the sea-bed rises gently to the beach behind which is a lake. The sea-bed is weed on mud, there being convenient anchorage in depths of 5 fathoms. Good shelter though within the lagoon is a fetch of 2 miles towards N.E. Anchorage inside the winding creek is impossible, but a small yacht can anchor in the little inlet to the N.E. taking a line ashore. Behind this anchorage is a most attractive valley well worth exploring.

There is no sign of habitation, and a yacht could spend a pleasant day or two underwater fishing.

On the southern shores of the Gulf from Yedi Adalari as far as its mouth are some open coves; but no further anchorages are worth mentioning and one follows the northern coast of the great Dorian Peninsula for 30 miles towards its western extremity. Here at the N.W. tip of a small cliff-bound peninsula is Cape Krio; a low, sandy isthmus joins it to the tall mainland range (1,800 ft). This cape, dividing the gulf of Kos from the gulf of Doris, forms on its S.E. side a most useful port of shelter:

Cape Krio with **Büyük Limani** affords shelter to local craft in this very windy corner of the Aegean. This anchorage is sheltered from the Meltemi

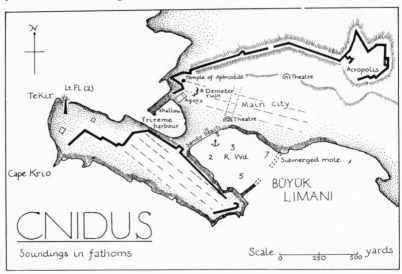

by the low narrow isthmus, and from the Sirocco by the two ancient moles—
'carried to a depth of nearly 100 feet', wrote Captain Beaufort during his survey
150 years ago, 'one of them is almost perfect, the other which is more exposed
to the S.W. swell can only be seen under water.'

Approach and Berth. By day this is easy, and a vessel may pass in deep water 20 yds off
the extremity of the S.W. mole. Keeping in the centre of the bay, the sea-bed rises slowly
to 3 fathoms with a bottom of heavy weed on sand and sometimes boulders. It is extremely
difficult to get a plough anchor to hold. Though there is perfect shelter from the sea, strong
gusts blow from N.W. by day and from N.N.E. by night during Meltemi periods. Off the
Cape itself very violent gusts make it advisable to lower sails before entering harbour.
General. There is an outpost of a dozen Turkish soldiers who may insist on seeing ship's
papers. The crew-list with passport numbers should be prepared to forestall a demand to
retain one's passport.
Facilities. A water tap by a jetty at the head of the bay. Two modest cafés.

Ancient Cnidus. Round the harbour are the terraced walls of large stone blocks
often rising from the water's edge to the ridge above. Nothing except the lower
theatre can be seen from the anchorage, but one must land to explore the ruins
on the north side of the harbour.

Near the top of the ridge stands part of the large theatre, more than half
having collapsed. Westward of its base is the ruined temple of Demeter, one of
whose statues was carried off by the archaeologist Newton (with the help of
the Navy) in the middle of the last century, and brought to London for the
British Museum. The most exciting excavation in recent years has been by
the Americans who found on the slope overlooking the isthmus the podium of
the Temple of Aphrodite. They also found the base of a statue which they have
reason to believe was made for the famous Aphrodite by Praxiteles—described
by Pliny as being 'not only the finest of Praxiteles' works, but the finest in all the
world'. Close above the harbour is another theatre with 35 rows of seats estimated
to accommodate about 8,000 people.

On the south side of the harbour there is not so much to see, but near where the
lighthouse now stands, Newton dug out a fine 12-ton lion—the symbol for
valour—which now stands proudly aloof in the British Museum. It was probably
a naval war memorial, and one likes to think that it was this lion which inspired
Thucydides to write these words:

> *The whole earth is the tomb of heroic men*
> *and their story is not graven only on stone*
> *over their clay but abides everywhere*
> *without visible symbol, woven into the stuff*
> *of other men's lives.*

The Scots chose this inscription for their war memorial at Edinburgh.

The ancient trireme harbour described by Strabo as 'a station for 20 vessels' has silted, and is now too shallow to serve any purpose today.

The Gulf of Doris or Hisarönü Körfezi

(Gulf of Fortresses)

See Chart 1604 and note that many hilltops are marked with the ruin of some early defensive work.

Entering the Gulf near Cape Krio (Iskandil Burnu) a vessel should follow the tall, barren Dorian promontory towards the wooded shores at its head. The mountain ridge (with a rough road from Cape Krio at its foot) slowly descends to the Plain of Datcha. There is very little traffic in the Gulf—the occasional trading caique or sponge-boat may be seen. Much of the countryside is deserted.

Datcha. An exposed anchorage at the head of a cove with a substantial village standing on the hillside.

> **Anchorage.** Let go in 5 fathoms in the southern cove opposite a landing place. A prevailing breeze off the land is from N.N.W. Should the wind shift to the eastern quadrants a yacht should make for Aiak Adasi, four miles to the N.E., and anchor behind the islets where shelter is good.
>
> **Officials.** As for a Port of Entry. Customs and Immigration are close to the landing place.
>
> **Facilities.** Fresh water at a tap on the quay or on application to 'bureau' at the head of cove, a small hotel, and limited provisions in the hamlet including a bakery.

Datcha was the original capital of the Cnidian Peninsula. The ruins of the acropolis stand on the hill by the shore about one mile north of the castle. After the Persian invasion in the 4th century B.C., the Cnidians again settled down but, because of the recent increase in sea trade, they realized the importance of the strategic position of Cape Krio, and built their harbours and the new city there. By doing so they abandoned the agricultural plain supporting Datcha, but the sea trade compensated for the arid land adjoining the new city.

In very recent times the port of Datcha has begun to recover something of its former importance; the present modern hamlet has been tidied-up and the place has a certain attraction. The village of Datcha lies 1½ miles inland on the hillside and is approached by a road.

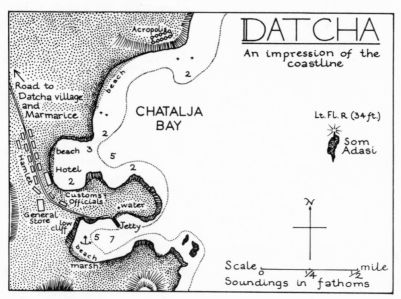

Miliontes Bay which is attractive and sheltered, lies close southward; unfortunately the depths are too great for convenient anchorage.

Kuruca Bükü (Kocini Bay) is a sheltered anchorage in pleasant wooded surroundings.

Anchorage. Let go off the N.W. beach in 5 or 6 fathoms on a mud bottom, being careful to avoid patches of heavy weed. It may be desirable to run out a warp to the shore.

The nearest habitation is a farm across the pinewoods on the isthmus. Sponge-boats sometimes put in here.

Göktas Bay, on the west of Kezil Head, appears to be worth exploring.

Bençik (Penzik) is a winding narrow inlet, wooded and well-sheltered.

Approach. *Sailing Directions* give warning of a sunken rock ⅓ mile before head of the inlet. **Anchorage** is at the head in 4–7 fathoms, shortly before reaching the marsh where it narrows; a warp ashore may be desirable.

A few scattered farmsteads can be seen from the anchorage. The only objection to the place is mosquitoes.

When Commander Graves was making his survey for the chart in 1844 he discovered traces of ancient cuttings in the rocks where evidently an attempt had been made to dig a canal across the mile-wide isthmus which marks the end of the Cnidian peninsula. In a description of this excavation written by Herodotus twenty-three centuries earlier there is mentioned that, at the time of the threatened Persian invasion, the Cnidians set to work to dig a defensive canal; but the diggers, being continually wounded and cut in the eye by flying chips of rock, began to wonder if their work was really necessary. Accordingly, priests were sent to consult the oracle at Delphi and returned with the following answer:

> Dig not the isthmus nor build a tower,
> Zeus would have made an island had he wished it.

The undertaking was abandoned, and later when the Cnidians were attacked they surrendered to the Persian invaders.

Thiaspori Cove (N. of islet) is entered by the eastern channel.

Anchorage is in N.W. corner in 5 to 7 fathoms, good holding and excellent shelter in attractive surroundings.

Keyif Cove, the westernmost of two coves near the head of the gulf (36° 47.3 N, 28° 7.5 E) provides a pleasant anchorage in fine scenery among wooded surroundings.

Anchorage. Let go off the centre of the beach in 5 fathoms, on a bottom of mud and thin weed.

At the head of the beach is a waterhole which attracts wild boar at night and roaming cattle by day. A short climb through the maquis takes one to the top of the ridge. Here, especially in the cool of the evening, when surrounded by a variety of sweet-smelling shrubs (rosemary, rue, thyme, sage, bay-leaves and myrtle), one can enjoy the view across the Gulf of Kerme.

About 2 miles eastward is the head of the Gulf, with a small river mouth. Nearby is a Customs Post and on the hilltops can be seen the ruins of ancient defences.

Along the south-east shore of the gulf the coast continues to be green and indented, but usually the heads of inlets are inconveniently deep for anchoring. This applies to the inlets of Port Losta and the anchorage under the islets of Karamea and Kaloyeré.

Port Kiervasili (Keçi Bükü) is a narrow sheltered inlet with a hamlet one mile from its head.

Approach. A mile inside the inlet you pass an islet crowned by a ruined fort. There were reported to be 9-ft depths between the islet and the western shore.

Anchorage. A small shallow draft yacht may anchor close under the islet in 1½ fathoms, but a larger yacht should anchor at the head of the creek in depths of 6 fathoms where shelter is better.

The valley is cultivated with scattered farmsteads. At the hamlet, half-an-hour's walk, one can buy small quantities of fruit and vegetables. The fort on the islet is interesting to visit, also the theatre and temple near Arin Dagh—a long walk. Mini buses convey one to Marmaris, a frequent service, taking 40 minutes.

Port Dirsek, an attractive sheltered inlet with an anchorage at its head in depths of 4 to 7 fathoms. A warp led ashore is sometimes advisable.

In the adjacent cove eastward (marked 'well' on chart) there is also a lovely anchorage off the beach with a deserted farmhouse. Fish and a few provisions may be obtained from local fishermen.

Turning into the smaller **Gulf of Symi** (Simi) is

Bozburnu Limani. Here a yacht may anchor in convenient depths off the village, but towards the head of the inlet it is shallow; alternatively anchor in the remote N.W. cove. If crossing over from one to the other care should be taken to avoid the shoal which appears to have extended.

Although there is no longer activity in the port, it was formerly the centre of the Turkish sponge-gathering industry; their Greek rivals were established at Symi. Nowadays a few fishing boats are built here.

Officials. Port Captain and Customs board a yacht on arrival.

Facilities are few: a couple of poor shops and some modest restaurants.

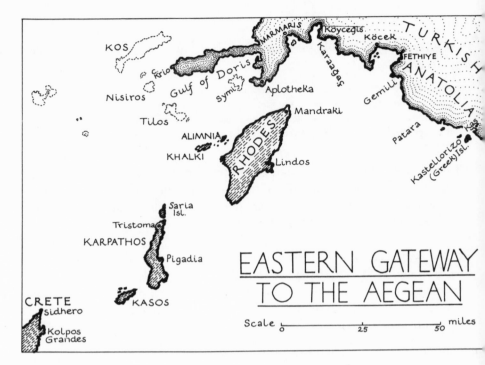

EASTERN GATEWAY
TO THE AEGEAN

Scale 0 ——— 25 ——— 50 miles

GREEK ISLANDS	ANATOLIAN COAST
Island of Rhodes	*Rhodes to Kekova Roads*
Mandraki	Port Aplotheka
Lindos	Marmaris (Marmarice)
Other anchorages	Karaağaç with Yörük Cove
Cape Istros	Köyceğiz Bay—Ekinçik
Cape Vigli	Dalyan Islet (for Anct. Caunus)
Island of Alimnia	GULF OF FETHIYE
Island of Khalki (Halki)	Skopea Limani
Island of Karpathos	Tersani Adasi
	Köcek
Pigadia (Port Karpathos)	Fethiye
Tristoma	Gemili Island
Other anchorages including:	Yorğun Köyü
Amorphos Bay	Patara
Island of Kasos	Kalkan
Ofris	
Makronisi	Island of Kastellorizo (Greek)
Kasos Strait	Kaş

7

Eastern Gateway to the Aegean

THE ISLAND BRIDGE
BETWEEN TURKEY AND CRETE

Island of Rhodes (Rodos)

Green and mountainous, is the largest and most historically interesting island, the capital of the Dodecanese. By the commercial port the inhabited medieval walled city makes a strange contrast with the large modern tourist resort spreading out from the old harbour of Mandraki.

Mandraki. Chart 1666 with harbour plan. This is the yacht harbour of the island and during the summer months it is invariably crowded with yachts—large and small. Adding to the general confusion during berthing movements is a number of local ferry-boats which also operate from here. This modern activity makes a strange contrast to the peaceful scene shown in the sketch—only fifteen years ago.

> **Approach.** Entering the approaches to Mandraki harbour, the extensive medieval walls of the old city come into view as well as the modern pseudo-Venetian buildings close to the quayside.

By day there is no difficulty in the approach. By night, however, if coming from south-ward along the coast caution is necessary to ensure clearing off-lying shoals, and on no account should the port be entered in strong southerly winds.

The light on Fort St Nicholas can be clearly distinguished from afar; but the weaker light marking the extremity of the dangerous, rocky point on the north side of the approach has, on a number of occasions, been washed away by winter gales and subsequently replaced. The last time it was washed away was before the loss of the yacht *Trenchemer* (Robert Somer-set) in a S.E. gale during darkness on the night of 27 February 1965. The light was eventually set up on a safer site a few yards further inshore and was still in position in 1974. Its present characteristics: Qk. Fl. G. shows over the arc of the approach and red through an arc towards west. Characteristics of the other lights can be found in *The Light List*.

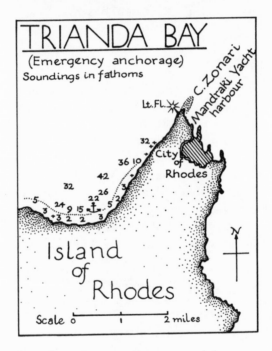

In strong E. to S.E. winds a yacht is strongly recommended not to try to enter Mandraki; instead, she should anchor off the beach in Trianda Bay, 3 miles S.W. of Cape Zonari.

Berth. Yachts usually berth beyond the second T-shaped jetty on the western shore, stern to the quay and bows east. The bottom is mud and the water rather foul. (Although complete-ly enclosed, there can be an uncomfortable surge in the harbour during winter gales from the S.E., when heavy seas sometimes surmount the breakwater.)

Officials. Health, Customs, Immigration and Harbour Master, this being a Port of Entry.

Port Facilities. Water is laid on by a hydrant near the root of the jetty: its supply and a hose can be arranged by the Harbour Master. Petrol and diesel fuel are available at the Fina Filling Station. Many shops are close at hand, especially at the white, octagonal market. There are numerous modern hotels, several restaurants of various standards, a number of banks, and wine in the old town near the harbour gate.

Winter lay-up and repairs, including hauling out, painting, shipwright and joinery work, engineering and electrical repairs can be undertaken at the yard of Petros Halkitis in Akandia Harbour. Although the draft of a vessel wishing to be hauled out is limited to 6 ft, tonnage up to 200 can be accommodated. Maestro Petros is a capable and reliable person with experience in building caiques and repairing local craft; he speaks Italian and his wife, a Cypriot, good English; correspondence should be sent to his home address, Odos Koloproni 20, Rhodes.

The 20-knot steamers from Piraeus run five times a week (about 20 hours) and berth in Emborikos Harbour. There is an air service to and from Athens several times a day; also air communication with Cyprus once a week.

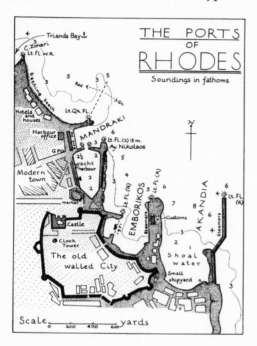

The Town. Rhodes has had many conquerors during its remarkable history. The modern resort of today was started by the Italians during their domination between the two World Wars. Not only did they erect the pseudo-Venetian buildings of the new town and lay out the avenues of flowering trees, but they restored the medieval city. The architecture of the Knights of St John of the 14th and 15th centuries is to be seen everywhere in the Old City, where almost until the First World War the old Turkish custom still continued of tolling a bell every night at sunset to denote the closing of the city gates. Only Turks and Jews might then remain within, while visitors from the west had to be content with accommodation provided outside in a little Greek inn. In half a century things had completely changed. Although the Italians promoted tourism it was not until after World War II that Rhodes became one of the principal resorts of the Mediterranean. In 1969 there were 120 hotels, most of them modern.

No one can visit Rhodes without noticing the large stone balls which have been neatly stacked in piles near the city walls. Many of them are believed to be the missiles used in the siege of 305 B.C. when Demetrius Poliorcetes of Syria hurled these monsters from the catapults of his fleet at the city's defences. As the siege was responsible both for these missiles and for the Colossus, a brief account extracted from the history by Diodorus Siculus is of interest:

Historical Note. Known as the Besieger, Demetrius, a claimant to the Empire of Alexander, had already had success in battle againt Ptolemy and Cassander. He wanted to consolidate these conquests and realized that Rhodes with its great trading fleet lay astride the main sea route to the Aegean: since it could at any time threaten Demetrius's communications, he decided to destroy this little 'maritime empire'. A vast expeditionary force of 200 warships and nearly as many transports was prepared, and with 50,000 men they set off for Rhodes.

The most remarkable vessels in the expedition were the 'Great Tortoises' or huge monitors, carrying large catapults and high towers intended to overshoot and destroy the Rhodian defence towers guarding the moles of the port. The siege was a tough one, and the Rhodians, although outnumbered, held their fortress. Reluctantly forced to withdraw, Demetrius returned to Antioch and having redesigned his equipment, again returned to the challenge.

This time his new attacking craft was the Helepolis described by Diodorus Siculus as having a large square base and a huge nine-storey tower—higher than any Rhodian watch-tower, and fitted with enormous catapults and drawbridges. Manned by 3–4,000 men, it was supported by 'tortoises', and when sighted by the Rhodian look-outs, it must have presented a formidable appearance. This was the master siege-weapon of all time, and it is known that catapults at that period could hurl stones weighing more than half a ton.

The result of the siege depended very much upon the effectiveness of the Helepolis which, despite repeated assaults on the harbour and defences, was only partially successful. Meanwhile messages from Syria demanded the immediate return of Demetrius. Reluctantly obeying, he was forced to make terms with the Rhodians; abandoning siege weapons and equipment, he agreed that a colossal war memorial should be built with the proceeds to commemorate this great event. Hence, there came about the erection of the great Colossus cast in bronze and 105 ft high dedicated to Helion, only to be overturned half a century later by the destructive earthquake of 227 B.C.

Afterwards the broken metal lay in the shallow water for nearly nine hundred years, and it was in this state when Pliny, impressed by its immensity, wrote: 'Even lying on the ground it is a marvel. Few people can make their arms meet round the thumb, and the fingers are larger than most statues'.

Now all is gone, the scrap metal, bought by a Levantine Jew, going back to Syria where it was first moulded: but among the piles of huge stone balls still lying by the city walls, some perhaps are the remaining relics of this great siege.

For some centuries local people thought that the great statue stood *astride* the harbour entrance, as shown on the tourist post-cards; but there is no evidence of this from the early descriptions. In Roman days many distinguished citizens came here to study, including Scipio the younger, Caesar, Brutus, Cassius and Sulla.

The fine medieval walled city built by the Knights of St John more than six centuries ago is largely intact. After they had been driven from Palestine at the end of the 13th century, the Knights captured this island from the Byzantines and soon began to build their city. With the support of the Venetians and the Genoese they were established in a key position to plunder Turkish shipping and exercise control of commerce in Levant waters. The building of fortresses at Halicarnassus, Kos and Kastellorizo, helped them in these activities which lasted more or less continuously until 1522, when the Knights, having withstood two sieges from the Turks, finally capitulated. They were however treated with great consideration, being allowed to evacuate the island with their arms and belongings, sailing first for Cyprus and finally after a period in Tripoli, making Malta their ultimate home. The best of the Knight's architecture remaining today is the Street of the Knights, and the 14th century hospital, now the museum. Most remarkable too are the very broad walls, more than 2 miles in length and surrounded by a moat 50 ft deep, hewn from the rock.

On leaving the town, the sight of the green countryside with its pleasant villages soon restores the feeling of being in Greece. Lindos, 20 miles down the S.E. coast, should not be missed, nor should the Hellenic city of Kamiros and the Castro of the Knights on the north-west coast. The scenery, particularly in the southern part of the island, is very fine.

Lindos, one of the three Hellenic cities, lies at the top of a high headland whose sides fall abruptly into the sea. Beneath it is Port Lindos, a sheltered summer anchorage from which one may conveniently land to visit the Acropolis. Lindos makes a pleasant day's sail from the town of Rhodes and back during the Meltemi season when there should be a broad reach and smooth water both ways.

Approach. Chart 1666, plan. There are no harbour lights, so that except under a bright moon and with previous knowledge, entry by night would be difficult.

Anchorage. Let go in 5 fathoms under the cliffs in the N.W. corner of the bay, where holding is best. The nature of the bottom varies, being in some places mud or sand on flat rock and occasional ridges of weed which would afford poor holding. There is good shelter except between E. and S.E.

Port Facilities. There are two restaurants by the beach which at night dispense loud music. This nuisance has encouraged yachts to shift berth to the south side of the citadel and anchor inside Ak. Ay. Apostoloi near St Barnabas' church in 2½ fathoms. This is recommended only in settled weather. A road leads up to the village which has some small restaurants, and a few provision shops. There is bus communication with Rhodes.

The Acropolis of Lindos, set on a rock high above the sea, is one of the most spectacular sites in Greece. Here is evidence of the whole history of the island, more dramatically and lucidly displayed than at any similar site in Greece. There is the classical Greek colonnade which caps the high platform of the Acropolis with the temple of Athena Lindos, the ruined Byzantine church and the castle of the Knights. Even the Turks have left a fortification to round off this long record of history.

Beneath it is the modern village, becoming spoilt with many tourist shops; but it is still pleasant to wander among the little white houses off the beaten track. Lindos was once famous for its pottery, and a few old pieces can still be seen in some of the houses.

The walk to Cleobolus's tomb is well worth it for the view of the acropolis and the bay.

The citadel opens on weekdays at 0800 (Sundays and holidays 1000) closing at sundown. Coaches bring tourists from Rhodes who overrun the place most of the day. If landing from a yacht it is therefore advisable to land early or late. The interior of the Church of the Virgin is also worth a visit.

Other Anchorages. *Sailing Directions* refer to a number of places in open bays off this coast suitable according to the weather. The south-east coast of Rhodes, which is mostly steep and hilly, provides some sheltered anchorages under a good lee during summer conditions. Among them are:

Cape Istros with a jetty on the S.W. shore. Caiques sometimes anchor here.

Cape Vigli, recognized by its ruined tower, has a good anchorage on sand N.E. of the point.

When leaving Rhodes to cross to Karpathos and Crete it may be necessary to anchor and wait for the weather to moderate. There are two convenient coves with excellent shelter and holding close to the southern cape of Nisos, where a vessel can await the opportunity for crossing. It is also necessary to bear in mind the impeding short sea that is sometimes whipped up over the shallow bank extending south-westward from the extremity of Rhodes.

A few miles off the N.W. coast of Rhodes are two outlying islands, Alimnia and Khalki. Though of little interest themselves, it is worth sailing from Mandraki to Alimnia for the view of the castles of the Knights perched in prominent positions on the Rhodian coast.

Island of Alimnia has a well-sheltered bay rather deep for anchoring. In unsettled weather there is a choice of two convenient coves where, with a warp ashore, a small vessel can lie in a hard blow from any direction.

Approach and Anchorage. Chart 1667. There is no difficulty by day, though it would not be advisable to enter at night. At the head of the bay a slight lee is provided by the remains of a breakwater extending from a small projection of the shore on which is built a little church.

In a southerly gale the caiques, seeking shelter, prefer to anchor in the small square bay, the south-east corner of the harbour, but the bottom shelves steeply and one should run out a warp to the beach.

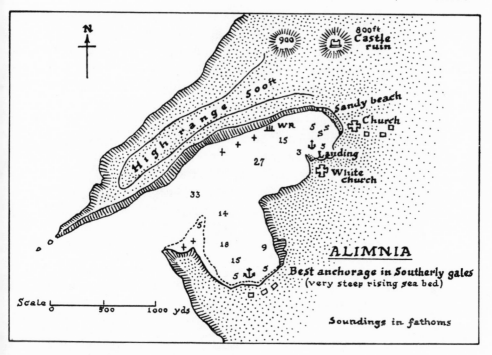

General. Although the castle is in ruins, the view from the hilltop is magnificent. Only twenty-five people live in this little hamlet and they communicate with Rhodes by caique, landing sometimes at Castella.

Island of Khalki is mountainous with the partially sheltered Emborio Bay and a village at the water's edge.

Berth. Chart 1667. The mail-boats berth at the new pier; but caiques and visiting yachts berth at its extremity or off the pierhead by the centre of the village with a stern warp ashore. This is not a desirable place to bring up in a yacht except in very settled weather. The holding is poor—mud with stones.

The Castle of the Knights lies in a dramatic setting on a peak, 2,000 ft up, behind the village.

The houses of the village appear to be in a state of disrepair and largely empty. Though the island had a population of over 3,000, agriculture seems to be almost abandoned. Communication is maintained with the main island of Rhodes by caique which runs daily to Longonia on the opposite coast.

Island of Karpathos (Scarpanto)

with Kasos forms the bridge between Rhodes and Crete; Karpathos, long, mountainous and narrow, Kasos small and insignificant. Neither has an adequately sheltered harbour suitable in the summer months.

Karpathos's best sheltered harbour, Tristoma, is closed all the summer and autumn months because of the dangerous sea breaking at its mouth. The only port of call then is Pigadia on the south-eastern shore where the mail steamer puts in, berthing alongside a substantial quay.

The tall mountain range forming the spine of the island runs from end to end. During Meltemi conditions hard gusts sweep down to the shores along the S.E. coast. Hence there are only a few places where landing is possible: in addition to Pigadia and some small sandy bays at the S.W. end of the island, there is a landing place at Palatia in the north, on the little island of Saria.

General Information. There are a number of small villages scattered around on the mountain slopes, but the island produces hardly any exports.

One of the reasons for visiting Karpathos is to see the interesting national dress worn by the women in the north of the island; long boots and white breeches under a long white skirt which is looped up when working, in a similar manner to that adopted by the Dalmatian women at Zlarin in Yugoslavia. They may be seen in the fields any day of the week wearing this picturesque costume.

Pigadia, the principal village of the island, has recently had some quays and a short mole constructed and is now known as Port Karpathos. The few inhabitants are mostly fishermen.

Approach and Anchorage. Chart 2824. Berth off a very short mole which runs in a westerly direction from a small projection on the north side of the town; but provides less shelter than one could wish. Alternatively berth in front of harbour office with anchor to the N.W. and secure stern to the quay (with a long warp) provided there is no strong Meltemi. Depths are about 4 fathoms nearly half way along the mole, and the bottom is mud. Shelter is poor and there is often a swell. It is occasionally necessary to anchor in the northern corner of the bay as suggested in *Sailing Directions*.

Facilities. There are provision shops, and spring water can be obtained from some of the houses. Fuel is available in the port. A restaurant, a small hotel, one or two tavernas are by the port. The mail-boat calls twice a week. This little port has recently been much improved with fair restaurants and good shops.

Tristoma is an attractive and out-of-the-way harbour with half a dozen houses, 3 hours by mule from nearest village. It cannot be used during the Meltemi season or during strong onshore winds.

Approach and Anchorage. The plan on Chart 1666 gives detailed information. In offshore winds very strong squalls blow out of the harbour between South Islet and Tristoma bluff, making entrance under sail impossible. Under engine-power one may use the northern entrance (50 yds wide) keeping in the middle.

Note. (a) The ruined church shown on chart, north of Church Point, no longer exists;

(b) a flashing light has been established on South Islet.

Anchor as suggested in Admiralty plan on Chart 2824, bearing in mind the possibility of strong squalls during onshore winds.

Facilities. There are no shops, but small quantities of bread, milk, fruit and vegetables may be bought locally.

Other Anchorages on Karpathos. (a) A good lee during strong N.W. winds is to be had in a sandy bay near the southern tip of the island; this is much used by small vessels on passage to Crete. (b) Good shelter has also been reported in **Amorphos Bay** where Cape Volocas bears 100° and the little white chapel on the island bears 220°. Here is good anchorage in 2½ fathoms, but open between S. and E.; it is also exposed to mountain gusts during the Meltemi.

Island of Kasos, the mountainous and barren-looking little island lying between Karpathos and Crete, has half a dozen hamlets, mostly in the N.W. A small amount of agricultural produce is sent away to Rhodes by the mail steamer which now berths behind a short mole near the village of **Ofris** on the north side of the island; this harbour is so small that there is only just room for her to berth inside. During a strong Meltemi the mail steamer cannot enter but must disembark her passengers under the lee of the island usually west of Stam Avlaki.

On the S.W. corner of the island is the deep bay of **Khelatros** where one may anchor at its head in 5 fathoms and run out a warp to the northern shore. It is planned to make this bay into the main port of the island, work having been started in 1973. A new road to the main village has already been built.

The north coast of the island is entirely exposed; if caught by bad weather, and there is no room in the harbour, caiques sometimes shelter under the lee of the islets north of Kasos. The low-lying islet of **Makronisi** is claimed to be the best choice; here shelter is good and there are convenient depths on a sandy bottom.

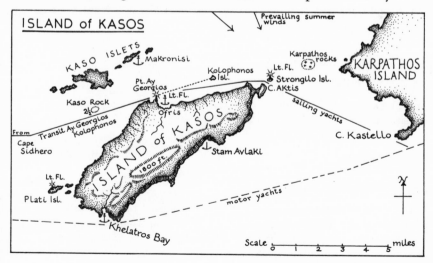

If approaching from the south-west the transit of Cape Ayios Georgios light with Kolophonos Islet clears the Kaso rock.

The Kasos Strait, Chart 3679, between Kasos and Crete is 25 miles across; there is occasional Levant and coastal traffic. If seeking shelter under the east coast of Crete, the safest place to make for is Kolpos Grandes—see Chart 1677. Though open to east Dhaskalia anchorage or those recommended by *Sailing Directions* are safer to approach than Sidhero Cove (Ayios Ioannis) which should only be attempted by day and during calm weather (see Chapter 8, 'Crete').

ANATOLIAN COAST FROM RHODES TO DALYAN

When crossing from Rhodes harbour to the Turkish mainland, the nearest anchorage is the old Rhodian settlement of Loryma on the coast immediately opposite.

Port Aplotheka is a sheltered inlet, quite deserted, with suitable anchorage at its head. A few ruins of Loryma are scattered on the hill slopes and a magnificent Hellenic fortress, with massive stonework still in place, guards the entrance.

Following the coast north-eastwards towards Marmaris are some pleasant coves suitable for temporary anchorage; all are about 6 miles apart.

Serce Bükü, Chart 1604, a deserted, land locked anchorage on a sandy patch near the head of the cove.

Arap Adasi has anchorage in 3 fathoms on a sandy patch behind the islet, but is of no particular interest. Open to S.E.

Giftlik Bükü, Chart 1545, has fine scenery and some cultivation, but no dwellings in sight.

> **Anchorage** at the head of the bay on a sandy bottom in 2½ fathoms. Mountain gusts are not uncomfortable. Open to E. and S.E.

Marmaris (Marmarice) is a delightful green, mountainous fjord with an interesting small town at its head.

> **Anchorage.** Chart 1545. In settled weather a yacht drawing not more than 7 ft may berth stern to the quay on the water-front close to the small port. The anchorage off the pier is rather exposed for a small yacht especially when autumn squalls sometimes sweep down from the mountains. In unsettled weather the best anchorage is in the N.E. corner off the castle. There is room for two or three yachts to berth inside the quay.

Outside the fjord is temporary anchorage in two bays: Kumlu Bükü, and Turunç Bükü (weed on sand) which is the more sheltered of the two.

Officials. A Port of Entry. Immigration, Health, Customs, and Harbour officials.

Facilities. A number of small shops for provisions and a market. Ice can be bought. Two modern hotels have grown up by the shore outside the town. Fresh water (untested) is laid on to the quay, and by tap at stairway N. side.

Marmaris, a small town of 4,000 inhabitants has been much improved in recent years with its built-up water-front and modern shops which now cater for tourists who come across from Rhodes in ferry-steamers. The winding streets at the back of the town leading to the old castle are interesting and from here the view across the fjord is beautiful.

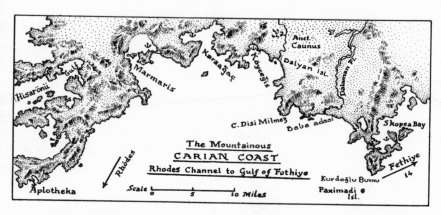

The Mountainous
CARIAN COAST
Rhodes Channel to Gulf of Fethiye

In sailing ship days the British Admiralty recommended Marmaris and the large bays of Karaağaç and Vathy for 'the many islands and snug coves contained in them; these are suited to the various purposes of airing stores, stretching rigging, repairing boats, erecting tents for carpenters, armourers and coopers, and for unloading and carrying transports and prizes.' At the beginning of the century this large fjord was visited annually by the British and Austrian fleets. Nowadays, in addition to the tourists, a few yachts and caiques call, a weekly mail steamer ·and the occasional cruise liner. Property developers have been busy setting up summer cottages round the shores, for the place makes a great appeal to all foreign visitors.

Karaağaç, ancient Cresse, another large inlet, has a deserted and attractive anchorage in **Yörük Cove,** with all-round shelter, but the depths are great and the sea-bed rises steeply.

Anchorage is close offshore in 8–10 fathoms, mud bottom; suitable for large yachts.

Köyceğiz Bay—Ekinçik. Shelter can be sought when anchoring near the head of the bay, either

(a) In a cove on the E. side below a ruined fountain, with a warp to a rock.
(b) North of the jetty in the N.W. corner with a warp to a pine-tree.

To this bay a small motor fishing-boat may come and offer to take one to the ruins of Caunus. This excursion from the shelter of Ekinçik, is preferable to taking the yacht to the somewhat exposed

Dalyan Islet, under whose limited lee is an anchorage for those wishing to proceed by boat up-river to visit the ruins of ancient Caunus.

The river leading to Caunus has a shallow entrance (2 ft on the bar) with its approach channel, difficult to discern, passing between the red-faced cliff and a white hut by the beach. The river then meanders among reeds and bamboos to Caunus (2¼ miles) and to the modern village, 1¼ miles further. In Strabo's time ships used to berth at the port of Caunus which can still be seen, overlooked by the ruins, today. There are fish-traps across the stream, gilthead and whitebream being caught, some sent by lorry to Izmir and much sent abroad. Small fishing craft are continually entering and leaving the river; it is sometimes convenient when wishing to visit the ruins to hail one of these boats and take advantage of their local knowledge—a bargain can be made—the trip taking about 3 to 4 hrs.

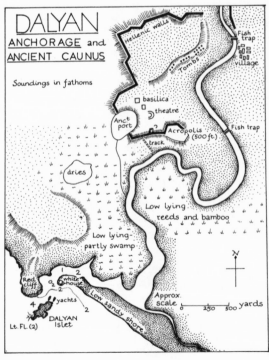

The ruins of *ancient Caunus* are well worth a visit, mostly for the lovely site of the old city and for the remarkable column or 'temple' tombs cut into the face of the rock towards the village. On the steep hill behind the old port stands the acropolis surrounded by a wall with towers of medieval origin, but on the summit—about 500 ft up—are the remains of the Hellenic fort. Near the foot of the acropolis is the fine Greco-Roman theatre with 34 rows of seats, also other buildings including a basilica, all looking down upon the ancient port where excavation work continues. The long wall, much of it still standing and surrounding the whole area, is of Hellenic origin.

Historians believe that this city was the Heraklion captured by Ptolemy in 309 B.C. At this time there was a prosperous trade in salt and slaves.

The village's 3,000 inhabitants are mostly cotton-growers and fishermen. Bread and fruit may be bought; a modest bar and restaurant are by the quay.

Dalyan Islet Anchorage. See Chart 1886 and *Sailing Directions*. In order to derive shelter from the prevailing S.W. swell a yacht should anchor off the N.E. end of the islet where depths of 2½ fathoms extend from the islet towards the shore for 150 yds. The width of the islet, however, being so narrow and thus presenting a limited barrier against the swell, compels a yacht to anchor as close to it as possible and run out a warp to the rocks. Suitable only for small to medium-sized yachts.

Continuing southward and rounding the tall Disi Milmez Burnu (1,340 ft) one comes to Baba Adasi, a low island crowned by a disintegrating brick tomb-pyramid; behind it is a temporary anchorage off some ruins on the low-lying mainland. Close N.E. the fast flowing Dalaman river from the Western Taurus debouches into the sea. (See photograph, fac. p. 189.)

Beyond the cape of Kurdoglu Burnu is the Gulf of Fethiye with the commercial port of Fethiye in the eastern corner.

GULF OF FETHIYE

On the west side of the gulf is **Skopea Limani,** the 10-mile stretch of coast protected by wooded islands with many charming but rather deep anchorages. The following have convenient depths:

Tersani Adasi has a well-sheltered inlet on the N.W. coast. Chart 1886 shows the inlet running in a S.E. direction.

Anchorage is in 3½ fathoms where the inlet opens into a basin. Here is room to swing and almost all-round shelter. Above the shore are a number of ruined houses which once formed a hamlet, but now only two modern cottages remain and a few grazing cattle may be seen.

Köcek lies at the head of Skopea Bay in attractive wooded surroundings—a small hamlet and an extensive deep-water quay (Paterson's Wharf) whence ore shipments are made. The new works detract considerably from the former beauty of the place.

Anchorage is in the S.W. corner of the bay in 5 to 6 fathoms on a bottom of mud—a warp run ashore to trees on the S.E. shore may be helpful. Excellent shelter.

The island of Domuz is owned by Prince Abd el Moneim, but apart from the prince's residence there is no habitation nor is there anchorage.

Fethiye is a small commercial port adjoining some chrome mines with a growing town of 9,000 people. It lies in the heart of a mountainous setting at the foot of the Taurus ranges.

Approach. Chart 1886 with harbour plan. The approach is easy day or night. The narrow island of Fethiye Adasi with a long line of new villas makes it easy to distinguish against the low shores of the harbour. On entering the inner harbour one should note that there is only one stone pier and not two as shown on latest chart. The pier lies to the west of the town and the medieval walls of the citadel can be seen on the hillside to the east.

Anchorage. Either anchor near the pier in 5 fathoms or berth stern-to off the inner part of the pier. Holding is firm sand, or mud and clay. (Steamers berth either side at the outer extremity of the pier.)

Officials. A Port of Entry with Health, Customs, Police and Harbour Master. Port Office is at the root of the pier.

Facilities. Water is laid on at the pier, both by tap and hydrant, now on the town supply. Provisions, fuel and ice can be bought. One or two modest hotels and some restaurants—mail steamers from Istanbul call weekly.

Fethiye is still expanding and is the centre of a large though somewhat primitive agricultural area The town is of no interest except for the Lycian tombs and Byzantine city walls visible from seaward. One can make a most interesting motor excursion to the old Lycian capital Xanthus and its port of Patara. Driving through a charming countryside of mountain rivers and cultivated plains with oak and pine woods one reaches the ancient Lycian capital—a 6-hr expedition. Both cities are incompletely excavated, and by far the most impressive building of Xanthus is the beautiful Nereid Monument carried off by the archaeologist Fellows in the last century and now very recently re-erected in its own hall in the

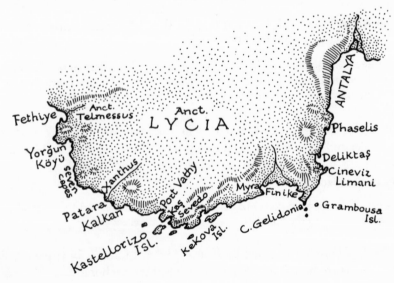

British Museum. More than a century ago Fethiye was a port of call for 'government expresses and travellers for Egypt'; small British warships, brigs and sloops put in for shelter, their captains complaining of the ill-effects of 'this mean little port on the men's health'—malaria was then the scourge.

Of ancient Telmessus (Fethiye's name in classical times) there now survive only a few rock tombs; much of the ancient remains have been quarried for modern building and even the theatre has been plundered.

Fethiye was the western boundary of the former kingdom of Lycia. Following the coast eastwards beneath the foothills of the Taurus the nature of the scenery continues to be equally attractive. Sometimes the great forests stand out against a background of tall mountains many of fascinating shape seldom equalled in the Mediterranean.

This coast was first accurately shown on the charts at the beginning of the last century when Captain Beaufort, hydrographer and archaeologist, moved along the shores and into the hinterland, recording, surveying, and identifying all he found. It was not always easy to determine the setting of each ruined site, for names had changed throughout the centuries, and the illiterate Turks whose tribes had been settled near these places since the 12th century had no knowledge to impart. Only by a study of the classical writers and the reading of such Greek inscriptions as were found, could these sites be identified and accurately located on the modern maps and charts.

Lycian tombs, which are remarkable at several places along this coast, are also to be seen at Fethiye. On a steep cliff-face above the town are three Lycian tombs still in a reasonable state of preservation. The most interesting, with its classical facade, has two well-proportioned columns and drooping Ionic capitals supporting an ample entablature. There are stone panels on the face of these tombs, which have long since been broken into and robbed.

The rock into which these tombs were cut is impregnated with iron and in the course of time the stone has 'wept'. In the evening light the whole cliff-face assumes a golden tint with veins of red and brown.

Continuing southwards along the Lycian shores you come to two small islands close off the peninsula of Ilbiz Burnu: Karaca Ören and **Gemili**. They are closely packed with the ruins of medieval buildings. There is no anchorage other than a small cove opposite Gemili, unless one wants to examine the submerged ruined houses in the channel. One should then moor fore and aft in about 3 fathoms, but only temporarily.

Two miles eastward of Gemili is the deep lake of

Yorğun Köyü (Olü Deniz) entered by a narrow channel only 25 ft wide and 2½ fathoms deep. It lies among steep green mountains and is very deep.

Approach. The entrance is invisible from seaward. One should steer for a white house at the northern end of a long white beach and keep a small rocky promontory close to port. After passing this promontory, less than a cable from the surf, one will see the entrance channel which closely follows the side of the small rocky peninsula; on opening into the lake, is a low above-water rock now marked by a perch.

Anchorage is at either end of the lake where at the far end the sandy bottom rises less steeply. It is advisable to run out a warp and secure it to a tree.

It is a place of great beauty. Apart from a small bar which sells drinks, fish and eggs, the shores are almost deserted. There are the ruins of a chapel, houses and a cistern on the north shore and some underwater remains of a building.

Patara. Continuing southward past the Seven Capes the ruins of the old Lycian capital Xanthus lie inland, but the mouth of the Xanthus River and the ancient port of Patara are still in evidence on the coast. From seaward one can hardly distinguish the theatre but some Greek columns and the city gate can be seen; in calm weather it is easy to land on the sandy beach. To the southward are huge piles of sand blown up by winter gales in the course of centuries, and to seaward half a mile off shore are whirls of dirty sandy water, evidently from the Xanthus River forced up under pressure from the sea-bed.

It was at Patara where St Paul, having made a fast passage down the Aegean in A.D. 55 'found a ship crossing to Phoenicia, went on board and set sail'.

Kalkan is a large exposed bay with a poor village at its head.

Anchorage is off the village in 4 to 5 fathoms on a sandy bottom—stern warps should be secured to boulders ashore.

Very little can be obtained in the village which was badly damaged by an earthquake in 1968. Caiques from Istanbul sometimes call for shipments of timber.

Should the swell be too uncomfortable off the village, anchorage can be found in a cove in the N.W. corner of the bay. Let go close to the 42-fathom sounding on the chart in a depth of about 6 fathoms on a bottom of sand. Suitable for a small yacht in settled weather.

Island of Kastellorizo

an outpost of Greece close off the Turkish Anatolian coast, is a scorched, barren little island with a decaying port, which affords good protection for a yacht.

Approach. Chart 2188. On entering the port, anchor as convenient and haul in the stern to the quay. Bottom is largely shingle.

Port Facilities. At the rather bare café, ouzo and a little wine may be obtained, but food thanks to refrigeration and imports of tinned provisions has much improved. Fresh water is very limited, and is collected in private cisterns. Diesel fuel out of bond is available.

Although it has an appeal, the little town, tucked under the eastern arm of the bay, is largely uninhabited. Damaged by fire during British occupation in the last war, the lack of trade has driven away the inhabitants.

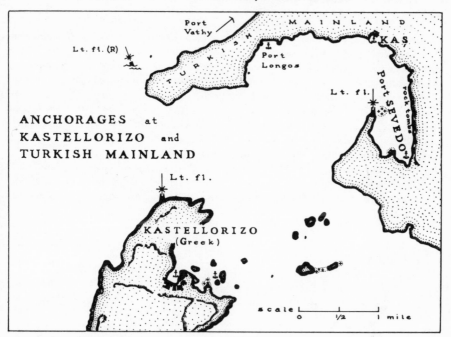

Formerly Castel Rosso of the Genoese, it is known as Meis by the Turks today. Before the 1914–18 war, when part of Turkey, this small island had a population of nearly 20,000 Greeks and at that time it was an important pilot station and its trade was sufficient to merit more than one European consul. Only 500 people live here today and many of them are looking forward to emigrating to the States and Australia.

On the hill overlooking the harbour is the large white church with Corinthian columns brought in some past century from an ancient Greek temple at Patara. Close to the church is a Greek school, also far too large for present requirements; both these buildings now strike one as a reminder of the island's more prosperous days. There are still some ruins of a fortress on the summit, probably erected originally by the Knights of St John who held the island until 1440.

On the east side of the island is a remarkable Blue Grotto, best visited by a local boat—an excursion of just over an hour.

Kastellorizo's only connection with the outside world is now maintained by the steamer which plies weekly from Rhodes. This 72-mile voyage is her lifeline, yet within hailing distance are the green shores of Turkey with its richly timbered hinterland which until recent years provided such valuable commerce for both Greek and Turk alike.

Kaş. A simple village by a small harbour, formed by its ancient Greek mole, lies in a mountainous setting.

Approach. Though no mention is made of this place either on the chart or in *Sailing Directions*, it is of some interest. The place may be recognized by the cluster of white houses forming the small village, and by the Greek theatre on the hill to the northward. The harbour mole has recently been built up. The entrance is about 60 yds wide and there is a depth of at least 5 fathoms until close to the centre of the harbour.

Berth. Let go in 4 fathoms where there is a patch of sand and run out a warp to the landing-steps. There is just room to swing. Shelter is relatively good, and some of the small craft lie here all the year round; they tuck into the N.W. corner of the harbour.

Officials. A Port of Entry. Health, Customs, Police and Harbour Master.

Port Facilities. There are some landing steps, yet nowhere to leave a dinghy. Though some fruit may be bought in the market, there are no provision shops, only a poor restaurant; sometimes ice is obtainable. Fresh water is piped from a mountain stream, but people complain of the calcium.

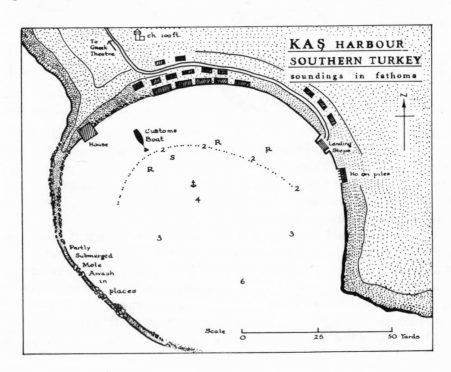

19 Island of Patmos: view from the monastery. *See p.* 136

20 Near Fethiye. One of the coves among attractive and sheltered surroundings. *See p.* 185

Kaş is a little village of a thousand people, formerly called Andiphilo. Close to the shore just beyond stands a well-preserved Greek theatre with twenty-six rows of seats southward and affording the audience a fine view over the fjords. Outside the village are a number of Lycian tombs, sarcophagi lying on the slopes, the rock-tombs cut into the cliffs above. The modern village, built by its pre-war Greek population when the port did a flourishing trade in the export of timber, appears to be slowly recovering. The recently established road communication with Fethiye and other coastal towns has given the place new life.

Ascending the northern side of the ridge behind the village, one looks down upon

Port Vathy, a long steep-to gulf with a sandy shore at its head. Here occasional Turkish caiques bring up to the beach to load their cargoes.

The depths are too great to provide suitable anchorage for a yacht, but larger vessels sometimes make use of the shelter. In the Second World War British destroyers used this anchorage for operations against the German-held Kastel-lorizo.

Port Sevedo. A spacious and completely deserted bay with high steep-to cliffs, excellent shelter; but very deep—a useful undisturbed anchorage.

Approach. Chart 2188 and *Sailing Directions* are all that are necessary for a daylight approach. The ledge which extends underwater from the northern point of the entrance (Lt. Fl.) was evidently a substantial breakwater in the early nineteenth century; Beaufort describes it as suitable for 'heaving down ships of the line'.
Anchorage. There is 5 to 6 fathoms in the S.E. corner of the bay with barely room to swing. It is well to run a warp from the stern to the rocks. The holding is mud, and the shelter from southerly and westerly winds is good—a slight swell enters.

The tall brown cliffs, honeycombed with Lycian tombs, look very fine in the evening light. There is no visible habitation in the bay, though a few farmsteads are not far away. Wild boar sometimes come down at night seeking water by the dried-up torrent.

'Port' Longos is not a port, but an open anchorage with a sandy bottom, well sheltered from north and westerly winds.

The coast now trends towards Kekova Island, Finike, Cape Gelidonya and the Gulf of Antalya. *See Southern Turkey, the Levant and Cyprus* (John Murray, 1973).

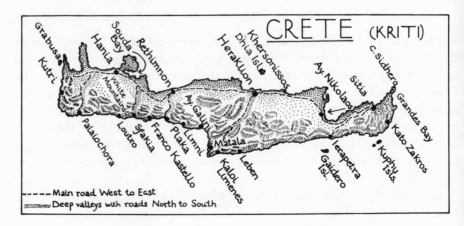

Main road West to East
Deep valleys with roads North to South

NORTH-EAST CORNER	NORTH COAST
Sidhero (Ayios Ioannis)	Sitia
Dhaskalia Bay	Ayios Nikolaos
Erimoupolis	Spinalonga
	Khersonissos Bay
	Heraklion (Iraklion)
	Mount Ida
	Island of Standia (Dhia)
	Rethimnon
	Souda Bay
	Hania (Chania)
	Island of Grabusa

Southern Crete is described in 'Ionian Islands to Rhodes' by H. M. Denham (John Murray).

8

North Coast of Crete

Knossus, her capital of high command;
Where sceptred Minos with impartial hand
Divided right . . .;

ODYSSEY XIX

Known as **Kriti** to the Greeks, this large island was once the centre of the western world and the home of the first European civilization.

It is Greece's longest and tallest island, being 140 miles in length: Mount Ida is in the centre of the great chain of high mountains (rising to more than 8,000 ft) forming a spine through which half a dozen valleys provide the only communication between the north coast and the south.

Crete at the peak of the Bronze Age was the leading maritime power. According to Diodorus 'Crete lay very favourably for voyages all over the world' (i.e., the Greek world of the Eastern Mediterranean). At the time of the disastrous Santorin eruption about 1500 B.C., the eastern half of the island suddenly became depopulated and the Minoan hegemony declined almost overnight. Recent geological surveys have proved that the whole surface of eastern Crete was coated with a layer of pumice powder which had been blown by the prevailing wind from Santorin; it had destroyed all cultivation and compelled the population to abandon this part of the island for many years to come.

Rich finds of the early Minoan and Mycenean civilization are admirably displayed at Heraklion, Knossos and Phaestos. The medieval architecture still surviving is Venetian, and the houses and streets of the larger towns are the legacy of the Turks. They held the island for two and a half centuries, having wrested it from the Venetians after the twenty-year siege of Heraklion in 1669, and they ruled it until the Greco-Turkish war, when in 1913 Crete was handed back to Greece. Since then some good roads have been built and the towns have been improved with many modern hotels and houses.

The country scenery is grand; although more than half the island is impossible to cultivate, the northern slopes of the mountains and the elevated plains are rich with vines, olives and farm produce. There are areas of forests, but no rivers; the rain water runs away in torrents.

The half-million inhabitants who live in the villages and small towns, mainly on the northern coast, differ from the mainland Greeks. Though St Paul complains of their being 'always liars, evil beasts, slow bellies', these people today are certainly in a different category and though very independent by nature are pleasant to strangers visiting Crete.

The Winds off Northern Crete. During the summer months north-westerly winds may be expected generally.

From the eastern end of Crete as far as Heraklion winds are almost invariably N.W., but in the Souda Bay–Hania area they become north; and in the Kithera Channel westerlies predominate with periods of N.E.

Although the northern shores are open to the prevailing wind all the summer there is sufficient shelter for a yacht at most of the ports listed.

The N.E. Corner of Crete

If approaching from the direction of Rhodes with the normal summer wind (W. to N.W.), sheltered anchorage may be found on the S.E. side of Cape Sidhero. In fine weather there is

Sidhero (Ayios Ioannis on Admiralty Charts) a minute 2-fathom cove close under Cape Sidhero affording shelter in all weather except S.E.

Approach and Anchorage. Chart 1677, plan. 'Wreck Rock' is most dangerous as it protrudes only one or two feet above water and is difficult to see: this anchorage should be approached in daylight only.

The bottom is of firm sand, has a constant depth of 2 fathoms when inside, but there is not room to swing. Moor fore-and-aft, S.E.–N.W. A rocky shelf extends about 60 yds from the shore; it is covered by a depth of only one fathom.

There are no facilities of any kind, the only inhabitants being the crew of four for the lighthouse, and a fisherman with his family.

If Wreck Rock cannot be seen it is advisable to make for

Dhaskalia Bay about a mile to the S.W. Alternatively in bad weather, especially N.W. winds, a yacht should make for

Erimoupolis and anchor in good shelter off a sandy beach. Ashore can be seen some Greco-Roman ruins and the remains of an early Christian church. Close by can be seen a valley with dwarf palm-trees reaching down to the sandy shore.

Note. Local craft sometimes shift to the restricted anchorage on the west side of Sidhero at Kiriamadhi.

NORTH COAST—Charts 3677 and 3678

(The South Coast is described in *Ionian Islands to Rhodes*)

After rounding Cape Sidhero the first port on the north coast is

Sitia, a small town with a protecting mole, of no particular interest except that an excursion can be made from there by car to the old monastery of Toplou.

Approach. Chart 1677, plan. The mole has recently been extended from close S.W. of Akri Kokkina in a E.S.E. direction for 170 yds; its root is less than a cable S.W. of the small light tower (Fl. G.). Here are depths of 3 fathoms for some 20 yds inshore, after which they decrease rapidly; if preferring to anchor off, there are suitable steps at the quay to land by dinghy. Very uncomfortable in N.E. winds.

Facilities. Fresh provisions and ice can be obtained at shops on the quay. Water from a tap at the root of the mole. Bus services ply to neighbouring villages and to Ayios Nikolaos. There are two small hotels, many restaurants and cafés.

The town's population has recently increased to about 5,000, owing to the development of the farming country in the neighbouring valley.

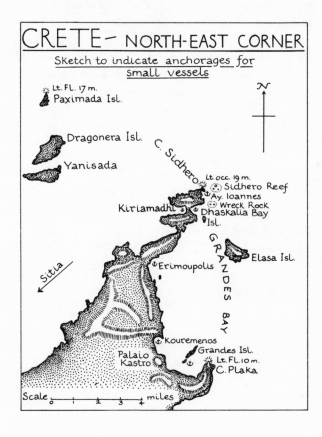

Ayios Nikolaos. A fishing port (with a protecting mole) becoming a major tourist resort.

The Port

Approach. Chart 1677 (Plan). A mole, recently constructed, runs from the N.W. eminence of Mandraki Point in a direction W.N.W. and then N.W. for nearly 100 yds. Its extremity is marked by a red flashing light. There are depths of 5 fathoms at the entrance and deep water all along. Yachts are advised to berth near the ramp at the root of the mole.

Shelter during a strong Meltemi is inadequate in the harbour, and vessels generally move to one of the undermentioned anchorages.

Officials. This is a Port of Entry with the usual authorities.

Facilities. Ayios Nikolaos is the capital of Lassithi province, and has banks, hospital etc. Water, though laid on to the quay, is not always available but it may be bought from a lorry at a reasonable price. There are some restaurants, cafés and hotels. The Minos Beach Hotel with its many facilities is said to be one of the best in Greece; more hotels have grown up recently. There is a bus service to Heraklion.

Other Anchorages

(a) The narrow cove off the hotel is well-sheltered and a pleasant place to be; the depths are slightly more than those marked on the chart. Small yachts have reported wintering here quite comfortably.

(b) Khandros Kavos is claimed to have a well-sheltered anchorage in the bay close southward, and during the Meltemi the gusts are less strong. The soundings on the chart are accurate and one can anchor close to the shore and run out a warp.

A car may be hired to drive to the Minoan town of Gurnia, the Byzantine church at Kritsa, and the monastery of Faneromeni.

Spinalonga. A shallow lagoon formed by an island, well-sheltered from the sea. The approach can be dangerous during the Meltemi on account of violent squalls from the high land close above. See also Porou—Chart 1677, plan.

Approach and Anchorage. Chart 2536 B gives sufficient information. Pass north of Leper's Island and if proceeding to the top of the shallow fjord keep one third over from the eastern shore. There is also anchorage off the place styled 'Turkish Cemetery' in 2½ fathoms. Excellent holding, but violent gusts come down the mountain during the Meltemi, and in this case a sailing yacht of moderate draft is strongly advised to anchor at the top of the fjord.

Port Facilities. At Elunta village provisions can be obtained and there is a bus service to St Nikolo. The whole area is under tourist development.

Spinalonga was used by Imperial Airways during the thirties for seaplanes routed to Egypt and India. There is now a small hamlet at 'Turkish Cemetery' with a daily bus service to Ayios Nikolaos. On the island of Spinalonga (Leper's Island) the old Venetian and Turkish buildings remain, but the island is uninhabited.

Khersonissos Bay (Chart 1677, plan) has a mole, only recently completed, extending for 220 yds from the ancient port. At the extremity is a short right-angled arm pointing shorewards. The root meets the shore by the ancient mole which gives it some protection. Behind the new mole is good shelter, and the land here being flat the Meltemi is less gusty.

The **village** has only about 500 people, many being employed at the brick factory. A modest taverna, one or two shops are close at hand.

Falconer the sailor-poet, at that time second mate in one of the British Levant Co. ships, a hundred years after the great Siege of Candia wrote:

—*the shore with mournful prospects, crown'd;*
The rampart torn with many a fatal wound
The ruin'd bulwark tottering o'er the strand;
Bewail the stroke of War's tremendous hand.

Heraklion (Iraklion)

A well-sheltered steamer port with an unattractive town, but a useful centre for visiting Knossos.

Approach and Berth. Chart 1658 is quite explicit—A yacht should proceed into the Venetian basin. Opposite the Venetian fortress turn to port and berth stern to eastern mole, bows W.N.W. in 2 fathoms. Mud bottom. Here it is well-sheltered; only a limited surge may be expected with northerly gales. The castle provides excellent shelter from a strong Meltemi. The long breakwater has recently been extended by 400 yds.

Officials. A Port of Entry with Customs, Health, Immigration and Harbour authorities close by, where weather forecasts may also be obtained.

Port Facilities. There are now some first-class hotels, and a half dozen more modest ones; also many small restaurants in the centre of the town where, in a street of their own, good food is served at a reasonable price. Provisions can be bought at the market at the top of the main street. Ice may be obtained at a store by the Museum Square (the road running eastward from the Port). Good water is available by hose from the steamer quay by prior arrangement with the Harbour Master and ice from a factory opposite the Harbour Office.

Air communication with Athens, several flights daily in summer; Piraeus steamers also call daily.

Sight-seeing Notes. Knossos, Heraklion Museum and Phaestos, should be visited.

Knossos. 5 kilometres from Heraklion. Bus every 20 min. from Kornaru Square. Allow 2 hrs there.

Heraklion Museum—allow 1 to 2 hrs.
open Sundays   1000–1300
      Mondays 0800–1300
other days   0800–1300, 1500–1800

Phaestos, etc. Travel agents run bus excursions costing 200 drachmae per person without lunch (250 drs. with lunch). A self-drive car costs about 500 drs. and a taxi (after bargaining) to Phaestos, Hagia Triada, bathing beach, and Gortys between 500 and 600 drs.

Known until recent years by its Venetian name of Candia, Heraklion has a population of 70,000. It is a useful centre for making excursions into the island. Taxis may be hired and most drivers know the country well. The Tourist Police will answer any queries regarding excursions or tourist amenities and will arrange a guide for Knossos where neither guides nor guide-books are always available.

The Ascent of Mount Ida (Psiloritis), about 8,100 ft, can easily be made in a pleasant three-day expedition.

There are four alternative routes, each with a place convenient to spend a night during either the ascent or descent: these are

> Anoyeia 33 kilometres from Heraklion
> Gergeri 39 kilometres from Heraklion
> Voutsari 41 kilometres from Rethimnon
> Kamares 53 kilometres from Heraklion

All these can be reached by bus.

If one chooses the Kamares route a bed may be found there before starting off with a guide (about £3) next morning. A visit should be made to Kamares Cave where the famous Minyan pottery, named after it, was recovered and sent to Heraklion. From the cave to the western summit takes about five hours. On the summit is the little Stavros church, where a night can be spent.

Descending the following day, the Nidha plateau (3,300 ft) can be reached in three hours and if desired the night may be spent here with the shepherds: food must be taken, and it is useful when setting off to carry also a supply of cigarettes and sweets—gifts for men and children—for those people living all summer in high altitudes are completely cut off.

From the Nidha plateau the Idean Cave where Minyan pottery was also discovered should be visited, and from there the descent to Anoyeia takes about five hours. In one of these villages El Greco, the painter, was born.

Island of Dhia (Standia), an off-lying island, is 6 miles to the N.N.E. It is hilly and barren. Of the two coves in Ormos Mesarios, that lying to the N.E. affords useful anchorage in northerly winds. Sometimes used by fishermen (Chart 1671).

Rethimnon is a very small walled Venetian port with a recently built outer breakwater.

Approach and Berth. Chart 1658. The new breakwater extends in an easterly direction from the seaward approach to the old port. Off the quay on the S. side are convenient depths for berthing.
Facilities. Fuel, water and provisions are available. Bus service Heraklion to Hania.

Rethimnon was one of the Venetian defended trading ports and still has its old narrow streets and a few Venetian-style houses.

Souda Bay (Chart 1658) provides the best shelter in Crete and for many years was used by large fleets as a base for exercises: it was used in the Second World War for the evacuation of British Forces from Greece. Tall mountains rise steeply either side of the bay, and during strong winds gusts sometimes sweep down the slopes into the bay.

This is the main commercial port for Hania and Western Crete, but the greater part of the harbour facilities are administered by the Greek navy, since Souda Bay is the second naval base for the Greek fleet.

Approach. The entire northern coast of the bay is taken up with naval installations and any approach is strictly prohibited. The commercial port is formed behind the long mole at the head of the bay. The Piraeus car ferry berths alongside this mole every day.

Berth. It is advisable to ask the harbour authority regarding berthing instructions. There are depths of 25 to 30 ft at the quay which was recently extended. As regards shelter, there are sometimes strong gusts from W. and N.W.

Facilities. Local shops are adequate, but Hania is barely 3 miles distant. Bus services to Hania and Heraklion.

During the early part of the Second World War the disastrous Cretan expedition and its evacuation cost the British 15,750 casualties after only 3 weeks' fighting. Naval casualties were enormous, and 209 aircraft were destroyed.

Hania (hitherto spelt Khania and recently Chania), though smaller than Heraklion is the capital of Crete, with a population of 40,000 people.

Its small harbour was built by the Venetians and, though picturesque, is a poor little place for a yacht.

Approach and Berth. Chart 1658. During strong northerly winds entry should not be attempted, and under moderate conditions the mole-head should be given a generous offing. The quay by the galley sheds (now warehouses) is the best place to berth, though this is very inadequate. The depths here are about 2 fathoms, but the bottom is hard, smooth rock on which no anchor will bite sufficiently to hold off a yacht during adverse conditions. A swell enters the port during fresh onshore winds. Improvements are planned to build new quays, and to dredge where necessary, but the maximum draft allowed is 10 ft.

Officials. Though no steamer calls, this is a Port of Entry, with the usual organization of officials.

Port Facilities. Some slipways are maintained for hauling out coasting craft and there is a 5-ton and a 3-ton crane. There is a number of restaurants around the quay and plenty of shops nearby. The town is pleasant and unspoilt by tourists; a motor road now connects it with Heraklion and other places on the north coast.

Excursions. By bus to the monastery of Ayia Triada, hence on foot to Gouberneto and a mountain cave.

Kissamos, an insignificant village with a dilapidated Venetian fortress overlooking a cliff. From here a mole extending 100 yds has recently been completed and the boat harbour cleared; but the depths are believed to be shallow, and Kissamos is considered suitable only as a boat harbour.

Island of Grabusa (Chart 1631) is an isolated island, with an insecure anchorage, beneath steep cliffs, on the N.W. of Crete. Still used occasionally by coasting craft, it has been neglected since the last century when British frigates used to anchor here in the course of stamping out piracy.* In the two years prior to the subjugation of Grabusa, the pirates' base, a total of 155 ships were plundered and their cargoes disposed of; 28 of them wore the English flag. The Venetian fortifications still remain, but the only inhabitants are a few shepherds.

With northerly winds there is good shelter, but should the wind shift to W. or S.W. one should clear out. Grabusa can be reached by caique from Kissamos.

---

* In February 1828 H.M.S. *Cambria*, a brig, when in pursuit of pirates missed stays and struck the reef, becoming a total loss. Some fittings from her rigging have recently been recovered from the bottom.

9
The Cyclades

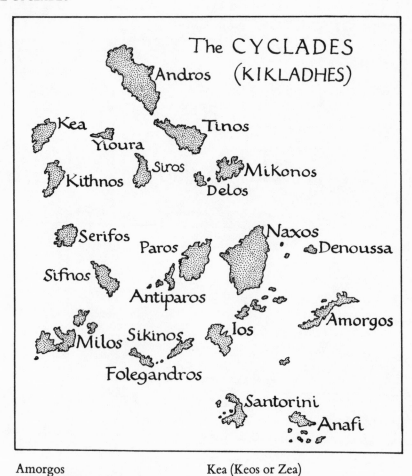

The CYCLADES (KIKLADHES)

Amorgos
    Katapola—the Port
Antiparos (*see after Paros*)
    Despotico
Andros
    Gavrion
    Batsi Bay
    Palaioupoleos
    Port Kastro
Delos
    The Pier
    Fourni Bay
Ios
    The Port
    Manganari Bay

Kea (Keos or Zea)
    Ayios Nikolaos
    Vourkari Bay
    Livadhi Bay
    Pisa Bay
    Kavia Bay
    Polais Bay

Kithnos (Thermia)
    Merika Bay
    Episkopi
    Apokrousis
    Fikiada
    Loutra
    Ayios Stefanos

Mikonos (Mykonos)
    The Port
    Ormos Ornos
Milos
    Adamas
Naxos
    The Port
    Kouroupa Point
    Cape Prokopis
    Cape Moutsouna
    Kalando Bay
    Apollona Bay
Koufo Islands (dependencies of Naxos)
    Ekhinousa Island, Myrsini Bay
    Iraklia Island
Paros
    Paroikia
    Naoussa
Santorini (Thira)
    The Port
    South Anchorage
Serifos
    Koutala Bay
    Livadhi Bay
Sifnos
    Kastro
    Faros
    Plati Yialos
    Fikiada
    Vathy

    Kamares Bay
    Vourlithia
    Ayios Georgios
Siros (Syra)
    Port Siros
    Ormos Megas
    Foinikos
Tinos
    The Port
    Kolimbithra
    Panormos

THE LESSER ISLANDS

Anafi Group
Denoussa
    Dhendro Bay
    Roussa Anchorage
The 'Dry Islands'
    Sikinos
    Folegandros
        Karavostasi
        Vathy Bay
Kimolos
    Psathi Bay
Kinaros, Pnigo Creek
Levitha Islands
    Levitha Inlet
Yioura or Ghiaros

9

The Cyclades

Ah! lonely isles, fragments of earth, that with his thunder
The wild Aegean girdles, like a belt about you thrown . . .
Antipater of Thessaloniki trans. F. L. LUCAS

INTRODUCTION

According to *Sailing Directions* there are nineteen islands encircling Delos, once a holy city and centre of the Confederacy. Some of these islands are small or unimportant and nearly all are largely barren, for they lack water and vegetation and produce little in excess of their actual needs. In ancient days, the best of the marble used in statuary and architecture was hewn in some of these islands and minerals also were obtained. Today there is a small export of cattle, honey, oil, olives and wine, and the standard of living is low. The life-line of these islanders is the bi-weekly steamer to Piraeus as well as the ubiquitous caique which plies among the islands. Though poor, they are a friendly people with great poise and dignity.

The character of each differs from that of its neighbour although they have a common pattern, the heterogeneous styles in architecture betraying the variety of their previous rulers. The houses are mostly built in the form of a cube and painted a dazzling white, with a flat roof, in contrast to the eastern islands such as, Samos, Khios, and parts of Mytilene, whose villages are in the Turkish style, with red tile roofs and projecting balconies. In Santorin and Naxos is some Venetian influence.

The principal town, or Chora, is usually known by the same name as the island. The Chora was often in a high position on a hill, originally built (for defence against pirates) with the stronger outer walls of the house side by side and without openings. Sometimes the houses were grouped closely together outside the castle, which in case of attack became a refuge for the inhabitants. Very occasionally the village of the port has also been the capital, and examples of this kind are Mikonos and Paros; but nearly always the ever-latent fear of piracy drove the people of these Aegean islands to the safer alternative of establishing their Chora inland. To augment this natural form of self-preservation, the land-owners sometimes built fortified towers, and though these have largely disappeared, traces of them could be found recently in Andros, Khios, Kithnos, and Amorgos.

Only a strong navy could suppress piracy and it was not until a final effort was made by British frigates in the early part of the 19th century that these islanders, after many centuries of fear and suffering, at last felt their safety assured. This had its influence on the ports, for from then onward the life of the port began to overshadow that of the inland Chora.

The great excitement in the port nowadays is the arrival of the Piraeus steamer whose approach is heralded well in advance by the port authority. People appear from nowhere and immediately assemble, closely-packed, on the quay, the departing travellers encumbered with boxes, suitcases, baskets, children and chickens. This event may take place at any time during the day or night and, as everyone knows the steamer will not wait, they jostle along, unable to suppress their excitement at the prospect of a glimpse of the outside world. At most of the better-developed islands there are berthing-quays where the steamer may lie snugly alongside; but at some places she anchors outside the harbour and the intending passengers must pile into boats which when closely packed, then proceed to the waiting ship. Very often the state of the sea at the anchorage is far from smooth and everyone gets splashed by the spray. Once alongside the steamer travellers must scramble up a narrow rickety accommodation ladder; old and young with children, baggage, and chickens are constantly urged to hurry by the sailors. As few of these people can afford any sheltered accommodation on board they huddle together at night on deck which, during the cold winter weather, must be the height of discomfort.

The boats then return with passengers who have disembarked from the steamer. For them the discomfort of the voyage is over; sea-sickness forgotten, as well as the indignity of being bundled down the ladders into a plunging boat—now the whole family is seen waiting on the quay to welcome them back from Athens. If the arrival is in the day-time they all pause at the cake-shop—for the men a glass of ouzo and *mezes* (cheese, olives, gherkins) or *dolmades* (meat and rice in vine leaves) or *garides* (prawns)—for the women probably *baklava* and for the children *loukoumi* (Turkish Delight) from Syra or Andros. All will like fruit. Then there is coffee, served in the Turkish manner with a glass of cold water.

Among the people living in the Chora, one invariably comes upon the 'American' type. He is generally to be recognized by the broad-brimmed hat, gold teeth and a massive gold ring, some of whom may call out 'Hey Johnny' to the passing Englishman or American though others of a quieter nature politely offer to interpret and to help with the shopping. In every island a number of the young men migrate to America, Canada and Australia. A surprisingly large proportion return to their native island in their old age in order to spend the last years of their lives among the quiet, simple surroundings of their boyhood. For the visitor they are often a great help in elucidating unknown facts about the people and the place, and thus contribute to the understanding of the local people.

Island of Amorgos is long and narrow with tall bare mountains and precipitous cliffs; it is primitive and quite unspoilt. The small hamlet of the port lines the quayside at the head of **Katapola Bay**:

The Port

Approach and Berth. Chart 1663. If approaching from east or south the monastery of Knozoviotissa stands out in white many miles away. When in the vicinity of Katapola Bay one should head for the S.E. corner.

Proceed nearly to the head of the bay where there is a sandy beach and a small bridge. After passing a point where the quay diverges towards the N.W., 'let go' in about 7 fathoms; bottom is weed on sand, poor holding. The stern may then be hauled in to the quay where there is 10 ft depth and normally very clear water.

The lee formed by the divergence of the quay is most effective, especially with a west wind, when a warp should be run out to hold up a vessel's bow. It is claimed that even a strong westerly does not endanger a vessel in this berth.

Port Facilities. A yacht station has been established near the root of the quay. Fuel and water are laid on, and nearby small shops where fresh provisions may be bought—fruit and vegetables come from Naxos. There is a bar, and in summer a small restaurant.

Fuel may be bought from drums. A bus runs up the hill to the Chora. The Pireaus steamer calls.

From Katapola a road ascends to the Chora—a typical Cycladic village of white houses clustered round the old Castro on the mountain spur. As one approaches, a number of very small churches with barrel roofs are to be seen near the roadside.

The visit to Khozoviotissa Monastery—half-an-hour's walk along a mule track from the Chora*—is the main object of a call here. This small eleventh-century monastery partly built into a cavern is supported by its massive white buttresses projecting upon a vertical cliff-face. Far below, the waves of the blue Aegean can be seen beating against the rocks. When the traveller, Bent, came here in the latter part of the last century he had to enter by a drawbridge 'with fortifications against pirates'. He described the whole setting as being 'truly awful'. Unoccupied for some years, during which period many of its treasures were removed elsewhere, the monastery was inhabited by two monks in 1973.

A century ago the island of Amorgos had a population of nearly 4,000; it has

* In 1974 a road was under construction.

since been slowly dwindling. The neglected terraces on the seaward slopes are witness of the declining agriculture, and of the many young men leaving to seek a more profitable living elsewhere.

Island of Andros

one of the largest and most northerly of the Cyclades, has a mountain ridge with peaks rising to over 3,000 ft. Though from the coast the rising slopes appear barren much of the interior is green and wooded; the small town and villages support a population of 17,000.

The south-west coast of Andros is mainly bare and monotonous, and of interest from seaward only for the remarkable walls which divide the barren properties—slabs of slate standing on end separated by horizontal layers of stone. Low woolly clouds lying on the high mountain ridge are an indication of strong north winds. Towards the N.W. end of this coast is

Gavrion, a spacious port, well-sheltered, with a small hamlet on the water-front.

Approach and Anchorage. Chart 1833, plan. There is no difficulty making up for the harbour entrance though caution is necessary at night to avoid the Vovi shoal. In seeking shelter during the Meltemi strong gusts are experienced when beating into the harbour and once inside it is best to anchor off the village in 3 fathoms. At the seaward end of the quay which has recently been extended to accommodate the ferry, there is sufficient depth for a yacht to lie stern-to with the anchor to the north or south. A yacht drawing less than 6 ft can anchor beyond the jetty, which is much used by car-ferries loaded with lorries of local mineral water.

Facilities. Fresh supplies are obtainable. There are one or two hotels, bars and modest restaurants. Regular steamer communication with the mainland by ferry from Rafina.

The three miles of coast between Gavrion and Batsi has some small bays with excellent sandy bathing beaches. These are now being exploited by the Tourist organization; hotels and restaurants are springing up everywhere.

Batsi Bay, three miles S.E. of Gavrion has recently become popular as a small summer resort for Athenians.

Approach. Passing S.E. of Megalo Islet the entrance to the bay, with its small white houses, opens up. A flashing light is now established on the rocky point on the west side of the entrance.

Anchorage and Berth. Anchor on the N. side of the bay in convenient depths on a sandy bottom. Alternatively there is just sufficient room for a medium-sized yacht to berth stern to the quay projecting from the S. end of the village.

The quay extends only for 70 yds in a N.W. direction and its outer half is used by the car-ferry. Two yards off there are depths of 10 ft. Shelter in summer is good but in winter during southerly gales the harbour is untenable, although the mole was recently extended. **Facilities.** Water hydrant is available at the quay by arrangement with the Harbour Master. Fuel can be obtained in cans from Shell. Restaurant, tavernas and provision shops are on the water-front. A bus service runs to Gavrion and to Kastro twice daily.

Batsi is a relatively new place lying in an attractive setting. Hitherto the island was known only for its ship-owning families, but now with the quick connection to Athens an increasing number of people come here in summer. The shores of the bay are surprisingly green with lemon trees and mulberries; there are a number of fresh-water springs.

About 4 miles S.E. of Batsi are a few scattered ruins of the ancient capital **Palaioupoleos.** Modern villas sprinkled on either side of an attractive steep green valley make the place easy to distinguish from seaward; but the anchorage is very open and the holding insecure. Of the ancient moles shown on Captain Graves's chart of 1844 only 2 or 3 yds of the S. mole now remain above water. A few architectural remains can be seen standing above some lines of cypresses—portions of ancient walls and an arch. The site is best visited by bus from Batsi.

Port Kastro on the N.E. side of the island has become important on account of the main village adjoining it. The harbour with its short breakwater affords only limited protection, and though the holding is good the port is quite un-tenable in strong N.E. winds.

Island of Delos

The extensive ruins of Delos, former head of the Delian Confederacy, are of great interest. Barren, low-lying and uninhabited (except for the museum care-takers) the island is visited daily by hundreds of tourists. They come in cruise ships or from Piraeus by steamer to Mikonos and thence by caique to Delos; having seen the ruins they are ferried back in the afternoon to their steamers. Facilities and conditions for a yacht at Delos are poor.

Anchorages. Chart 1647. The main channel is inadvisable on account of the foul nature of the bottom. There is a choice of two places providing other yachts are not also here:

The S.E. side of the pier. A small yacht not exceeding 7-ft draught can berth stern to a very small jetty and there are 9-ft depths at the concrete end of the pier. Ferry-caiques also use this pier.

Fourni Bay, suitable for nothing larger than 20 tons, is much the best place to anchor, clear sandy bottom, good holding and a sheltered beach on which to haul out the dinghy when landing. There is, however, scarcely room for a yacht to swing.

The north wind whistles through this strait all day reaching a strength of

Force 6 or 7 during Meltemi conditions. Should the wind shift to south good shelter may be found on the island of Rhenea in a cove on the southern end of Skhinos Bay.

By the main site of the ruined temples is the museum and a small hostel with a shop selling local handicrafts. A guide may be hired. All round are drums of columns, plinths of broken colonnades and foundations of vanished temples all broken off at a low level; only the terrace of lions in white Naxian marble (seventh century B.C.) stands out, forming an impressive approach to the temple as one comes from the port. Appearing considerably less robust than lions of today, their lean bodies may perhaps have been sculptor's licence; apart from these the rest of the ruins are Hellenistic. Close by is the dried-up sacred lake and the bases of columns which once formed the Temple of Apollo.

Winding up the hillside is a narrow cobbled street leading to the theatre, on either side are the stone walls of once elegant houses with little niches to take the lanterns which lit the street.

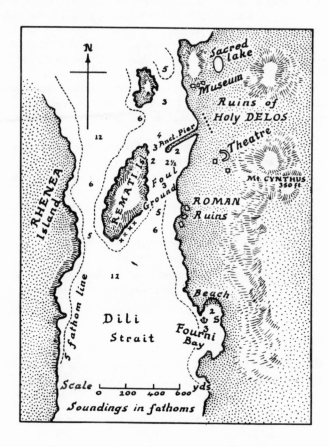

The restored private houses are in much better state than the remains of the temples themselves; here are terra-cotta stoves, marble tables, and well-heads, some inner courtyards with colonnaded verandahs, portions of paintings and stuccos (resembling those at Pompeii) and some remarkably complete and interesting mosaic pavements.

Brief History. Early legends tell of Delos rising from the sea to become the refuge of the pregnant Latona and so the birthplace of Apollo and Artemis. As a holy shrine it was respected in later years by some of its conquerors; Polycrates of Samos is said to have secured the Holy Island to its neighbour Rhenea with a chain. During the Peloponnesan War Athens removed all tombs to Rhenea and forbade birth or death in Delos, thus completing the purification begun by Peristrates. Delos took no part in the Persian War, but fear of the Phoenicians led to the establishment of the Delian Confederacy, almost immediately dominated by Athens. It was independent in Macedonian times but later again placed under Athens by Rome. It is perhaps best known for the yearly Theoria, or pilgrimage, and the choir of Delian maidens.

In the early Roman era this island was made into a free port, and though destroyed later by Mithridates's admirals it became, according to Strabo, a great centre of commerce, 'thousands of slaves changing masters in a day'; they were provided by pirates to satisfy the needs of Rome, and both the kings of Egypt and of Syria co-operated in this trade.

In the later centuries Delos was plundered many times. Randolph writing in 1687, stated 'The ruins are carried away by all ships who come to anchor there, so as part are in England, France, Holland and mostly Venice.' Those making the Grand Tour a century later, would, as a matter of course, help themselves to what they could remove.

French archaeologists claim to have excavated a slipway longer than any found in Piraeus. Perhaps this discovery may lend support to an observation by Pausanias—'I have yet to hear that any man has built a larger vessel than the one at Delos which is banked for 9 banks of oars.'

A stone stairway ascends to the top of Mount Cynthus, and from here one has the clearest impression of the island. In the cool of the evening, when the north wind abates, a peaceful quiet descends upon the island and one can see the ruins reflecting something of their strange, eventful history. Most impressive of all is to land when the moon is full; shining brilliantly on the white marble lions, they appear quite ghostlike in an eerie stillness broken only by the occasional bark from a shepherd's dog.

> *Les fêtes et les gloires étaient passées; le silence*
> *était égal sur la terre et sur la mer; plus*
> *d'acclamations, plus de chants, plus de pompes sur le rivage*
> CHATEAUBRIAND: *Itinéraires*

Island of Ios

a barren, though inviting island of gentle slopes, has three or four sheltered inlets as well as the attractive Ios Bay close to the island's capital.

The Port
Approach and Berth. Chart 1832, plan. Ios Bay can be entered by night as well as by day.

There is good holding and shelter 150 yds from landing quay in 4 fathoms (see plan). Small yachts also berth with stern to the quay by the Port Office where there are depths of 8 ft. The yacht station at the extension of this quay is very shallow, but yachts usually run out a warp. (See photograph, fac. p. 224.)

Facilities. There are some hotel-restaurants and tavernas (where ice is sometimes obtainable) and several shops. Bus to the Chora. Water hydrant on the quay. The Piraeus steamer calls two to three times a week, and a few caiques from neighbouring islands are often in the port.

The small village, 20 minutes' walk up the hill, is attractive with its flagstone paving, the edge of each stone being carefully outlined in white. Among the little white houses are one or two where provisions can be bought. There is nothing of antiquity on the island save the site of one of the many tombs of Homer, but both village and country have much charm.

Known to the Turks as 'Little Malta' on account of the good shelter, this bay was once used by some of Britain's anti-piracy ships for careening.

A memorable incident occurred in 1692 when His Majesty's hired ship, the galley *Arcana*, sank as she was being careened. Mr Roberts,* who had saved himself but lost all his possessions, described how he was captured by Corsairs and made to work for them on board as gunner for many months, suffering great hardship. He writes '. . . twelve rogues . . . laid hold of me, and carrying me on board on the starboard side, when I no sooner ascended but came a fellow and clapped a chain on my leg, and no-one spoke to me one word.'

Manganari Bay on the south coast is another suitable anchorage but rather exposed to gusts of wind during Meltemi. Two small hotels have recently been built here.

Island of Kea (also Keos or Zea)

is a mountainous island supporting nearly four thousand people, but of little importance today. Its shape and contours are remarkable especially when seen from the air; there is a high central ridge (1,800 ft) with deep-cut, barren valleys which fall symmetrically away on either coast.

Ayios Nikolaos (Chart 1833) is Kea's only good harbour. It was once of some importance as a coaling station for steamers plying between west European ports and the Black Sea. This spacious sheltered bay has two arms, the northern one,

Vourkari Bay, has good anchorage in convenient depths and excellent shelter under all conditions. A small yacht may berth stern to the quay off the hamlet in fine weather; but the

---

* Mr Roberts' *Adventures among the Corsairs of the Levant*, 1699.

sea-bed rises steeply and the depths, close off, are shallow. (On no account should the yacht station be used because of the shoal water.) Two restaurants on the water front.

The southern arm of the bay,

Livadhi Bay, with a quay off Korissia hamlet, has a short protecting mole projecting eastwards. In strong northerly winds however a big swell comes in and makes the bay untenable, but when the mole has been extended as planned (1974) shelter should improve.

Of the two hamlets Korissia is the more important. It has an hotel, restaurant and provision shops; a ferry steamer operates to Lavrion but not during adverse weather. Some stretches of sandy beach round the bay attract a few summer visitors from Athens.

From Korissia a motor-road ascends to Kea village, the island capital, standing 1,000 ft above the bay. This is an interesting example of a mountain village with narrow white-washed paths separating little white houses which seem to stand almost on top of one another. The medieval village was built on the site of the early Greek city Iulis, among whose ruins some of the Arundel marbles were recovered.

Passing through the village and walking in an easterly direction for about 20 minutes one comes to a colossal lion, 20 ft in length, hewn from the rock-face and standing on the side of a valley. Its presence may lend support to the legend that the island was once inhabited by nymphs who were frightened away by a lion and fled the island.

The most impressive feature of the steep mountainous countryside is the ubiquitous terracing. Hardly a slope is without it, yet today nearly all is neglected, for only the older men remain in the island, the young men go abroad seeking more profitable occupations elsewhere. Even the valona oaks no longer contribute to the acorn exports (for tanning) and the vineyards are mostly uncared for.

The following temporary anchorages may be found convenient in summer weather:

Pisa Bay where a landing may be made to ascend the torrent bed to Ayia Marina, a small church beside a remarkable three-storey medieval tower, now largely fallen apart. The anchorages is exposed to S. and the holding uncertain.

Kavia Bay. There is anchorage off some small houses at the head of the bay where some fishing boats are kept. There is nothing here of interest.

Polais Bay, on the S.E. coast, is much exposed to the swell, but it attracts keen underwater fishermen who sometimes land large fish. The remains of the ancient town of Karthea can be found close by, together with a few inscriptions. Cut in a large block of marble are the impressions of two enormous feet.

Island of Kithnos

formerly Thermia, a largely barren island of some 2,500 people is of no particular interest, though it has a number of inlets suitable for summer anchorages:

On the *West Coast* are

Merika Bay, the port for the mail steamer which in the past has been poorly sheltered and of no particular attraction, is likely to have a new look. Harbour works are expected to be completed 1975–76.

Anchorage. Chart 1825 gives a choice of anchorage. Open to W.N.W.; a swell often rolls in, but with the mole extended to 100 yds (1972) shelter is better.

A new hotel has been built in the port, and a motor-road connects with Kithnos, the principal village, where adequate provisions are obtainable.

North of Merika are three other anchorages shown on Chart 1825. Of these **Episkopi** is similar to Merika as regards shelter. **Apokrousis,** a deserted bay further north, is much better sheltered.

Fikiada, also a deserted bay, but smaller than the others affords almost all-round shelter. There is no land communication here; only one summer villa stands by the shore with a short pier.

Anchorage. See plan; let go on a sandy patch as convenient. Bottom is coarse sand with long weed through which a plough anchor does not always cut and dig itself in.

On the *East Coast* are:

Loutra, an uninteresting anchorage with partial shelter, off a former 'Cure Resort', on the N.E. side of the island.

Approach and Anchorage. The white Hydro and small houses are visible some distance to seaward. The most convenient anchorage is in the S.E. creek where half-way along are depths of 3 fathoms on a sandy bottom (also some weed and small stones). There are one or two bollards for warps on the northern shore. A heavy mooring-chain runs along the bottom from the white bollard to the opposite shore. Shelter is reasonably good.
Facilities. Limited provisions may be bought locally and there are one or two bars and a restaurant in the small hamlet. The Piraeus steamer calls once a week in the summer months. Kithnos village is 40 minutes' walk along a road.

Though not many visitors come to this place, the old thermal baths establishment, built for Greece's first king, Otto of Bavaria, is still kept open.

An ore-tip and a mooring buoy in the exposed bay are relics of a mining concern no longer in operation.

Another bay, but at the S. end of the east coast,

Ayios Stefanos is well-sheltered, being slightly open to S.E. but always tenable as an anchorage. (See plan, Chart 1825.) Only three or four small houses stand by the beach, and a couple of fishing boats usually base themselves here.

Caution: The rocky shoal two cables south of the entrance point can usually be recognized by the discoloured water.

Island of Mikonos

or Mykonos, lying close to northward of Delos is largely barren. It has become a tourist resort with modern hotels. Its port serves as a base when tourists arrive in the steamers from Piraeus, and are then ferried by the local caiques to Delos.

The Port

The North Mole has been extended, and though the red buoy beyond it is still in position, the pierhead light had not been exhibited by 1973.

Anchorage. Yachts sometimes berth among the caiques in the S.W. corner, which is conveniently close to shops and restaurants; however, the Meltemi can make the southern part of the harbour most uncomfortable. More sheltered and agreeable berths, also suitable for bathing are:

1. Off the inner wider portion of the North Mole, with anchor S.S.E.
2. Stern to the new quay which runs S.S.E. from the root of the North Mole, see plan.

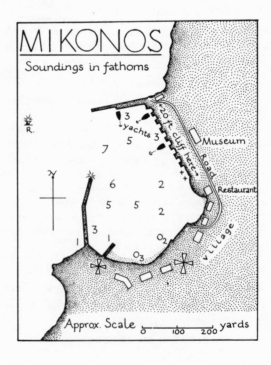

MIKONOS

Soundings in fathoms

Approx. Scale 0 100 200 yards

Facilities. Water by tanker-lorry. Fresh provisions, good reastaurants, tavernas, some modern hotels. There is a daily steamer to Piraeus and an air-service to Athens. In the season it is very crowded with holiday-makers of all classes and with visitors off anchored cruise ships.

White houses line the harbour with the small town rising on the slopes behind. Along the ridge above the slopes are the white-painted windmills which continue to grind the corn of the island.

Though the countryside is almost barren and without interest, the town is charming with its dazzling white houses—sometimes of two or three stories—with doors and shutters in green, and little churches with blue domes. The narrow winding streets are pleasant to wander through, having the occasional attraction of a small square, a Venetian well-head, or an outside stairway. The Museum of Antiquities on the sea front contains objects brought from Delos and Rhenea.

There is practically no history attached to the island. Strabo mentions that the islanders become bald at an early age and Pliny writes that the children were often born without hair. Today they appear to be quite normal.

The local industry is cotton-weaving and clothing, such as shirts, skirts, and belts, attractively displayed for sale to tourists and many 'boutiques'.

Ormos Ornos, a bay on the south side of the island is sometimes used as a yacht anchorage, the depths being convenient, and shelter good. During the strong Meltemi gusts it is recommended to make use of the mooring buoy in the N. corner of the bay. Tourists have begun to appreciate its attraction as a bathing resort; one can, however, find two unfrequented bays lying further eastward; the first, Psarou, is the more secure. These have pleasant anchorages on a sandy bottom, but are open to the south. There are tavernas at each of them.

For yachts making eastward, it may be useful to anchor for the night in the small bay in the S.E. corner (N 36° 26.25, E 25° 25.5) close to fishermen's houses. The rocks marked on the chart are easily identified and the anchorage has almost all round shelter. The holding is sand on rock.

Island of Milos

a volcanic island with mountains forming a circle round a huge bay, with its port.

The Port (Adamas)

Approach and Berth. Chart 1832, makes pilotage easy, and lights having now been established on Lakida Point and Bombarda, entry by night presents no difficulty. Two jetties not shown on the chart have now been built out extending southwards from the shore at Adamas. The westernmost is used by the mail steamer and small freighters which berth alongside. A yacht may berth at the extremity of the eastern pier in depths of 2 fathoms or anchor off. The bay being large would not afford much shelter to a small yacht in the event of a blow from the southern quadrant; but it is one of the best harbours among the islands for small steamers. The holding on the sandy bottom is good.

Port Facilities. The unattractive port of Adamas is of recent development; it has a modern hotel and a few shops and a modest restaurant. Limited fresh provisions are available. There is no tap-water, but a tank lorry may be obtained if given notice. Ice can be bought. The Piraeus steamers call.

Half-an-hour's drive takes one to the Chora, attractively built upon the hill over Hellenic remains, with a Greek theatre. Within 200 yds of this theatre the famous Venus—now in the Louvre—was found in 1820. A Venetian castle stands on the summit. The village, which is interesting and still unspoilt, affords fine views over the surrounding fjords and nearby islands.

The island's population of nearly 7,000 is mostly occupied in mining sulphur, bensonite, barium etc. There are some villages connected by roads. The lower slopes of the mountains are largely covered with scrub, and there is some cultivation.

Earlier History. During the centuries of Turkish domination, the island enjoyed much prosperity, and so long as it paid tribute to the Pasha no force was ever used to prevent its harbour from being used as a great base for pirates. It was here they brought their prizes for disposal and consequently the port grew rich as a mercantile transhipment centre.
(See adjacent island of Kimolos (Psathi Bay), page 234.)

Island of Naxos

is the largest and most mountainous island of the Cyclades. '*La plus grande et la plus belle*', says the *Guide Bleu*. Because of its agriculture and the activity in the harbour it gives the impression of having a brisk trade. The quayside is usually animated with café life, restaurants and tavernas, buses and taxis, steamers coming and going, and caiques loading and unloading.

The Port

Approach and Berth. Chart 1832. The harbour is easy to find day or night, but in strong northerly winds the main breakwater is inadequate and seas surmount its low wall, setting up a surge within. The inner mole has recently been extended with quays to enable the Piraeus steamers to berth alongside. A yacht station has been established on the N. side of the inner mole at which yachts may anchor with bow facing N., stern to the quay.

Facilities. Shops, tavernas and small hotels are on the water-front. Water, which is very good can be obtained from a tap on the quay; fuel and ice are also available. Taxis can be hired for pleasant drives to country villages as recommended by the Tourist Office on the quay. The mail steamers call almost daily during summer. An airport has been built.

Above the port are the few interesting remains of the old Venetian town standing on the side of the hill. Extending round the quay is an old winding street crossed by arches; Venetian doorways, pediments, and occasional coats of arms can be found.

A number of monasteries date from the 15th century, and the Frankish castle behind the town has now become a convent school. Altogether nearly 20,000 people live on the island.

In the country, perhaps the most interesting drive is to the colossal Apollo (34 ft tall), cut in marble some 2,000 years ago, at the northern end of the island S.E. of Cape Stavros. It was intended for Delos and would have been taken on rollers down to Apollona Bay, and thence by sea. At the last moment it was decided that the quality of the marble was poor, and so the statue was abandoned without ever being detached from its bed. The white marble used by sculptors is one of the Naxian exports today, but emery and lemons are more profitable.

In very early days Naxos was famous for its wine and it was here that Dionysos (Bacchus) is reputed to have found Ariadne (daughter of the Cretan king) after her desertion by Theseus. The Venetians made good use of the island early in the 13th century when Marco Sanudo, taking advantage of the decadence of the Byzantine Empire, captured it. The descendants of this great adventurer, who set themselves up as Dukes of Naxos, ruled this island and others of the Cyclades for 350 years until overwhelmed by the Turks in 1566. The islands were not restored to Greece until after the liberation of 1832.

Other anchorages off Naxos. Chart 1663. (See sketch plan, p. 220.)

On the West Coast (where, along its northern shores, pilotage should be treated with caution) are two anchorages referred to in *Sailing Directions*. They can be useful to a yacht working up the Naxos Strait against strong winds, impeding sea and consequent adverse current.

Kouroupa Point. Lying 2 cables eastward of the cape is a delightful sandy bay with excellent holding in 3 fathoms. A hotel at the head of the bay makes a good distinguishing mark.

Cape Prokopis, nearer the port, also affords a good lee.

Both the above anchorages are under the lee of low-lying land which allows the wind to blow at constant strength.

On the East Coast is a lee under

Cape Moutsouna. In a bay on the south side is fair anchorage near a jetty used by lighters when shipments of emery are being taken away.

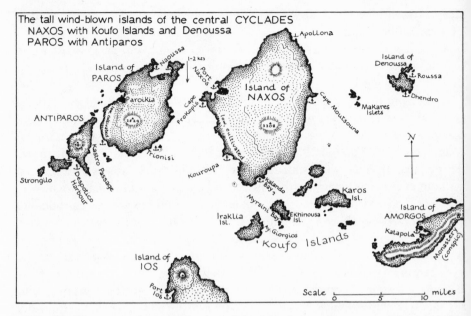

The tall wind-blown islands of the central CYCLADES
NAXOS with Koufo Islands and Denoussa
PAROS with Antiparos

Kalando Bay, near the south point of the island, is rather open and susceptible to a reflected swell as well as mountain gusts. Good holding (fine weed on sand) in 3-fathom depths. The shores are deserted.

Apollona Bay, on the N.E. Coast with its hamlet of about 260 people, can hardly be recommended as an anchorage. If wishing to visit the great Apollo by sea, a yacht should choose calm weather. The anchorage is in 3 fathoms on a sandy bottom 80 yds S.E. of the hamlet where a quay provides slight protection from the prevailing wind. The Apollo statue lies 200 yds inland in the old quarry. Under usual summer conditions it is preferable to drive here by the new road from Port Naxos.

The small Koufo Islands lying close S.E. of Naxos are mostly large enough to support village communities:

Ekhinousa Island, relatively low-lying has a narrow inlet, Myrsini, on the south side affording good shelter.

Myrsini Bay is actually a creek with a small stone quay and a road leading to the hamlet on the hill.

> **Approach.** The entrance can be distinguished by a small light tower (Lt. Fl. W. 4) on the west side of the creek.

Berth. The inlet runs N.N.E. and near its head a small bay opens on the eastern side. On the northern side of this bay is a shallow quay where small fishing boats moor. On the southern side is a quay to which a yacht can go stern-to with depths of 7–8 ft at its western end; towards the other inland end the depths diminish rapidly. Sea-bed is irregular; boulders and sandy patches.

Facilities. Fruit, bread and vegetables can be bought at the hamlet—15 minutes' walk.

Life on this small island is simple, but the standard of the people is the same as in the larger communities. Some of the Kalymnian sponge-boats base themselves here in summer.

Iraklia Island has an inlet, unnamed on the new chart but once called Ayios Giorgios, on the N.E. corner. It can be recognized by a few white houses lining the water-front.

Anchorage is at the head of the creek in 3 to 5 fathoms on a sandy bottom with room for a medium-sized yacht to swing. A swell sometimes rolls in. This anchorage is not as sheltered as Myrsini Bay.

One or two hamlets can be seen inland and there are a few farmsteads on the slopes.

Island of Paros

half the size of Naxos, has a population of about 10,000 who live in the three main villages of Paroikia, Naoussa and Marmora and in scattered farmsteads. The mountains being lower and the contours more gentle, shelter under the lee of Paros during strong north winds is less blustery than at Naxos.

Paroikia, the principal port, consists of two quays and a pleasant village where supplies and provisions can be obtained.

Berth and Anchorage. Chart 1832 and plan p. 222. A yacht may berth off the extremity of one of the moles, or anchor off. In strong north winds it is recommended to anchor at the head of the bay where there is also good holding and better shelter. Apart from the natural shelter provided by the bay it is very exposed for a yacht to berth off the town quays. The considerations are the change of weather and the busy traffic, for small steamers, ferries and caiques are constantly arriving and leaving.

Facilities. In the village is a wide choice of modern shops, small summer hotels, restaurants and tavernas. Water and fuel were being laid on at the new mole in 1970. A local retsina and a red wine are produced, both quite palatable. Ice at the factory. One or two engineering shops, banks and taxis in the village. Car ferry from Piraeus calls daily and connects with Naxos. A caique ferry runs to Antiparos.

Officials. The Harbour Office beside the Post Office faces the public gardens.

The village (3,000 inhabitants) has much charm. The narrow winding streets with little white houses are attractive. Many of the older ones retain their frontage but are being converted into modern shops or flats—all are scrupulously clean being whitewashed every year and even the flagstones of the streets are outlined in white as in other of the Cyclades.

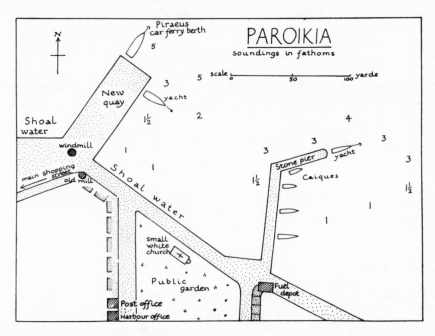

The principal object of interest here is the Katapoliani or Ekatopiliani (Church of the Hundred Gates). The church is, in fact, three churches in one, the main structure being of Byzantine conception with an early basilica (partly built of columns from a Greek temple) and a baptistry. It is all of much interest and should be visited as well as the small museum close by.

In the village is the tower of the Venetian Kastro—a medieval structure of long marble blocks, drums of columns and plinths collected from early Greek temples and fitted together to form a tower.

About 5 miles eastward of the village and reached by taxi are the ancient marble quarries. The seam of transparent white marble which formed the medium for Praxiteles's work and for the Parian Chronicle (now at Oxford among the Arundel collection) is no longer worked. After being quarried for long periods during the early centuries the place was abandoned until the last century when some of this marble was required in 1844 to form part of Napoleon's tomb. The quarry, once more abandoned, can be visited by scrambling down a steep gulley, but as much of the tunnelling is underground a torch is necessary.

Naoussa is a substantial village in the centre of a broad inlet. A very shallow caique port (5 to 6 ft) lies close by, but two sheltered anchorages suitable for yachts are under each headland of the approach. The shores are largely deserted.

> **Anchorage.** Chart 1832 shows an excellent plan and indicates the anchorages suitable for a yacht in the N.W. and N.E. corners of this large bay. Though protected from sea and wind there is sometimes the reflection of a swell during the Meltemi.

This place used to be severely afflicted with malaria. Once a main base for the Russian fleet under Alexis Orloff after 1770, it had large shore installations and gun defences on the western headland; but after a few years the base had to be hurriedly abandoned on account of the declining state of health among the sailors.

There is also good shelter towards the southern shore of Paros both close westward of Trionisi and by the southern approach to the shallow pass of Kastro. Chart 1837.

Island of Antiparos is a flat little island with the hamlet of Kastro and a famous grotto. Its interest for a yacht lies mainly in the 14-ft passage between Paros and Antiparos, and the harbour of **Despotico.**

> **Approach.** Chart 1837, made from recent Greek surveys shows that the two shallow channels between Paros and Antiparos have changed considerably since Commander Graves's survey in 1842. His original '14-foot passage' now called the Pass of Kastro is shown as having a minimum depth of only 8 ft whereas the N.E.–S.W. passage is reputed to have 13 ft. A yacht would naturally choose the deeper water, but examination of the sea-bed showed the bottom to be irregular, at one point with a depth of only 9 ft over a reef. Although the water is very clear the passage should not be attempted except in calm weather and even then a deep draught yacht is recommended not to accept the risk.
>
> **Anchorage.** The harbour of Despotico is frequented by caiques and has the reputation of being a good all-weather port. It has convenient depths and good holding. Formerly, in the 16th and 17th centuries, it was the laying-up port for all the pirate vessels, including Genoese, French and Maltese galleys.

The grotto, which lies 1½ miles from the sea and 4 from the village, is now electrically lit in order to attract the tourists who visit the island from Paros. It is recorded that in 1673 the French Ambassador to the Porte came here with five hundred followers, and celebrated the Christmas Mass. He afterwards removed several of the statues which had been hidden in the grotto and took them to Paris: some of them may be seen in the Louvre today.

Island of Santorini (Thira or Santorin)

appearing in the distance as a peakless cone, is, in fact, an ancient volcano forming a circular island which has been split in two by a tremendous eruption; possibly the same great upheaval, with attendant earthquakes and tidal waves, that some consider to have destroyed the Minoan palaces of Crete in Mycenean times. There has been a number of severe eruptions since those days, one alluded to by Strabo in the second century B.C. when 'flames rushed forth from the sea for a space of four days, causing the whole of it to boil and be on fire'. This tall cone, Mt Prophet Elias, nearly 2,000 ft, is crowned by a remarkable white monastery and a radar station.

Entering the wide, sheltered strait among the islands, a broad ribbon of white houses appears on the skyline above the sheer, brown cliffs. This is Thira, the capital.

To the southward is the lava islet of Nea Caemene where caiques are often to be seen moored to the rocks in the sulphurous water above the little crater which still spews out its sulphur fumes through the sea-bed beneath. Taking advantage of this natural benefit provided gratuitously by the sea-bed, these vessels remain here for a day or two after which their bottoms are foul no longer.

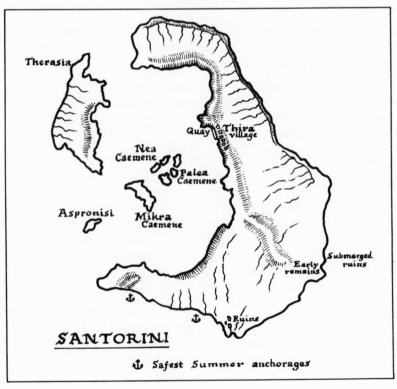

SANTORINI

⚓ *Safest Summer anchorages*

The Port

Berth. Chart 2043. The small quay beneath the main village of Thira is easily distinguished by day. Though there are depths of 6 to 10 ft, the sea-bed falls away very steeply. There is a big mooring buoy for yachts close to the quay, and several further out for steamers. In the event of a swell or unsettled conditions a yacht should proceed to the south of the island and anchor where indicated in the plan.

Facilities. On the quay there are now two small tavernas where basic provisions can be bought, but normal fresh provisions must be got at Thira and brought down by mule. The owners of these beasts, whose numbers appear to be inexhaustible, make a lucrative trade carrying tourists up and down between the landing and Thira. There is air communication with Athens.

When berthing off the quay it is an awe-inspiring sight to find oneself lying beside the crater-wall of a gigantic volcano. Beneath the water is a drop of 1,000 ft, and opposite are the three islets—the remains of the volcano's shattered walls.

The mule-track zigzags up the 700 ft precipitous slope. The sides of the cliff, once the interior of the crater, are sometimes ash-red and even black; often corrugated as if with pillars, interspersed here and there are troglodyte dwellings.

The long narrow town of Thira clings to the top of the ridge. Its two streets lined with white houses, and often spanned by arches, are attractive. There is a cathedral and several churches, and the peal of bells is sometimes to be heard. (See photographs opposite.)

The view from the top is magnificent, for one appears to be standing almost directly above the quay with probably one or two yachts and caiques moored beneath. This high plateau is agreeably peaceful after the disturbing impression left by the nether regions of the port. Across the deep blue water are the steep, brown cliffs rising vertically from the depths, and in the distance can be seen other islands of the archipelago.

One of Santorin's difficulties is shortage of water. Though rainwater is collected and run into the numerous cisterns at Thira, supplies are insufficient, and during the summer months a tanker from Piraeus must sometimes augment them.

The tourist trade contributes considerably to the resources of this island, there being a number of excursions to places of archaeological interest. In addition, there is an export of pumice and wine, tomatoes, barley and beans.

Early History. It was about the time of the Exodus of the Israelites when the Bronze Age was at its height that both Santorin and Minoan civilization in Crete disappeared almost over-night.

Great interest has been taken in recent years to cut through the lava rock and examine remains of Minoan type houses and other relics of the Minoan age on the site marked Ruins on the map. It can be reached by taxi from Thira village. The frescoes recovered from here are now displayed in the National Archaeological Museum at Athens. These discoveries have involved difficult excavation beneath the lowest layer of rose-coloured pumice rock. The powder of this pumice has been located in layers on the seabed in the S.E. and over eastern Crete whither it was blown by the prevailing wind at the period of the great eruption about 1500 B.C.

Island of Serifos

is mountainous and barren, with two large bays on the south coast:

Koutala Bay, a former ore port both for the ancients as well as the modern Greeks, is an unattractive anchorage largely because of the disused ore tips and the iron mines which disfigure the whole countryside.

> **Anchorage.** Chart 1833 shows clearly the choice of where to anchor. The large mooring buoys shown on the plan have now been removed.

The only dwellings are those connected with the old iron-ore workings.

Livadhi Bay provides good shelter in agreeable surroundings at the foot of the mountain village of Livadhi.

> The new mole extending eastwards from Ak. Poundi is marked by a small light structure at its extremity. (The light formerly on the cape has been moved 100 yds east.)
> **Berth.** Yachts sometimes berth inshore of the ferry berth at the quay (about 8 ft depth) or anchor in the bay which is rather deep until it shelves towards the shore. The holding of soft mud may grip a CQR anchor, but during strong gusts with northerly winds a fisherman's anchor usually drags.
> **Facilities** have recently been improved; most of the fruit and vegetables being brought by ferry. Fresh water from a nearby tap, a small summer hotel and some restaurants by the port

The village of Livadhi clings to the hill immediately above the port; its little houses of dazzling white standing out prominently against the barren hillside can be seen many miles away. The ascent up a mule track is a steep, but rewarding experience taking at least 1½ hours to the top and back. There is also an occasional bus which climbs the new winding road to the top.

The harbour, which is very shut-in by the surrounding mountains, can be remarkably hot in summer, but the sandy shore attracts visitors, and villas are springing up.

The abandoned iron-ore workings to be seen on many hillsides of the island were started by the Romans and continued throughout the Middle Ages until recent years. When the Venetian conquerors came their seamen complained of their 'compass needles being disturbed by the iron ore'. Today there is very little employment and the population of the island is declining; at Livadhi it is only about 200.

Island of Sifnos

appears from seaward as mountainous and barren; but inland it is fertile with two main inland villages, Apollonia and Artemon. On the coast are a number of inviting anchorages suitable for yachts.

On the East Coast:

Kastro, the most beautiful, is a shallow cove overlooked by a crumbling Venetian citadel with its high white walls and old houses clinging to the top of a conical hill. Unfortunately there is no proper harbour, and only in settled weather can a yacht anchor under the lee of Cape Eftamartiros or in the entrance to the cove (see plan, Chart 1825). A road leads up to Apollonia, the principal village, standing on the plateau above.

SIFNOS

Scale 0 1 2 miles

Faros. A charming inlet affording sheltered anchorage for a medium-sized yacht.

> **Anchorage.** Chart 1825. Let go in 5 fathoms one hundred yards off the centre of the hamlet; sandy bottom. The anchorage is open, only through a narrow sector, to south.
> **Facilities** are almost nil. A café and a dozen small houses line the shore from which a motor-road leads over the hills to Apollonia. A few fishing boats work from the port.

Plati Yialos. See Chart 1825. This is an open bay in attractive surroundings and a suitable anchorage for a large yacht. It has a reputation for violent squalls which sometimes sweep down from the mountains with strong N. winds.

A few little houses are spread round the shores of the bay and there are two small summer hotels. A road leads up to Apollonia.

> *Note.* After a strong northerly blow the passage across to Antiparos should not be attempted by small vessels on account of dangerous breaking seas.

On the West Coast:

Fikiada, a deserted inlet with good shelter.

> **Anchorage.** Chart 1825. Proceed near the head of the creek and let go in 3 to 4 fathoms on a sandy bottom with patches of weed. Room for medium-sized yachts to swing. Open to W.S.W.

There are no facilities or dwellings at Fikiada; only the attractive little white domed church of Ayios Georgios standing on a rocky slope, completely cut off, on the north side of the entrance.

Vathy. An attractive well-sheltered anchorage in the midst of mountainous surroundings. A number of little white houses spread themselves along the shore.

> **Anchorage.** Chart 1825. Let go where indicated on the plan; sandy bottom with fine weed and shelter nearly all round.
> **Facilities.** Only a café and basic provisions.

Vathy is the best harbour in the island and is always practical even in bad weather. There is room for a large yacht to anchor, or for a number of medium-sized yachts. A poor road (not for vehicles) leads to Apollonia.

Kamares Bay, the mail-steamer port, is both the least attractive and least sheltered of all.

> **Anchorage.** Chart 1833. Anchor in convenient depths at the head of the bay. Bottom appears to be hard sand into which anchors do not readily dig in; holding is most unreliable. The bay is exposed to west and a swell usually rolls in. The stone pier has depths of only about 6 ft at its extremity.

21 Island of Ios: the anchorage. *See p. 212*

22 Santorini:
The summit of
Thira

23 Santorini:
looking down
at the small
quay from the
village of Thira
800 ft above

Facilities. A few local shops can provide fresh provisions. Fuel and water are available, but facilities for embarking them are lacking. A bus runs (to a schedule) to Apollonia.

Other anchorages off Sifnos:

The following two inlets lying towards the northern tip of the island have suitable anchorages for small yachts:

Vourlithia. A deserted creek with convenient anchorage in 3 to 5 fathoms near its head. The bottom is sandy and the creek is open between W. and S.W. The mountainous sides rise rather steeply and in strong winds gusts could be expected.

Ayios Georgios has anchorage at the head of a sheltered creek for a small to medium-sized yacht.

Anchorage. Let go in 3 fathoms where the small houses begin. Run out a warp to the small quay (3-ft depths). Bottom is hard sand and one cannot be sure that a plough anchor will easily dig in. Excellent shelter, almost all round. The sides of the creek not being high strong winds should not cause discomforting gusts.

The houses of the small hamlet are mostly abandoned and only half a dozen are still occupied. The local people are all old, occupied with pottery, fishing and grazing goats. Communication is by boat with Kamares and track to Artemon village.

Though of little importance today, in ancient times Sifnos was rich on account of its gold mines, and witness of this period is the splendid marble treasury still to be seen nearly intact at Delphi.

Island of Siros (Syra)

Capital of the Cyclades, has a town of more than 20,000 people; the commercial activity in its spacious port, which made the island so important in the last century, declined between the two World Wars.

The two main villages, the catholic Ano-Syra and the Greek Orthodox Ermoupolis are each perched on a hill beyond the harbour, their white houses reaching down to the port. Here is the small town with an impressive 18th-century square complete with public buildings and a small opera house—the most striking 'city centre' of the Aegean and quite un-Greek in appearance. In the port the presence of a floating dock, some quays busy with loading and unloading caiques and small steamers, the establishment of two training schools for the merchant navy as well as some large vessels refitting, all tend to suggest a revival of activity. Tourists know Syra for the manufacture of Loukoumi (Turkish Delight).

The Port

Approach and Berth. Chart 1833, plan. A yacht should proceed to the farthest quay, berthing stern-to and bows towards the entrance. This berth is among the caiques and is not a salubrious corner of the harbour; but the main quay is often occupied with commercial vessels. The harbour is well-sheltered, though not clean. In 1968 a new quay had been completed on the inner side of the new mole at Nisaki.

Facilities. Most things can be obtained close by on the quayside. Water is difficult to obtain and can only be bought expensively from a tank-cart. There is a number of tavernas. It is possible for a yacht to slip on a skid cradle at the shipyard. There is an airport. The Piraeus steamer calls three times a week. In the summer a bus runs to Krasi Bay where there is a bathing beach.

Officials. A Port of Entry; there is the usual quota of officials.

Other anchorages off Siros recommended for a temporary stay:

Ormos Megas (Chart 1639). This *T*-headed bay has good holding on a sandy bottom in the N.W. corner in convenient depths of 2 to 3 fathoms. The headland called Akri Grammatica is composed of marble slabs on which sheltering mariners during past centuries have scratched their names and dates.

Foinikos lies on the S.W. corner and Krasi Bay is a pleasant place to bring up

Approach. Chart 1825, plan. A high rocky point marks the N. entrance, and the low-lying Psakhonisi islet must be passed with care.

Anchorage in the N.E. corner of the bay in 3 fathoms off a small quay good holding. Open between S. and W., but in the S. part of the bay is shelter from a S. wind.

Facilities. At the hamlet fresh provisions are obtainable. A taverna. A bus service runs to the town of Siros.

Historical Note. The British interest in Syra began after the founding of the Levant company in the reign of Queen Elizabeth, but its real prosperity was during the last century in the early days of steam.

After gaining her freedom from the Turks together with the rest of Greece in 1829, Syra found herself in a fortunate situation. Her commodious port lay in a strategic position on the trade route between the Black Sea, Levant and western ports. In those days steamers could proceed only limited distance without bunkering, and Sira's geographical position was in the precise locality to suit most routes. Thus the packet service, Egypt-Constantinople, Austro-Lloyd from Piraeus, Trieste and Brindisi, and the French Messageries ships, Biddy Line, etc., all called here for bunkering; it became in consequence a market for British coal. With its growing commercial importance consular representation was established; in addition to the British Consul there were nine consulates of other nations, and a British church and chaplain.

Siros has never been devastated by foreign invaders nor persecuted by the

Turks as has happened to other islands. It was fortunate in having had a Capuchin mission which for centuries had the protection of France, and the Turks never molested them. It seems that this happy state of security attracted refugees who had fled from other islands, and thus at the time of the boom in shipping the manpower was available to help develop the resources of the port.

At the beginning of this century when oil began to take the place of coal, the importance of Syros declined and today there seems only limited activity in the port, mostly confined to repair work.

Here, as in so many of these islands, the interest is entirely in the port, for the countryside is unwelcoming. The bleak mountains of Syros with their lower slopes now so barren and tree-less bear no resemblance to their description nearly three thousand years ago by Homer:

> 'Of soil divine,
> a good land teeming with fertility,
> Rich with green pastures, feeding flocks and kine
> a fair land with streams, a land of corn and wine.'
> ODYSSEY XV

Island of Tinos

The island is remarkable today as being the 'Lourdes of Greece'. Its well-sheltered port with an interesting town in mountainous surroundings should be visited.

Since 1822, when the miraculous icon of the Panaghia was discovered, pilgrims from Greece have flocked to Tinos every year to attend the great feast of Our Lady on August 15. Tinos has thus become a place of pilgrimage and the local inhabitants have prospered as a result.

The Port
Approach and Berth. Chart 1833, plan. Secure stern to the northern quay with anchor towards entrance. (Eastwards of the second bollard from the west it has been dredged.) A new quay has been built south of the main quay and the mole extended (1970).
Facilities. Water, said to be the purest in Greece, is supplied by a tap close by. Plenty of provisions are available close to the quay; there are modest hotels, restaurants and tavernas. The two filling stations for fuel on the quay do not supply out of bond. Ice can be bought in the early morning only, off Platera Taxiarchon. The local weaving industry has some good examples in a shop up the hill. Mail steamers leave for Piraeus daily.

The harbour is large and the quayside usually animated with caiques loading and unloading, and many Greek visitors frequent the tavernas and restaurants.

From the quay, walking towards the hill, one soon approaches the large white Greek Orthodox church. Although of no architectural merit, the forecourt is attractive, as well as the courtyard of the convent whose glaring white walls are softened by the shadows of the dark cypresses.

Inside the church is the icon itself with typical Byzantine silver-work almost covering the painting of 'the great and gracious Lady'. Pilgrims are often wheeled in and the priests may be seen reciting their supplications, at the same time treating the pilgrims in no gentle manner as they twist them about, apparently to draw the Virgin's attention to that part of their anatomy they are beseeching her to cure. Hung from the roof of the church are many models often in silver—the votive offerings given by those who have been saved from a violent death by the intervention of the Virgin. Perhaps one of the more curious is that of a caique which had been holed and was about to sink, but was saved by the timely arrival of a benign fish, which swam into the hole and so sealed it from the inrushing water. The hull, the sails and even the fish are skilfully and realistically worked in silver.

In Tinos church, a votive offering

In the little crypt are two chapels, one marking the site of the discovery of the icon, and the other a memorial to the dead sailors of the Greek cruiser *Elli*. On 15 August 1940, when Greece was at peace with all nations, their cruiser *Elli* had been sent to attend the usual celebrations of Our Lady of Tinos and lay at anchor outside the port. She had dressed the ship in honour of the occasion and many of her ship's company were ashore. An Italian submarine operating under orders from Rome fired a torpedo, sinking *Elli* and many of the crew—an outrage the Greeks cannot easily forget.

The shores of the S.W. coast rise to a chain of mountains (more than 2,000 ft), their monotony being relieved by a number of mountain villages whose little white houses form a pleasant contrast to the bare, sombre mountain sides. These villages, where the people are employed in farming, have spring water at heights of 1,000 ft. A number of Jersey herds are grazed, the cattle being shipped to Piraeus mainly in caiques.

A low woolly cloud lying on the ridge of this island and on Andros is a sign of strong north winds. They sweep down the mountain sides usually in violent gusts, and on the north-east or the weather side of the island the anchorages become quite untenable all the summer months. The two bays at the northern end of the island referred to in *Sailing Directions*, **Kolimbithra** with its deserted monastery and **Panormos** where the marble is shipped, can be most uncomfortable anchorages in summer.

THE LESSER ISLANDS

Anafi (Anaphi) **Islands** is a group of relatively flat and largely barren islands with very few inhabitants except for those living in the village on the south of the main island which is hilly. Here is an open anchorage where the mail boat calls, but there is no harbour—only a boat camber. Occasionally the island is overrun by a plague of partridges which cause havoc among the sparsely cultivated fields of the farmers.

Island of Denoussa, a small but relatively tall island with a hamlet in the south, has two anchorages:

Dhendro Bay (Chart 1663), on the south coast is distinguished by a white domed church standing in the middle of a small hamlet. The anchorage is on a sandy bottom in 5 fathoms open to the south. About 200 people live on the island which in addition to the hamlet has a few scattered farmsteads. There are no roads and the island is primitive. A few caiques, used for fishing, are often berthed off a small quay.

Roussa (Chart 1647) lying on the E. coast is partly sheltered by the islet of Skilonisi. The best anchorage is off the beach, for the sea-bed near the islet rises too steeply. Dhendro Bay anchorage is the better.

At the beginning of the First World War, Denoussa was the secret rendezvous for the German battle cruiser *Goeben* then being pursued by the British forces whilst escaping towards the Dardanelles. She urgently needed fuel and here a German collier was directed to await her arrival. Having topped up with coal *Goeben* steamed at full speed for the Dardanelles, and successfully eluding her pursuers reached Constantinople; her presence exerted considerable influence in forcing Turkey into the war as an ally of Germany.

The 'Dry Islands' of Sikinos and Folegandros are mountainous, barren and steep-to. They are very little visited, though both have open sandy bays and in summer they afford comfortable anchorage.

Island of Sikinos

Anchorage. There is 2 fathoms close in and room to swing; the bottom is fine sand. A landing quay is on the western side of the small bay. The Meltemi produces a few strong gusts; it is entirely open to south.

Facilities. A small taverna and one or two small houses are on the quay, and there is a fresh-water well 200 yds inland. Provisions must be obtained from the main village on the hill.

The Chora lies on the mountain ridge on the opposite side of the island—a village of 700 people. They are largely employed in cultivating the terraced vineyards and cornfields which cannot be seen from seaward. It is less than an hour's walk along an easy mule road to reach the village and is worth the effort. The local Orthodox church is another hour onward; this was built round the former temple of Apollo whose Ionic columns still stand.

Island of Folegandros has no port, but a weekly steamer calls, anchoring off the main village.

Anchorages

(a) Karavostasi, with the island village adjoining, may be approached with aid of Chart 1832. A stony road leads up to the Chora.

(b) Vathy Bay has convenient depths on a sandy bottom; but being rather open a swell creeps round the bay during northerly winds.

The island, with a population of only 500 people, offers nothing of particular interest, though a walk to the Chora is rewarding. The coastline is remarkable for its tall steep-to cliffs. Though cultivation cannot be seen from the sea, a number of terraces in the valleys leading up to the Chora are still farmed.

The remaining three islands of the Cyclades are seldom visited:

Island of Kimolos—a barren-looking island close north of Milos with one or two sheltered anchorages:

Psathi Bay has occasionally been used by yachts who report favourably on its attraction. At the landing place is a taverna; the Chora lies on the hill above—an easy climb from the anchorages (Chart 1832).

Kinaros, a smaller uninhabited island of this group has the narrow steep-sided

Pnigo Creek affording perfect protection for a medium-sized yacht. A beach is at the head of this creek and is sometimes used by small caiques.

> **Approach.** The creek is about 700 yds in length and without hazard until reaching a small patch of rocks on the western shore near the head of the creek. A shelf with depths beginning at 7 fathoms and slowly decreasing begins about half-way.
> **Anchorage.** There are 3-fathom depths between a distance of 50 ft to 8 ft off the beach. Bottom is sand on rock. A warp must be run out ashore.

Levitha Islands consists of a chain of small islands lying about E.N.E. from the north of Amorgos.

Levitha Inlet is in the middle of the southern shore of the main island. It extends in an easterly direction, being rather narrow at its head and rocky at the sides. Although it provides all-round shelter the sea-bed consists mostly of flat rock and stones on which no anchor can hold. One or more warps are essential.

Apart from the lighthouse-keeper there are no permanent inhabitants; only one or two patches of cultivation and spring grazing.

Island of Yioura (Ghiaros) is small and barren; sometimes still used, as it was by the Romans, as a penitentiary for prisoners. It is prohibited as a place of call.

Local Craft

The ubiquitous lugger of the Aegean carries the trade of the islands. Nowadays only
steadying sails are used, and the motor drives her along at 5 or 6 knots

Until a few years ago the whole of the Aegean was remarkable for the numerous and distinctive types of sailing craft. They were without motors until the
early 1920s but since then mechanical power has slowly displaced the need
for the original spread of sail, and many types of craft have now vanished.

In Greece some of the former hulls continue to be built today but they are to
be seen only under power with steadying sails—a poor apology for the handsome spread of canvas which once characterized them.

In Turkey the traditional types are hardly seen at all, and the modern caique
is definitely an ugly boat. Even steadying sails have been discarded and a strong
derrick is fitted permanently to plumb the hold.

The few old-timers among Greek sailors today are sometimes quite perplexed
at being confronted with photographs of Aegean vessels of half a century ago

and only after some hesitation will they recognize the type of hull. Then, with still more doubt, they may specify the rig, although sometimes that particular rig originates from a district with which they are not familiar.

The great majority of craft still to be seen in the Aegean are the *Perama* and *Trehandiri* hulls with *Bratsera* rig:

The Bratsera or Aegean Lugger. This ubiquitous vessel with standing-lug main and balance-lug foresail can carry cargoes of 50 to 150 tons, and more.

With an accentuated sheer and pronounced flare carried well aft, these boats have a wide beam at deck level. A shallow keel, without ballast and little draft, makes them poor performers to windward. The low waist, protected against spray by a canvas screen laced to a light spar supported by gunwhale-irons, is still a characteristic feature of all Aegean craft, except in the case of the large wine schooners. (See photograph, fac. p. 63.)

The Turks, who formerly shared with the Greeks considerably more of the Aegean coast than they do today, also built these vessels. Though constructed largely by Greek shipwrights, the older Turkish vessels still in service have a more accentuated sheer, giving them an almost crescent effect.

The origin of the hull and rig are difficult to determine, but there is good reason to believe that the rig is Italian, probably from the north Adriatic. Except for a few in trade with the Ionian islands, these vessels are not seen outside the Aegean.

Of the two types of hull used with these luggers the most common is the

Trehandiri which ranges from 100 tonners to quite small fishing craft of a couple of tons, although in this case the rig is usually of mainsail (lug or gaff) and jib.

It may be seen in the following sketches that the *Trehandiri* has a curved stem often projecting above the gunwhale.

The Perama has a straight inclined stem, forming at the stemhead a beak with an athwartships transom. The hull is thought to be a more efficient sailer than the *Trehandiri*.

Details of Perama beak, showing characteristic features of
pre-Nelson athwartship bulkhead and prominent bitts

A deeply laden Perama accentuates the wide beam

Until recently caiques were built in considerable numbers at Piraeus; they are also built at Siros, Samos, Ikaria, Volos and Skiathos, nearly all of pinewood from the forests of Samos, this timber being considered the most suitable for ship construction in the Aegean.

Planking-up starts from the covering board downwards and from the keel upwards at the same time, being fastened to doubled frames with galvanized nails. Instead of steaming the planks for an unwilling bend, they are usually soaked for a while in salt water. The gap where the planks meet sometimes requires a filling piece of most peculiar shape—quite horrifying to those un-versed in Greek construction. In the more primitive island yards no drawings are used, but one or two standardized moulds may sometimes be seen put away on the walls of the builder's store. When asked how he builds to a particular shape or design, the reply is usually 'I build like my father taught me'.

When the construction is complete, caulking is applied here and there; after a coat of red-lead, the boat is then painted, nowadays in gay colours, sometimes a white hull with red, light blue or vermilion gunwale. The priest is asked to bless her and she is then launched before the admiring eyes of the owner's family and friends. The owner is often only part-owner; as much as half the money is sometimes lent by the banks.

The Sponge-Boats (*Sfoungaradiko*) are small *Trehandiris* and are frequently seen in the summer months, both in the Greek islands and on the Turkish coast. In each country the boats are similar and with a length of only 33 to 43 ft; at sea when fishing they always appear to be terribly crowded, carrying about

A Sfoungaradiko

eight men. In Greece they are built at Kalimnos and Symi and in Turkey at Bodrum.

The **Sacoulevi**—the only survivor of the sprit rig remaining in the Mediterranean—can occasionally be seen but only in small boats. The rig has been illustrated in various forms, sculpture, drawings etc. since earliest times and as

A Sacoulevi

late as the First World War a few traders of about 100 tons were still operating under sail. An early French dictionary described them as being the 'coaster-ship of the Levant, with pronounced sheer and high stern. The *Sacouleves* sail fast.' A later English dictionary (Smyth) of 1867 gives a similar description, but refers to them as small craft. In the Azores similar rigs were also common in the last century.

Varkalas transom-stern schooners (or luggers), usually with Italian clipper bow, are related to the Arab *baggala*. They are also to be seen with *Perama* or *Trehandiri* hulls, but always with the transom stern. This is invariably carved to overcome monotony of such a large flat area. Sketch shows the more usual type of hull and rig to be seen in the Aegean today. Most of these craft are built at Samos and some at Symi.

In the foregoing description of caiques no attempt has been made to record types of vessels which were to be seen earlier in the century and are now no more.

Varkalas with Italian type hull and modern gaff ring

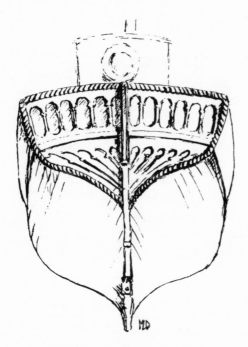

Detail of typical carved transom.
Vessel is on slipway with rudder and
propeller removed for repair.

No doubt the modern *Trehandiris* and *Peramas* with built-up bulwarks (instead of weather screens), steadying sails and powerful engines will continue to be constructed at the surviving shipyards for some years yet; but already one notices that on the longer Aegean shipping routes small steel coasters of the Dutch 'Gröningen' type are slowly creeping in.

> *And now the old ships and their men are gone;*
> *the new ships and the new men, many of them*
> *bearing the old auspicious names have taken up*
> *their watch on the stern and impartial sea.*
>   CONRAD—*The Mirror of the Sea*

Index